CW01261090

AIR WAR OVER EAST YORKSHIRE
IN WORLD WAR II

PAUL BRIGHT

FLIGHT RECORDER PUBLICATIONS

A passion for accuracy

First published in Great Britain in 2005 by
Flight Recorder Publications Ltd
Ashtree House, Station Road, Ottringham,
East Yorkshire, HU12 0BJ
Tel: 01964 624223
E-mail: beketley@dircon.co.uk
Website: www.flight-recorder.com
© 2005 Flight Recorder Publications Ltd

All rights reserved. Apart from any fair dealing for the purpose of private study, research, criticism or review, as permitted under the Copyright, Design and Patents Act 1988, no part of this publication may be reproduced, stored in a retrieval system, or transmitted in any form or by any means, electronic, electrical, chemical, mechanical, optical, photo-copying, recording or otherwise, without prior written permission. Paul Bright has asserted his moral right to be recognised as the author of this work. All enquiries should be directed to the publisher.

ISBN 0 9545605 7 4

Edited by Barry Ketley
Digital photography and scanning by
Eduard Winkler
Colour artwork by Jon Field, Aeroprints
Maps by Steve Longland
Design by Flight Recorder Publications Ltd
Printed in the EEC

Distribution & Marketing
in UK and Europe by
Midland Publishing
(a part of the Ian Allan Group)
4 Watling Drive, Sketchley Lane Industrial Estate,
Hinckley, Leics, LE10 3EY
Tel: 01455 233747 Fax: 01455 233737
E-mail: midlandbooks@compuserve.com

Distribution & Marketing
in USA & North America by
Specialty Press
39966 Grand Avenue, North Branch, MN 55056,
USA
Tel: 651 277 1400 Fax: 651 277 1203
E-mail: davida@cartechbooks.com

ALSO AVAILABLE

AUSTER
A Brief History of the Auster Aircraft in British Military Service
by
Barry Ketley
ISBN 0 9545605 6 6

THE LONG DRAG
A Short History of British Target Towing
by
Don Evans BEM
ISBN 0 9545605 4 X

KURT TANK'S PHOTO ALBUM 1940-1943
by
Roy Powell & Barry Ketley
ISBN 0 9545605 3 1

THE WARLORDS
US Eighth Air Force Fighter Colours of World War II
Volume 1
The 4th, 20th & 55th Fighter Groups
by
Barry & Ann Money
ISBN 0 9545605 1 5

A CIVILIAN AFFAIR
A Brief History of the Civilian Aircraft Company of Hedon
by
Eduard F. Winkler
ISBN 0 9545605 0 7

FORTHCOMING

WEKUSTA
Luftwaffe Weather Reconnaissance Units & Operations 1938-1945
by
John A. Kington & Franz Selinger
ISBN 0 9545605 8 2

RISE AND DEFEND
The USAF at Manston 1950-1958
by
Duncan Curtis
ISBN 0 9545605 5 8

THE WARLORDS
US Eighth Air Force Fighter Colours of World War II
Volume 2
The 56th, 78th & 339th Fighter Groups
by
Barry & Ann Money
ISBN 0 9545605 9 0

Caption to title page: A colourised picture of Hull burning during the Blitz of May 1941. Holy Trinity church and the Guildhall can both be seen, silhouetted against the glare from burning buildings in the city centre.

CONTENTS

Introduction		6
Chapter 1	1939: From 'Phoney War' to shooting war	8
Chapter 2	Early combats: The first bombs and a heroine at Aldborough	23
Chapter 3	Into the Battle of Britain: Coastal attacks and the Poles at Leconfield	39
Chapter 4	The 'Eagles' attack: Target — RAF Driffield	44
Chapter 5	After the battle: The cost	58
Chapter 6	Hit and run raids: Bridlington bombed and Spitfire funds	67
Chapter 7	Night battles 1941: The Blitz on Hull	77
Chapter 8	Baedeker 1942: The raids on Hull and York	100
Chapter 9	Coming in on a wing and a prayer: Drama in Filey Bay	114
Chapter 10	1943: Dorniers and Beaufighters down	119
Chapter 11	1944: A forced landing at Grindale — Flamborough Head's link to D-Day	136
Chapter 12	1945: Gisela — the Luftwaffe's final fling and the last air raid on Hull	148
Chapter 13	Epilogue: Emptying the bomb dumps — postscript	167
Ships lost to enemy action in the Humber and off the coast of East Yorkshire		165
East Riding Airfields in 1945		173
Index and Bibliography		174

Fortunately for those living in the East Riding, the ominous shape and sound of the V-1s or 'doodlebugs' was no more than a fleeting shadow. The one and only attempt to air-launch these weapons off the east coast by the Luftwaffe as an early Christmas 'present' on 24 December 1944 was an unmitigated disaster for the attackers. Few reached Manchester, their intended target; the four that fell in the East Riding caused little damage, but II./KG 53 discovered to their cost that the V-1 could explode as it was released...

ACKNOWLEDGEMENTS

There is no way in which I could have completed this book without the help and support of many knowledgeable and supportive people. To all of them I am very, very grateful.

For my primary sources, I relied heavily on the PRO (Public Record Office) at Kew; this excellent establishment is now named the National Archives. There, employees in the Reprographic Ordering Section did a sterling job on my behalf in locating and supplying me with copies of relevant RAF documents. Similarly, I have received outstanding input from the Royal Air Force Museum at Hendon. At the museum, Peter Elliott, Senior Keeper in the Department of Research and Information has been a tower of strength, always replying promptly to my queries, providing me with invaluable information, and often pointing me in the right direction. Thanks must also go to East Riding archivist Ian Mason and his well-informed and accommodating staff at the East Riding of Yorkshire Archives and Records Service in Beverley, for allowing me to publish Civil Defence documents. Similarly, I greatly appreciate the help and support received from the staff at the Air Historical Branch and Imperial War Museum in London.

With regard to secondary sources, I have assembled my own collection of books relating to various aspects of the air war over Britain in World War Two, but I have also depended to a considerable extent on the excellent libraries of East and North Yorkshire. In particular, I must acknowledge the efforts made on my behalf by the friendly and enthusiastic staff of my local library in Filey, and the staff at Hull Library (Local Studies Department), Beverley Library (Reference Section) and Bridlington Library (Reference Section). Two people in the library service who deserve a special mention are Susan McLaughlin in Bridlington Library, who helped with the selection and copying of wartime photographs of crashed German aircraft and bomb damage in Bridlington, and Alan Moir, the Libraries, Museums and Archives Manager of the East Riding of Yorkshire County Council, who gave his permission for the photographs to be reproduced in this book.

Next, a special world of thanks for the input which I have received from three established authors: Chris Goss, Bill Norman and Simon Parry. I have pestered them on many occasions and their responses have always been good-natured and obliging. The important contributions made by these three professional writers have been greatly appreciated by this raw, but enthusiastic, amateur.

In the course of my research and preparation for this book, I was most fortunate to make contact with a number of ex-RAF aircrew. First, it was John Goldby DFC, ex-bomb aimer with 78 and 640 squadrons, who was on board the Halifax which ditched in Filey Bay. I am deeply indebted to John for his unstinting co-operation, advice and support. It was the same when I met Harry Lomas DFM, former navigator with 158 Sqn, at his home in Driffield. Harry was particularly helpful when I was working on the Luftwaffe's last major operation over East Yorkshire. In March 2002, I was saddened to learn that Harry had died after a short illness; I had only known him for about two years but felt that I had lost a good friend. I last saw Harry shortly before he was taken into hospital and, although he was poorly at the time, he still displayed his usual twinkling sense of humour and, as ever, was most encouraging about my research and proposed publication. Anyone interested in the experiences of a Bomber Command airman in World War Two should read Harry Lomas's excellent book *One Wing High*. Harry kindly gave me permission to use quotes and a crew photograph from his book.

I have not met former RAF pilot Peter French, but have had a number of fascinating conversations with him over the telephone. Peter willingly answered my queries about his forced landing in East Yorkshire and has allowed me to quote from his article *It Started with an Oil Leak*. Other former RAF men who have helped me in one way or another are George Tuohy of Croydon, who was a mid-upper gunner with 158 Sqn at RAF Lissett, and Stuart Leslie of Scalby who served for a time at RAF Driffield with 1484 Flight.

I should also like to acknowledge the considerable input and encouragement I have received from the following individuals: Cec Mowthorpe of Hunmanby, an old family friend and local historian — it was Cec's own publication *A Village at War* which inspired me into embarking on my own literary effort; Lee Norgate of Filey, an aircraft crash site researcher, who has both provided relevant information and also had me along on some of his 'digs'; Charles Weston, former headteacher at Hunmanby County Primary School, who gave me access to the school's Log Book for the war years; Florence Jackson of Clitheroe and her son Michael Watson who passed on some invaluable material relating to Kenneth T. Watson DFC; Norman Cardwell, of Garton-on-the-Wolds, who was so helpful with regard to his mother's bravery; Flight Lieutenants Steve Beanlands, Dave Flett and Dave Gorringe who at various times were stationed at RAF Staxton Wold; Flight Lieutenant Jeremy Caley of 202 Squadron's 'E' Flight at RAF Leconfield; Peter Green, an affable and generous collector of aircraft photographs, of Irby in Lincolnshire;

Val Boyes of Filey, who speedily translated a number of Luftwaffe briefing documents; Anne Wood at the Evening Press in York, who supplied me with the photographs of bomb damage in York; Anne Brittain and Mandy Codd, librarians for the Hull Daily Mail; Barbara Jessop of Leconfield, who not only helped me to locate the grave of P/O R.A. Smith, but also did a marvellous job in cleaning and tidying up the grave in Saint Catherine's churchyard at Leconfield.

Other individuals who have made contributions to this publication are: Ted, Joyce and David Bradshaw of Reighton; J.H.B. 'Dick' Bradshaw of Skipsea; Jack Mallinson of Hunmanby; Chris Coleman of Speeton; Tony Rudd of Nafferton; Tony Harrison — Honorary Secretary of the Royal Air Force Association in Driffield; Bill Kelly — Secretary of the 219 Squadron Association; Tim Kitching of Altofts who has written a history of 219 Squadron; Filonians John Albin, David Baker, Geoff Cappleman, Bill Colling, Rodney Court, David Crimlisk, Michael Fearon, Dick and Jim Haxby, Horace Howard, Doris Marshall, George Smithson, Alan Staveley and Bob Watkinson; former Filonians Colin Ross and John Fleming who now live in Kent and Scotland respectively; Flamborians Norman Hall MBE and David Wilkinson; David Mooney of Bridlington; former Bridlingtonians Brian Colley (now in South Africa) and Bill Skelton (now in Scotland), Colin Cruddas (now in Dorset) Bill Milner who left Driffield for Canada; Irene Megginson of Bishop Wilton; Rodney Robinson of Hornsea; Arthur Credland of the Maritime Museum in Hull who kindly allowed me to use photographs of bomb damage to the city; Friedemann Schell of Germany who supplied much valuable information from Luftwaffe aircrew logbooks; Roy Powell for revealing the story of his top-secret Humberside radar operations and John Cottrell-Smith, who allowed me to use extracts from his diary/ memoirs of his childhood on the Alexandra Dock.

With regard to the final stages in the production of this book, I must sincerely thank my daughter Joanna for typing out the first half of the manuscript, and husband Eric for transferring the hard copy to a CD-Rom, and Denny Stubbs and Kath McLeod of Computer Troubleshooters in Filey for doing the same with the second half.

Last, but no means least, I shall be forever grateful to Barry Ketley, of Flight Recorder Publications in Ottringham, for accepting my book, editing it, providing extra information and photographs and publishing it.

Throughout the research and preparation for this book, my wife Val has tolerated the transformation of our dining room into a study-cum-office-cum-library; this was supposed to have been a temporary arrangement, but it has now prevailed for several years. Thanks Val!

Paul Bright
Filey
North Yorkshire
2005

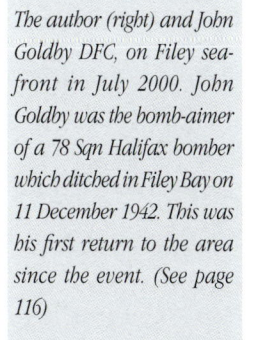

The author (right) and John Goldby DFC, on Filey seafront in July 2000. John Goldby was the bomb-aimer of a 78 Sqn Halifax bomber which ditched in Filey Bay on 11 December 1942. This was his first return to the area since the event. (See page 116)

INTRODUCTION

Memories of a wartime childhood

My primary school days, at the village school in Hunmanby, coincided almost exactly with the years of World War Two. I should have started school on Monday 4 September 1939, but Britain's declaration of war on Germany the previous morning led to the start of the 1939-40 school year in East Yorkshire schools being put back one week until Monday 11 September. When term did get underway, there was an influx of far more pupils into Hunmanby Council School than the headteacher, Mr W.S. Bray, had bargained for. This was due to the arrival in the village of more than 100 evacuees, children moved out of Hull and Middlesbrough – both likely to be attacked by German bombers – into the relative safety of the East Yorkshire countryside. So many boys and girls descended on Hunmanby from Hull (19) and Middlesbrough (86) that the local school had to operate a shift system from Monday 25 September: Hull and Hunmanby children attended school in the mornings while the Middlesbrough youngsters were in school for the afternoon sessions. Similar problems arose for schools in Hornsea (240 evacuees), Withernsea (140) and Aldbrough (55), to mention just a few of the East Riding schools affected by the arrival of large numbers of evacuee children.

When the anticipated air raids on Hull and Middlesbrough failed to materialise during the early months of the war, most of the evacuees returned to their families. After Whitsun 1940, most schools in the East Riding were back to a normal school day.

Sadly, the return home of these evacuees was distinctly premature, especially those from Hull, a city which was to be devastated by German bombs in 1941.

For those children fortunate enough to stay put in the countryside, the war years were, in the main, very interesting times, there was always something different going on. Signposts and railway station nameplates were suddenly taken down, removed so they couldn't aid the movement of spies so we were told. Iron railings were cut down, to become scrap for the war effort. A major event in our village was when the Army arrived to occupy Hunmanby Hall School, a Methodist independent boarding school for girls which had been hastily evacuated after Dunkirk. Soon, marching soldiers, a variety of military vehicles and bugle calls were very much part of village life. Later, outside the village, heavy tanks tore gaping holes in hedgerows while roaring across the Wolds between Hunmanby, Burton Fleming and Wold Newton as they prepared for D-Day and the subsequent advance over the rolling hills of Normandy. Then, of particular interest to local people, there was the arrival at Hunmanby railway station of hundreds of German and Italian prisoners of war, who were marched by armed British soldiers to prisoner of war camps at Burton Fleming and Butterwick.

Despite all these interesting goings-on, it was the aircraft which really caught my imagination during the war years. There always seemed to be aircraft overhead, and as my father was in charge of the village's AFS (Auxiliary Fire Service)[1] unit I had access to the fire station's aircraft recognition cards and wall charts. Although very young at the time, I soon knew the difference between a Hurricane and a Spitfire, a Whitley and a Hampden, and a Junkers 88 and a

4 Above: This is how many people first made their acquaintance with the Spitfire — via the coloured illustrations in packets of Player's cigarettes. These cards were eagerly collected by small boys (and grown-ups) and not only formed the basis of many an aircraft spotter's data base, but inspired others to obtain first hand experience of the aircraft in later years.

[1]*NFS (National Fire Service) as from May 1941.*

Heinkel 111. Also, I could soon distinguish the sound of a Luftwaffe bomber from 'one of ours'. An added bonus was that my father was a mechanic working for the Hunmanby Engineering Company, near the village railway station, and his work often took him to repair lorries which had broken down while engaged in airfield construction work in East Yorkshire. At weekends and in school holidays he would take me with him on airfield jobs and soon such names as Lissett, Melbourne, Holme-on-Spalding Moor and Carnaby became very familiar to me.

With this kind of background and with personal memories of air raid sirens, the sound of enemy bombers overhead, bomb craters and shrapnel, crashing and crashed aircraft, and the dreadful scenes of bomb damage in Hull after major air raids, I decided that one day I would try to find out what had really happened in the skies over East Yorkshire between 1939 and 1945.

When I eventually got my research underway, I quickly discovered that this was not going to be a straightforward short-term operation, especially when I investigated the Battle of Britain period as it affected East Yorkshire. After having read many books and articles on the Battle of Britain, I realised I would have to look beyond such secondary sources in order to obtain the full story. So many publications had completely ignored the air battles over East Yorkshire during the Battle of Britain, while others contained serious inaccuracies with reference to the region.

Eventually, thanks to access to primary sources of information: RAF records at the PRO (Public Record Office)[2] at Kew and the Royal Air Force Museum in Hendon, a number of Luftwaffe documents, and ARP/Police messages and reports held at the County Archives Office in Beverley, I felt that I had at last got much closer to the true story of what had happened in and over East Yorkshire during the Battle of Britain.

A similar situation prevailed when it came to researching certain aspects of RAF and Luftwaffe nighttime activity over the region. Again, it was back to primary sources.

What I have tried to do in this book is to examine the main phases in the air war over East Yorkshire – that is, the East Riding as it was in World War Two, Hull, York, and adjacent coastal waters. Also, to analyse some of the most memorable air dramas to unfold over the region, introduce the reader to some of the leading personalities caught up in the air war, and relate what happened on the ground during major air raids to what was going on in the air in the course of these attacks.

As far as I am aware, this approach has not been attempted before and therefore feel that this publication adds depth and accuracy to existing documentation of certain aspects of life in East Yorkshire during World War Two.

[2] Now the National Archives

5 Top right: *This is the original picture on which the Player's cigarette card illustration was based. It shows the first production Spitfire I, K9787 in 1938. It was later converted to a PR Mk III and was lost on operations on 30 June 1940.*

6 Right: *Many homes in the East Riding acquired a new piece of furniture at the outbreak of war — the Morrison-type air raid shelter. This was basically a steel cage inside which people could take shelter during a raid. It was usually located in a living room where, as here, it could be used as a shelf for the wireless and potted plants.*

1939

From 'Phoney War' to shooting war

The term 'Phoney War' was one coined by an American politician who saw the first six months of World War Two as a period of tedious inactivity. It was a glib, throwaway remark from someone who had apparently expected immediate German attacks on Britain following our declaration of war on Sunday 3 September 1939.

One group of young men who did not share the Senator's observation was the aircrew of 77 and 102 Squadrons flying Armstrong Whitworth Whitley bombers from RAF Driffield. Their first wartime operations over Germany during September and October 1939 were 'Nickel' (leaflet dropping) raids, which entailed dangerous flights of seven hours or more. They may only have been dropping sheets of printed propaganda material but once over enemy territory their aircraft were just as likely to be shot at by German fighters or flak (German anti-aircraft fire). The Driffield-based Whitley crews faced similar dangers when later switched to 'security patrols,' a mixture of reconnaissance flights over German ports and seaplane bases and attacks on enemy shipping. To the Whitley boys there was nothing phoney about these operations; this was real war.

It was well into March 1940 before the so-called 'Phoney War' came to an end following a Luftwaffe bombing raid on Scapa Flow in the Orkneys on 16 March, during which a civilian was killed and several others injured. Four days later, the Whitleys from RAF Driffield joined other Bomber Command Whitleys and Hampdens in attacking German seaplane bases in the Frisian Islands. The RAF bombing campaign against German land targets then intensified with raids on the towns and the cities of Germany's industrial heartland, the Ruhr.

Up to June 1940, only German reconnaissance and anti-shipping aircraft were active over the coast of East Yorkshire and adjacent coastal waters. Then, during the first week in June, Luftwaffe bombers attacked East Yorkshire for the first time in World War Two. The air war over the region was 'hotting up', and the Spitfire fighters of 616 Squadron at RAF Leconfield were soon to be engaged in aerial combat with enemy bombers.

7 Above: *The Observer Corps performed invaluable service throughout the war, visually identifying, tracking and reporting on aircraft movements. In exposed positions on cliffs, buildings and factories, aviation enthusiasts of all ages manned their posts, often for many hours, for they were the only means available for tracking enemy aircraft once they had penetrated the eastwards facing radar screen. Here the man on the left is using a standard Pullin & Co plotting instrument Mk 11B which has not yet been fitted with the Micklethwait Height Correction Attachment. This allowed heights to be corrected between two observer posts and was invented by a member whose name it bore.*
8: *A classic Player's cigarette card showing the Armstrong-Whitworth Whitley bomber in 1938-style camouflage and markings. The wing roundels were intended to be swiftly modified in the event of war.*

9: The winter of 1939-40 was one of the coldest in living memory. The crews of the unheated Whitley bombers suffered terribly from the intense cold — ground crews also as this iced-over aircraft (of 58 Sqn) shows.

10: Inside the cramped fuselage of a Whitley, packs of propaganda leaflets being prepared for dropping over Germany. Both 77 and 102 Squadrons made so many leaflet-dropping flights of this type that they became known as the 'Driffield Bumphleteers' by other Yorkshire-based squadrons.

11 Below: An aerial view of Leconfield looking south showing the main 'C' type hangars on the western side. The areas either side of the runway have been camouflaged to resemble fields.

12: *The Chain Home (CH) station at RAF Danby Beacon on the North York Moors showing the transmitting masts/aerials in the foreground and the receiving masts/aerials beyond. RAF Staxton Wold had a similar arrangement of masts but with three, not four, transmitting masts. (via RAF Staxton Wold).*

13: *RAF Staxton Wold as it looks today.*

14: *A lineup of Spitfire Mk Is immediately before the outbreak of war. These are actually from 19 Sqn, but Leconfield's two 'resident' fighter units during the war, 72 and 616 (South Yorkshire) Sqns would have looked very similar. Two Spitfire Mk Is known to have served with 616 Sqn were L1055 and N3269, also Mk IIa P7435 and P7732.*

Preparations for battle

Following the declaration of war, the immediate threat to East Yorkshire was from the air rather than the sea. Bombing raids by aircraft of the Luftwaffe on military, industrial and commercial targets in Hull and the East Riding appeared inevitable.

So, at the outbreak of World War Two, the question was how effective were the defences of East Yorkshire likely to be in confrontations with the bombers of the Third Reich?

In September 1939 there were three important airfields in East Yorkshire; at Driffield, Leconfield and Catfoss. There were plans to develop a fourth at Cottam, four miles north of Driffield, but the frequency of adverse weather conditions in the circuit over the Yorkshire Wolds led to the rejection of Cottam as an operational airfield.

RAF Driffield, situated a short distance to the west of Great Driffield and on the northern side of the A163 Driffield to Market Weighton road, had been developed and expanded during the 1930s. By September 1939 RAF Driffield was a well-established bomber base with five brick and steel C-type hangars, workshops, accommodation and administration blocks and grass runways. Two Whitley Mk. V bomber squadrons, 77 and 102, were in residence at the station which came under the control of 4 Group Bomber Command, whose HQ was at Heslington Hall near York. RAF Driffield was likely to be high up on the Luftwaffe's list of East Yorkshire targets.

RAF Leconfield, located some two miles north of Beverley and sandwiched between the A164 Beverley to Driffield road and the Hull to Scarborough railway line, had also been developed as a bomber base in the 1930s. However, when war broke out it was not operational having been placed on a care and maintenance footing. But, just one month into the war RAF Leconfield was transferred from 4 Group Bomber Command to 13 Group Fighter Command with 616 (South Yorkshire) Sqn and 72 Sqn in residence, both equipped with Spitfire Is.

RAF Catfoss, to the east of the A165 Hull to Bridlington road near Brandesburton, had functioned as a gunnery and bombing training airfield before the war, using the range off the coast at Skipsea. Rather surprisingly this function ceased when war broke out and the 1 Armament Training School moved on. From October 1939 until May 1940 the airfield was used from time to time by 616 Sqn Spitfires from nearby Leconfield and heavily involved in convoy patrols off the Yorkshire coast. During the Battle of Britain, however, no RAF squadron was based at, or operational from, RAF Catfoss.

Thus, for the early part of the war East Yorkshire had just one fighter station, at Leconfield, to take on any enemy bombers. Any major threat from the air necessitated calling on the fighter squadrons based at RAF Church Fenton in West Yorkshire, RAF Catterick in North Yorkshire or RAF Kirton-in-Lindsey and RAF Digby in Lincolnshire.

There was, however, one other RAF station in East Yorkshire, one which did play a significant part in the defence of the region against the aircraft of the Luftwaffe, but which has remained virtually unknown, namely RAF Staxton Wold.

For some months, people living within a considerable radius of Staxton village had been somewhat mystified by the array of tall masts, which had been constructed along the Wolds skyline at Staxton Wold. A story circulated locally that the masts were there to send out 'death rays' aimed at bringing down any incoming hostile aircraft. This theory was regarded as rubbish by many local folk, but it was in line with the thinking of some 'high ups' at the Air Ministry who were involved in formulating a defence strategy for Britain during the 1930s.

When, however, officials brought the 'death ray' concept to the attention of H.E. Wimperis, Director of Scientific Research at the Air Ministry, he immediately consulted Robert Watson Watt, Head of the Radio Department at the National Physical Laboratory. It did not take Watson Watt long to declare that such a concept was impractical, but he did have his own theory about the 'radio location' of aircraft, a theory which he was anxious to put to the test.

Eventually, on 26 February 1935, the very day when Hitler and Göring were gloating over the creation of the Luftwaffe, Robert Watson Watt and his assistant, Arnold Wilkins, were busy conducting experiments with a device which was to play a crucial part in the defeat of that organisation during the Battle of Britain. These early experiments, carried out in the Northamptonshire countryside at Weedon near Daventry, involved the BBC Daventry transmitter, a Heyford bomber from the Royal Aircraft Establishment at Farnborough in Hampshire and a cathode-ray tube. The exciting results obtained from the Daventry experiment were followed up in May 1935 at Bawdsey Manor, south of Orfordness on the Suffolk coast. By the outbreak of war with Germany on 3 September 1939 a chain of early warning aircraft location stations had been established to guard the southern and eastern coasts of Britain.

This brilliant innovation was initially called RDF (Radio Direction Finding). The term 'radar'[3] was not introduced until September 1943, by the Americans. RADAR is an acronym of RAdio Detection And Ranging. Throughout the remainder of this book we shall stick with 'radar', a word which people are now so familiar with throughout the world. The stations were referred to as RDF stations or Air Ministry Experimental Stations (AMES). Later, these powerful stations, with a range of up to 120 miles, became known as CH (Chain Home) stations.

The mysterious masts at the top of the northern scarp of the Yorkshire Wolds marked the location of the one CH station in East Yorkshire, RAF Staxton

[3] *In fact radar was conceived by a German scientist, Christian Hülsmeyer, as early as 1904 — and which he patented in England!*

15: Germany's Graf Zeppelin, photographed by an RAF pilot while the giant airship was on one of the earliest 'ELINT' (ELectronic INTelligence) gathering missions off the east coasts of England and Scotland, Thursday 3 August 1939.

Wold. At the station there were three 360ft tall steel masts carrying the transmitting aerials on the eastern side of the site and four 240ft wooden masts with receiving aerials to the west of them. There had originally been four steel masts, but one had been dismantled and transported for erection in the Shetland Isles as the Chain Home system was extended northwards. The transmitting and receiving equipment was housed in separate buildings close to their respective masts/aerials. Power was provided by electricity from the National Grid but the base also had emergency generators on site in the event of the mains supply being disrupted.

RAF Staxton Wold's first inkling of suspicious aerial activity off the coast of East Yorkshire actually materialised just one month before war was declared, on Thursday 3 August 1939. Around lunchtime on that day, a radar operator in the receiver block noticed an outsize 'blip' on his cathode-ray tube. Close observation over several minutes suggested that a very large object was flying slowly northwards and approximately 15 miles from the Yorkshire coast. CH stations as far south as the Thames Estuary had been picking up similar responses all morning. Reconnaissance flights by RAF aircraft revealed that it was the German LZ 130, *Graf Zeppelin II*, a 762ft long airship. It is now known that the airship was actually in use as a very well-equipped flying radio laboratory.

It was on a spying mission to investigate and report on any radio transmissions related to the tall masts which had sprung up close to the southern and eastern coasts of Britain, from the Isle of Wight to the north of Scotland. Fortunately for Britain the spy flight failed; as the system operated on different wavelengths to those being used by the Germans in their own embryonic radar systems, the German radio scientists on board the airship assumed that the masts in which they were so interested were normal radio transmitter towers.[4]

In the summer of 1940, a strange looking flying machine became a familiar sight in the sky over Filey Bay. This was an autogiro, based at Church Fenton and flown initially by P/O Westenra. The machine was actually carrying out calibration work for the radar station at Staxton Wold. But, because of its low speed and limited ceiling the autogiro was soon superseded by more conventional aircraft.

Although the CH stations like Staxton Wold were becoming increasingly efficient in detecting high-flying aircraft, they could not accurately detect the position of incoming low-flying planes. Hence the establishment of a second tier of radar stations, the Chain Home Low (CHL) or AMES 2 stations, whose function was to detect and report on any enemy aircraft coming in under the CH cover. In East Yorkshire, CHL stations were constructed on Bempton

[4]Following the disaster to the hydrogen-filled LZ 129 Hindenburg at Lakehurst, USA, on 6 May 1937, all passenger-carrying airship flights were forbidden. There was, therefore, little practical use for the remaining two Zeppelins and both were broken up in 1940 on the direct order of Hermann Göring.

16: In November 1939 it was decided that the vital work of calibration of the Chain Home radar system should be undertaken by the Cierva Autogiro Co, under the control of test pilot R.A. Brie. On 1 May 1940 the unit became 1448 Rota Calibration Flight and was attached to 19 Sqn at Duxford. The Cierva/Avro C.30A autogiros used by the unit were fitted with special tail aerials and a calibrating radio transmitter, as seen on this example at Duxford in July 1940. It is either K4232, k4233 or K4235.

17: *Britain's RDF (radar) network as it existed in the summer of 1940.*

◆ Chain Home stations
◆ Chain Home Low

Cliffs, just west of where the RSPB Reserve is now located, and at Easington on the low, flat Holderness coastline some twenty miles east-south-east of Hull.

To enable the radar operators at CH and CHL stations to distinguish between incoming enemy aircraft and RAF planes, the latter were fitted with IFF (Identification Friend or Foe) transmitters, which produced a distinctive elongated blip on the cathode-ray tube display. Plots of approaching enemy aircraft, referred to as 'hostiles', were passed by land line from radar stations to the Filter Room at Bentley Priory, Fighter Command HQ at Stanmore in Middlesex. There, all incoming information was swiftly analysed and important detail passed on to the relevant Fighter Command Group HQ and then the Sector HQ. With regard to East Yorkshire, prior to August 1940 details of enemy aircraft encroaching on the region went first to 13 Group HQ at Newcastle and then to the Sector HQ at Church Fenton from where orders would go out to the sector airfield at Leconfield. From August 1940, however, control switched to 12 Group which meant that Fighter Command HQ's first

13

contact was with 12 Group HQ at Watnall, north of Nottingham, before information was passed on to Church Fenton and Leconfield as before.

Reference must be made at this point to the invaluable work done by members of the Observer Corps (Royal Observer Corps from 1941). These were volunteers who regularly spent hours of considerable discomfort at their open posts – a cliff top, in the middle of a field, at the top of a church or some other kind of tower – plotting the movement of enemy aircraft after the latter had crossed our coastline inbound. Vital information was then relayed to the Regional Observer Corps HQ, which in the case of East Yorkshire was at York, who would then contact the Sector HQ airfield, Church Fenton.

It was highly probable that the two operational RAF airfields at Driffield and Leconfield, plus the radar base at Staxton Wold would become targets for the Luftwaffe bombers. Consequently, ground defences for these stations, provided initially by the Army, were vital and had been established before the first bombs fell on East Yorkshire. At RAF Driffield, there were four heavy 3.7inch AA (anti-aircraft) guns and two light 40mm AA guns manned by the Royal Artillery. In addition, there were two twin Lewis guns on the Station HQ roof and several machine gun posts around the perimeter of the airfield, all manned by first the Green Howards and then the East Yorkshire Regiment. There were three light AA quick-fire Bofors guns at RAF Leconfield and two at RAF Staxton Wold manned by the Royal Artillery and, as at Driffield, machine gun positions around the perimeters of both stations and manned during the early part of the war by troops from Yorkshire regiments.

Away from the RAF stations it was considered necessary to locate four light AA guns at Brough, eight miles west of Hull, to protect the important Blackburn Aircraft Company's factory and airstrip from aerial bombardment. But the greatest concentration of AA guns in the region was to the east of Hull which at that time was Britain's third port and, with its docks and warehouses, factories, flour mills and oil storage facilities, was likely to be a prime target for the German bombers. During the first few months of the war there were some forty AA guns protecting Hull but this number increased as the number of air raids escalated to a peak in 1941. The main AA batteries were close to Spurn Point, at Kilnsea, Sunk Island, Halsham, west of Rise, between Atwick and Hornsea and near Welwick, Preston and Hedon.

The AA batteries could handle daylight air attacks on their own, but at night they depended heavily on the searchlight units whose job was to illuminate enemy aircraft for the guns and our night fighters. There were also more than seventy barrage balloons around Hull raised to over 5,000 ft and designed to deter the Luftwaffe pilots from making low level attacks on the city. Most of these balloons were land-based, but some were also launched from vessels moored in the Humber.

We have already seen how priority was given to defending the region against attacks from the air, but this did not mean that coastal defences to counter any attempts at a seaborne invasion were completely overlooked. Although plans were afoot in 1939 for the construction of pillboxes and various anti-tank devices along the coast of East Yorkshire, work on such schemes did not get underway in earnest until the summer of 1940. Then, following the British evacuation from Dunkirk, the capitulation of France and the German occupation of the Channel Islands, an enemy invasion of the British mainland became a very real possibility.

The construction of such lines of defence along the coast and adjacent to roads leading inland, demanded a monumental effort and necessitated close co-operation between the Army and civilian building contractors. In East Yorkshire, from Filey Brigg south to Spurn Head, there was frantic activity as concrete pillboxes and gun emplacements were constructed

Facts:
Two of the most popular songs of 1939 were Vera Lynn's We'll Meet Again *and Flanagan and Allen's* We're Going to Hang Out the Washing on the Siegfried Line. *Clark Gable and Vivien Leigh starred in the classic film* Gone with the Wind. *Milk cost 3d (1.5p) per pint – and Yorkshire were County Cricket Champions.*

17: *In September 1939 there were 30 heavy anti-aircraft guns with the 2nd HAA Division, tasked with defending Hull and the Humber. By July 1940 there were 38. These were supported by batteries of searchlights such as shown here. This is a 90cm model, one of the three standard sizes in use in 1939-40; the others were the elderly 120cm and the modern 150cm type mounted on a four-wheel trailer. At first the lights were aimed by sound locators; radar-directed lights did not make an appearance until much later in the war.*

18: *Apart from guns and searchlights, Hull was also defended by a Balloon Barrage forming 942 Balloon Sqn. On 1 July 1940 this consisted of 36 balloons, spread between Hessle and Fort Paull, 14 of which were waterborne 'mobiles', as seen here on the barge* Norman Wade. *At the end of July there were 74 balloons, 24 of them waterborne. The crews of these vessels had the unenviable job of sitting out air raids in the middle of the Humber. By the end of 1941 many of the land-based crews consisted of women in the WAAF, who proved the equal of men in the task.*

19: *By mid-1940, even the Daily Mirror's comic heroine, Jane, had joined the Forces, but she still managed to regularly show plenty of leg, thereby raising the morale of many thousands of servicemen! Later still, her value was recognised by the American services magazine* Roundup, *which noted, 'Well sirs, you can go home now. Jane peeled a week ago. The British 36th Division immediately gained six miles.'*

20: *Probably the most effective 'light' anti-aircraft gun available to the British was the highly effective 40mm Swedish-designed Bofors gun seen here. In March 1940, however, there were only 108 in the entire country — some 4,000 short of what was felt to be necessary. On 11 July that year there were none at all defending Hull, but a few were found to protect the vital RAF stations at Driffield and Staxton Wold and the Blackburn Aircraft factory at Brough. Considerable numbers of light machine guns were, however, in use.*

15

21: Soldiers of the Royal Engineers building coastal defences. In 1940, these would have presented a far more formidable barrier to German forces attempting a landing when they lacked the many specialist armoured vehicles and equipment available to Allied forces who faced similar obstacles in France in June 1944.

22: The Humber was defended by two of the heaviest guns available in 1940; namely the Mk 9 or 10 9.2 inch coastal artillery pieces at Spurn Head. These dated from 1880, but were retained in use until 1956. Potentially highly effective counter-bombardment guns, they had a range of over 20 miles, firing a 380lb HE shell. As seen here, it took four men to carry the shell, although this was only as far as the ammunition store, loading being mechanical. Standing orders were not to open fire until any invaders were within 3-4 miles of the coast so as to give them as little time as possible to respond.

23: An aerial view of Spurn Head, a key landfall point for raiding Luftwaffe bombers. The two 9.2 inch guns were installed in rotating barbettes, emplaced in well camouflaged concrete pits, with the barrel just clearing a parapet. The remains of some of these defences can still be seen at Spurn Head today, although all guns have long since gone. (Simmons Aerofilms A214928)

24: Aircraft recognition was pitifully inadequate at the outbreak of war, being almost totally neglected by the armed forces. Indeed, it was so bad that the first aircraft shot down over this country in World War II were two Hurricanes of 56 Sqn shot down by Spitfires of 74 Sqn. There was a self-evident urgent need for everyone to be able to tell 'ours' from 'theirs' and the result was a number of books similar to this one from Real Photographs which gave fairly accurate information on aircraft of the time.

along cliff tops, while anti-tank blocks, coils of barbed wire and lengths of steel scaffolding were installed at the foot of cliffs and along beaches. Also, in some places, minefields were laid in the lower clay cliffs while many slipways to the beach were blown up. The construction of pillboxes, gun emplacements and anti-tank blocks was done by civilian building contractors, while the laying of the barbed wire and minefields, the erection of the scaffolding structures and the destruction of slipways was usually carried out by the Royal Engineers.

Army camps sprang up at regular intervals in the coastal zone, their troops manning the AA guns, searchlights, pillboxes and gun emplacements and carrying out patrols along the cliffs and beaches. Their numbers could be augmented at any time by local units of the Home Guard.

Then there were the coastal batteries, equipped with large heavy guns, to challenge any attack from the sea on the Humber area. These were located near Spurn Point, east of Kilnsea, at Sunk Island and on the two island forts at the mouth of the Humber. Most of their guns were of the 6 inch variety which could fire a 100lb shell more than 10 miles out to sea, but the most powerful guns in East Yorkshire were the two 9.2 inch monsters at the Godwin Battery near Kilnsea. They fired a 380lb shell and had a range of over 15 miles.

Brave contributions to the defence of the region were also made by local fishing crews. Although Royal Navy warships and RAF aircraft were constantly in action carrying out convoy patrols, providing protection for Merchant Navy ships bringing in vital supplies of food, fuel and raw materials, many Hull trawlers contributed to the cause by acting as minesweepers and clearing shipping lanes off the Yorkshire coast and in the Humber Estuary. Furthermore, the larger trawlers and drifters had light AA guns fitted to their decks thus enabling crews to retaliate against enemy aircraft. Many smaller fishing vessels were armed with less powerful weaponry so that they could 'hit back' whenever possible.

Finally, the contribution of the various Civil Defence services across the region should not be forgotten.

The train lurched to a halt at the platform, to the empty stares of a small group of soldiers, abjectly waiting in some shade provided by the station-master's office. Two of the group climbed wearily into our carriage, their infantry uniforms filthy with mud and oil. One man had no cap but carried a rifle and a crumpled paper bag; the other a half empty kit-bag. These men had just returned from Dunkirk and were on their way to their depot. The lad with the kit-bag was obviously strongly religious, for he rummaged in his bag and produced a Bible and started reading it. He then told my mother that he was sure that he would die soon, upon which both of my parents hastened to reassure him that he would not. The other soldier cheerfully told him to 'brighten up, 'cause things can't get any worse!'
A fussy woman in the corner enquired 'but what if they come over the Channel?'
'The navy'll stop the buggers, don't you worry', said the soldier with the rifle.

John Cottrell-Smith's diary

17

25: An outpost on an unidentified East Yorkshire cliff-top, manned by soldiers equipped with the excellent Bren light machine-gun. This had its origins in a Czech design, much developed by the Royal Small Arms Factory at Enfield which gave it its name (BRno in Czechoslovakia/ENfield). 30,000 were in service by 1940, although many were lost at Dunkirk. It was a superb gun: robust, reliable, easy to handle and maintain, not too heavy and capable of firing 500 rounds per minute at low-flying aircraft.

26: A closer view of the Bren Mk IV, introduced in 1944. It is almost identical to the Mk I seen above, apart from a simpler rear sight and a slightly shorter barrel. Some armies still use the Bren.

In the event of major air raids the efforts of Civil Defence workers, most of them part-time volunteers, were to prove invaluable to their communities.

Apart from full-time personnel in the police, fire service and medical services, thousands of ordinary civilians in East Yorkshire donned uniforms of one kind or another to 'do their bit'. This included enrolling as a Special Constable, joining the AFS (Auxiliary Fire Service) or LDV (Local Defence Volunteers) — later the Home Guard — or becoming an ARP (Air Raid Precautions) Warden or Rescue Worker. Some, with knowledge of first aid, joined a First Aid Party or became an ambulance driver, while others made their contributions as telephonists.

A voluntary organisation which was prepared to brave air raids and play a very active role on the Home Front was the WVS (Women's Voluntary Service). WVS members were ready to take on a wide range of duties, from operating mobile canteens and field kitchens to manning Rest Centres and Clothing Depots and caring for people who had been bombed out of their homes. Other voluntary organisations ready for action in the event of air raids included the British Red Cross, the Order of Saint John of Jerusalem and the Friends' Ambulance Unit.

Finally, there were the messengers, young people (some still at school) who by bicycle or on foot were to maintain contact between Civil Defence Services and Report Centres in the event of telephone lines being brought down in an air raid. These were remarkably courageous youngsters who proved to be prepared to risk their lives in delivering messages as bombs fell and exploded and buildings collapsed around them.

So, East Yorkshire was ready, but where and when would the Germans strike? Although a seaborne invasion was never ruled out, such a strategy seemed highly unlikely without the Luftwaffe first destroying the aircraft and airfields of the RAF.

The *Luftwaffe*, the new German Air Force, which had been created in 1935, was certain to play a major role in any conflict between Britain and Germany. But the question remained; how serious was the Luftwaffe threat to East Yorkshire? Which airfields would the enemy bombers fly from, which German aircraft would feature in an air offensive against the region and what types of bombs would they deliver?

27 Right: Young children being prepared for evacuation to the country, each carrying a bag of clothing, a gas mask in a box and an identity label.

28 Far right: Families building their Anderson air raid shelters — sheets of corrugated steel bolted together embedded in the garden and covered with soil.

Issued by the Ministry of Information in co-operation with the War Office and the Ministry of Home Security.

If the INVADER comes

WHAT TO DO — AND HOW TO DO IT

THE Germans threaten to invade Great Britain. If they do so they will be driven out by our Navy, our Army and our Air Force. Yet the ordinary men and women of the civilian population will also have their part to play. Hitler's invasions of Poland, Holland and Belgium were greatly helped by the fact that the civilian population was taken by surprise. They did not know what to do when the moment came. *You must not be taken by surprise.* This leaflet tells you what general line you should take. More detailed instructions will be given you when the danger comes nearer. Meanwhile, read these instructions carefully and be prepared to carry them out.

I

When Holland and Belgium were invaded, the civilian population fled from their homes. They crowded on the roads, in cars, in carts, on bicycles and on foot, and so helped the enemy by preventing their own armies from advancing against the invaders. You must not allow that to happen here. Your first rule, therefore, is :—

(1) IF THE GERMANS COME, BY PARACHUTE, AEROPLANE OR SHIP, YOU MUST REMAIN WHERE YOU ARE. THE ORDER IS "STAY PUT".

If the Commander in Chief decides that the place where you live must be evacuated, he will tell you when and how to leave. Until you receive such orders you must remain where you are. If you run away, you will be exposed to far greater danger because you will be machine-gunned from the air as were civilians in Holland and Belgium, and you will also block the roads by which our own armies will advance to turn the Germans out.

II

There is another method which the Germans adopt in their invasion. They make use of the civilian population in order to create confusion and panic. They spread false rumours and issue false instructions. In order to prevent this, you should obey the second rule, which is as follows :—

(2) DO NOT BELIEVE RUMOURS AND DO NOT SPREAD THEM. WHEN YOU RECEIVE AN ORDER, MAKE QUITE SURE THAT IT IS A TRUE ORDER AND NOT A FAKED ORDER. MOST OF YOU KNOW YOUR POLICEMEN AND YOUR A.R.P. WARDENS BY SIGHT, YOU CAN TRUST THEM. IF YOU KEEP YOUR HEADS, YOU CAN ALSO TELL WHETHER A MILITARY OFFICER IS REALLY BRITISH OR ONLY PRETENDING TO BE SO. IF IN DOUBT ASK THE POLICEMAN OR THE A.R.P. WARDEN. USE YOUR COMMON SENSE.

III

The Army, the Air Force and the Local Defence Volunteers cannot be everywhere at once. The ordinary man and woman must be on the watch. If you see anything suspicious, do not rush round telling your neighbours all about it. Go at once to the nearest policeman, police-station, or military officer and tell them exactly what you saw. Train yourself to notice the exact time and place where you saw anything suspicious, and try to give exact information. Try to check your facts. The sort of report which a military or police officer wants from you is something like this :—

"At 5.30 p.m. to-night I saw twenty cyclists come into Little Squashborough from the direction of Great Mudtown. They carried some sort of automatic rifle or gun. I did not see anything like artillery. They were in grey uniforms."

Be calm, quick and exact. The third rule, therefore, is as follows :—

(3) KEEP WATCH. IF YOU SEE ANYTHING SUSPICIOUS, NOTE IT CAREFULLY AND GO AT ONCE TO THE NEAREST POLICE OFFICER OR STATION, OR TO THE NEAREST MILITARY OFFICER. DO NOT RUSH ABOUT SPREADING VAGUE RUMOURS. GO QUICKLY TO THE NEAREST AUTHORITY AND GIVE HIM THE FACTS.

IV

Remember that if parachutists come down near your home, they will not be feeling at all brave. They will not know where they are, they will have no food, they will not know where their companions are. They will want you to give them food, means of transport and maps. They will want you to tell them where they have landed, where their comrades are, and where our own soldiers are. The fourth rule, therefore, is as follows :—

(4) DO NOT GIVE ANY GERMAN ANYTHING. DO NOT TELL HIM ANYTHING. HIDE YOUR FOOD AND YOUR BICYCLES. HIDE YOUR MAPS. SEE THAT THE ENEMY GETS NO PETROL. IF YOU HAVE A CAR OR MOTOR BICYCLE, PUT IT OUT OF ACTION WHEN NOT IN USE. IT IS NOT ENOUGH TO REMOVE THE IGNITION KEY; YOU MUST MAKE IT USELESS TO ANYONE EXCEPT YOURSELF.

IF YOU ARE A GARAGE PROPRIETOR, YOU MUST WORK OUT A PLAN TO PROTECT YOUR STOCK OF PETROL AND YOUR CUSTOMERS' CARS. REMEMBER THAT TRANSPORT AND PETROL WILL BE THE INVADER'S MAIN DIFFICULTIES. MAKE SURE THAT NO INVADER WILL BE ABLE TO GET HOLD OF YOUR CARS, PETROL, MAPS OR BICYCLES.

V

You may be asked by Army and Air Force officers to help in many ways. For instance, the time may come when you will receive orders to block roads or streets in order to prevent the enemy from advancing. Never block a road unless you are told which one you must block. Then you can help by felling trees, wiring them together or blocking the roads with cars. Here, therefore, is the fifth rule :—

(5) BE READY TO HELP THE MILITARY IN ANY WAY. BUT DO NOT BLOCK ROADS UNTIL ORDERED TO DO SO BY THE MILITARY OR L.D.V. AUTHORITIES.

VI

If you are in charge of a factory, store or other works, organise its defence at once. If you are a worker, make sure that you understand the system of defence that has been organised and know what part you have to play in it. Remember always that parachutists and fifth column men are powerless against any organised resistance. They can only succeed if they can create disorganisation. Make certain that no suspicious strangers enter your premises.

You must know in advance who is to take command, who is to be second in command, and how orders are to be transmitted. This chain of command must be built up and you will probably find that ex-officers or N.C.O.'s, who have been in emergencies before, are the best people to undertake such command. The sixth rule is therefore as follows :—

(6) IN FACTORIES AND SHOPS, ALL MANAGERS AND WORKMEN SHOULD ORGANISE SOME SYSTEM NOW BY WHICH A SUDDEN ATTACK CAN BE RESISTED.

VII

The six rules which you have now read give you a general idea of what to do in the event of invasion. More detailed instructions may, when the time comes, be given you by the Military and Police Authorities and by the Local Defence Volunteers; they will NOT be given over the wireless as that might convey information to the enemy. These instructions must be obeyed at once.

Remember always that the best defence of Great Britain is the courage of her men and women. Here is your seventh rule :—

(7) THINK BEFORE YOU ACT. BUT THINK ALWAYS OF YOUR COUNTRY BEFORE YOU THINK OF YOURSELF.

---

29 Above: Many civilians were removed from areas thought to be likely landing places of the Germans, but in June 1940, mindful of the chaos caused by fleeing refugees in France, the government here issued every household with this ominous leaflet.

30 Right: The members of Keyingham Home Guard. How they might have fared against the legions of the SS is, thankfully, a question that remains unanswered, but they provided a key element of the Home Forces.

31: From the beginning women played a vital role in the British war effort. Here members of the ATS — Auxiliary Territorial Service — the women's section of the army, deliver supplies to a camp 'somewhere in England.' Not long afterwards they took on far more aggressive roles, many manning (?) anti-aircraft and searchlight batteries, thereby freeing men for front-line roles. In fact to be on an AA gun emplacement in East Yorkshire under German bombs often was the front-line. Even HM Queen Elizabeth II was a member.

32: Another organisation in which many East Yorkshire women played an essential part was the Womens' Land Army, which took over much of the back-breaking agricultural work on local farms, traditionally done by men. Here a group of trainees are learning the art of ploughing with the aid of the ubiquitous Fordson tractor.

Following the collapse of France, the vast Luftwaffe organisation had been divided up into five huge *Luftflotten* (Air Fleets): Luftflotten 1 and 4 were based in Germany, Poland and Czechoslovakia and were unlikely to participate in air attacks on Britain; Luftflotte 2 controlled Luftwaffe activity from northern France, Belgium, Holland and northern Germany and had bombers capable of raiding targets in East Yorkshire. Luftflotte 3 was confined to north-west France and was likely to concentrate on strikes against London, south-east and south-west England. Luftflotte 5 was based in German-occupied Denmark and Norway and seemed the most likely to be involved in raiding Yorkshire.

The largest operational unit within the Luftwaffe was the Geschwader, which, in theory, could have 90–120 aircraft at its disposal. Due to technical problems, training accidents and operational losses, however, the number of a Geschwader's aircraft participating in a major operation could be greatly reduced. Often just two of the Gruppen would be operational.

Each Geschwader was given a prefix according to its particular function:
JG *Jagdgeschwader* Fighter Group
St.G *Stukageschwader* Dive-bombing Group
NJG *Nachtjagdgeschwader* Nightfighter Group
KG *Kampfgeschwader* Bomber Group
LG *Lehrgeschwader* Instructional/Technical Development Group
ZG *Zerstörergeschwader* Heavy fighter Group
Two smaller operational units were:
Aufkl.Gr *Aufklärungsgruppe* Reconnaissance Wing
Kü.Fl.Gr *Küstenfliegergruppe* Anti-shipping Wing (these were under the control of the German Navy)

Although the main threat to East Yorkshire undoubtedly came from the bomber units, some reconnaissance aircraft also carried bombs, which could be dropped along our coast at the end of a mission. Similarly, the maritime reconnaissance units were

33 Far right: The part played by women pilots in the ATA — Air Transport Auxiliary — which fetched and ferried every type of aircraft used by the RAF all over the country must also be mentioned. Among its ranks was Hull's most famous daughter, Amy Johnson, who lost her life in that service. The unknown lady seen here is carrying a standard RAF C-Type parachute.

34: The location of the main Luftwaffe bases and units which took part in attacks against East Yorkshire.

able and willing to bomb coastal targets if they had failed to locate any shipping to attack. Neither the fighters nor dive-bombers had the range to reach East Yorkshire. As for the *Zerstörer* ('destroyer' — heavy fighter) units, the Junkers Ju 88Cs were certain to be in action over the region, attacking RAF aircraft as they were taking off or landing and strafing their airfields. The Luftwaffe's principal heavy fighter at the outbreak of war, the Messerschmitt Bf 110C, was, however, destined not to play a significant part in the air war over East Yorkshire.

The accompanying map shows the main airfields from which the Luftwaffe bombers launched their first operations across East Yorkshire. KG 26, the *Löwen* (Lion) Geschwader, was based at Stavanger in Norway and equipped with Heinkel He 111H aircraft. Aalborg in Denmark was the home of KG 30, the *Adler* (Eagle) Geschwader, flying Ju 88As. The bombers of KG 4, the *General Wever* Geschwader, were based in Holland, the I Gruppe at Soesterberg with Heinkel He 111Hs, II Gruppe at Eindhoven with similar aircraft, and III Gruppe at Schipol (Amsterdam) using Ju 88As. KG 26 aircraft also operated briefly from airfields near Schleswig and Lübeck in northern Germany during the early years of the war.

With regard to German bomb loads, during the early part of the war Luftwaffe bomber units could select from 1 and 2kg incendiary bombs ('IBs') and 50, 250 and 500kg high explosive bombs ('HEs'). As the war progressed, the Luftwaffe acquired a far greater range of bombs, from small anti-personnel devices to highly destructive parachute mines. Perhaps the biggest uncertainty for the people of Britain was whether the Germans were prepared to launch poison gas attacks against the country's civilian population.

And so the highly-organised and well-equipped Luftwaffe was set to make its menacing appearance in the skies over East Yorkshire. Inevitably, this was to bring the Luftwaffe bombers into conflict with the fighters of the Royal Air Force.

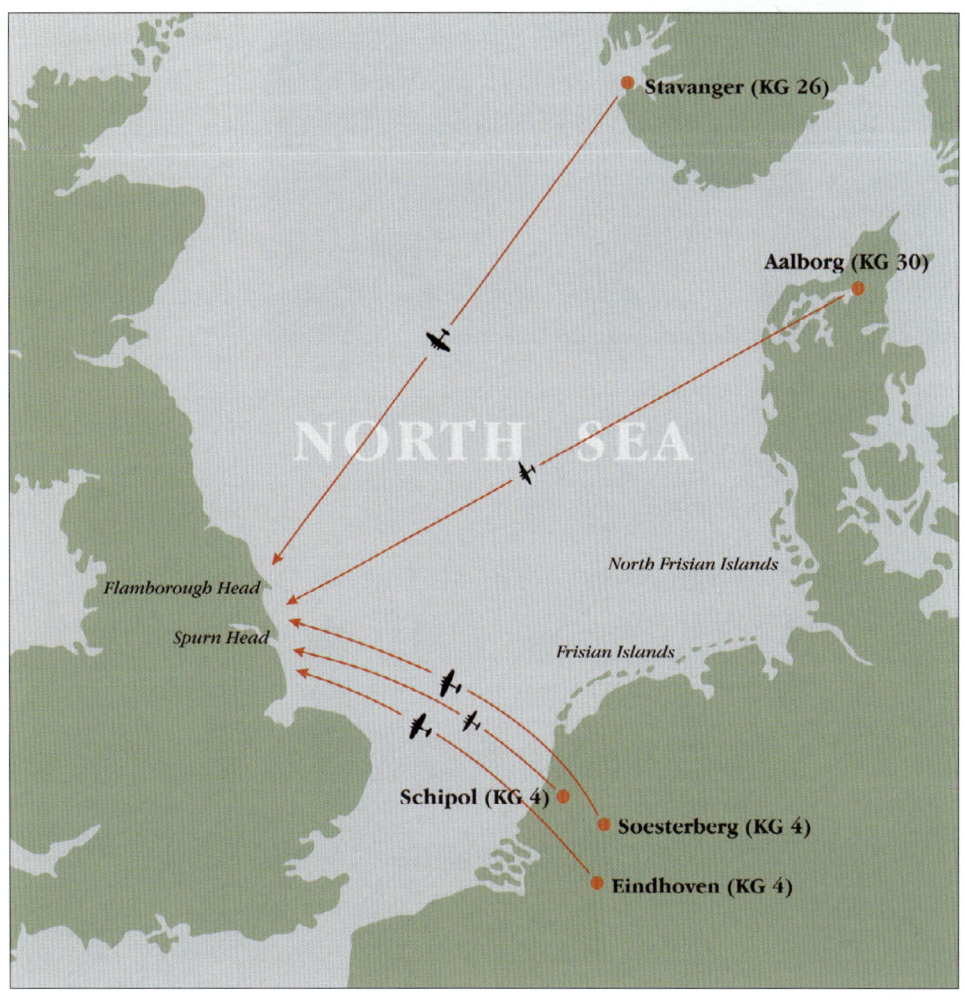

35: A Royal Navy mine demolition team removing the explosives from a German mine washed up on the Yorkshire coast. The mine seen here appears to be an EMD type.

Facts:
The Lewis gun was invented by an American, Col Isaac Lewis in 1912. It weighed 27lb (12.25kg). Rejected by the Americans, the first customer was the Belgian army. The British soon bought them and used many thousands by the end of World War I, when it was estimated that Lewis guns had caused 80% of German casualties. After Dunkirk stockpiled guns were issued to the army, Royal Navy, RAF, Home Guard and, as here, merchant ships and fishing vessels. They were declared obsolete in 1945.

36: Some smaller fishing vessels had a Lewis machine-gun mounted on deck as seen here on the steam drifter Silver Line. Seated at the gun is Tom Watkinson of Filey, possibly the first East Yorkshire civilian to 'have a go' at an enemy aircraft. This was on 3 April 1940 when he fired at a low-flying Heinkel He 111, which had already been critically damaged by a 41 Sqn Spitfire piloted by F/Lt. Norman Ryder. The five German airmen in the Heinkel were later rescued by the vessel and landed at Scarborough. With Tom Watkinson are fellow Filonians (from left to right), Ted Robinson, Bill Watkinson and Charlie Hunter.

37: The Humber ferry continued to operate the essential link between the north and south banks of the Humber throughout the war. Unlike many similar vessels on the south coast, the Humber paddle ferries were never requisitioned for naval use. This is Tattershall Castle. Her sister ship was the Wingfield Castle.

38 Above: *A Heinkel He 115C model, coded K6+EH, of 1./Kü.Fl.Gr 406 in flight off the Norwegian coastline. It is typical of the aircraft which made nocturnal visits to the Humber estuary to lay their deadly mines in the early years of the war. This version has a forward-firing 20mm cannon mounted under the nose, but earlier models were not so heavily armed. The battered paintwork is a result of the harsh conditions in which maritime aircraft in the North Sea had to operate.*

[5]*The difference in unit codes between the aircraft above and this one can be accounted for by a change in unit designations which took place in October 1939.*

39 Far right: *Flamborough policeman Thomas H. Loft of the East Riding Constabulary with a German sea mine (probably a UMB type), minus its deadly 'horns' – spikes which were supposed to detonate the mine when in contact with a ship. This mine was washed up at South Landing on Flamborough Head during the first year of World War II.*

EARLY COMBATS
The first bombs — and a heroine at Aldbrough

During the first few months of the war there was considerable enemy activity off the coast of East Yorkshire; shipping was attacked and mines were laid in the Humber Estuary. Also, German aircraft conducted regular reconnaissance flights over the region, photographing likely targets and probing our defences. As a result of all this Luftwaffe activity, the rising and falling wail of air raid sirens became a familiar sound, especially in Hull, although the expected air raids did not materialise in 1939.

On two occasions during the first three months of World War Two, people living on or close to the Holderness coast were startled and frightened by two very loud explosions. These were not caused by German bombs, however, but were the result of German sea mines washing up and exploding; one at Bridlington on Monday 30 October 1939 and the other at Aldbrough on Saturday 4 November 1939. In both instances there was some damage to property but no casualties. A number of sea mines also drifted ashore without detonating and were successfully dealt with by British bomb disposal teams.

The attacks on shipping and the mine-laying operations were carried out by Küstenfliegergruppe (literally coastal flying units) aircraft operating from Norway, Holland and northern Germany. The Küstenfliegergruppe was a branch of the Luftwaffe which worked very closely with the Kriegsmarine (German Navy); in fact many of the Kü.Fl.Gr. pilots were naval men attached to the Luftwaffe. The addition of *zur See* to an officer's rank, eg. *Leutnant zur See* Kemper, denoted a naval officer flying with the Luftwaffe.

It was hardly surprising that the first German aircraft to be destroyed off the coast of East Yorkshire was a Kü.Fl.Gr machine. This was during the afternoon of Saturday 21 October 1939 when a Heinkel He 115B float plane of 1./Kü.Fl.Gr 406, S4+EH[5], from List, was shot down off the Humber Estuary. There is some uncertainty as to which RAF pilot was responsible for the destruction of this aircraft. A brace of Spitfires from 72 Sqn's 'B' Flight at RAF Leconfield plus six Hurricanes of 46 Sqn's 'A' Flight, normally based at RAF Digby, but operating on this occasion from RAF North Coates on the Lincolnshire coast, were all engaged in combat with enemy floatplanes off Spurn Head and the Humber that afternoon. The fact that the Heinkel crashed into the sea at approximately 1500 hours, however, and the 46 Sqn Hurricanes were not involved in combat until after that time suggests that S4+EH fell to the guns of the Spitfires piloted by F/O Desmond Sheen (K9959) and F/

O Thomas Elsdon (K9940) of 72 Sqn. The Heinkel's crew of *Oblt zur See* Heinz Schlicht, *Lt* F. Meyer and *Uffz* B. Wessels were all killed in the crash.

The Heinkel He 115 float plane pilots were daring young men who frequently landed their aircraft in the Humber Estuary in order to ensure that their mines were accurately positioned in shipping lanes. These aircraft were, however, no match for British fighters and, after heavy losses, were quickly withdrawn from service with the Luftwaffe over the North Sea.

Across East Yorkshire, 1940 started as 1939 had ended…quietly. In fact the first six or seven weeks of the year constituted one of the quietest periods of the war as heavy snow swept across the region. Up on the Yorkshire Wolds, farms and villages were cut off for lengthy periods, and elsewhere main roads and the Hull to Scarborough railway line were blocked for a time. At RAF airfields in East Yorkshire, the Whitley bombers of 77 and 102 Squadrons were grounded at Driffield, as were the 616 Sqn Spitfires at Leconfield. The RAF station most seriously affected by the severity of the weather, however, was the Chain Home radar base at Staxton Wold. With Site 'A', the technical site, being located on a plateau high up on the Yorkshire Wolds and Site 'B', the domestic site, being situated at the foot of the chalk escarpment, movement between the two sites became a physical ordeal. The notorious Staxton Hill was frequently impassable to motor vehicles, resulting in supplies and equipment for the technical site having to be carried or dragged on sledges up the steep scarp slope by service personnel. Soldiers involved in ground defences at Site 'A' also had a miserable time, carrying out their foot patrols through knee-deep snow and having to endure the lowest temperatures in the region for more than fifty years.

Fortunately, across the North Sea, the bases of Luftflotte 5 had been similarly affected by adverse weather conditions and there was therefore little Luftwaffe activity over the North of England during that dreadful winter of 1940.

In early February 1940 there was, however, an incident which helped to temporarily lift the wintry misery and gloom for civilians and service personnel alike. This was on Saturday 3 February when a German bomber was shot down near Whitby. The aircraft, Arado-built Heinkel He 111H-3 1H+FM (*Werk Nr* 2323) of 4./KG 26, operating from Schleswig in northern Germany on an anti-shipping operation, had been detected by RAF Staxton Wold's sister CH radar station at Danby Beacon on the North York Moors. The Heinkel was quickly located and shot down by three Hurricanes of 43 Sqn's Yellow Section based at RAF Acklington in Northumberland. Blistering gunfire from the Hurricanes, piloted by F/Lt Peter Townsend, F/O 'Tiger' Folkes and Sgt Jim Hallowes[6], soon disabled the He 111 causing it to lose height and only just struggle over the roof tops at Whitby before coming down in a field. The bomber then slithered on its belly through deep snow before smashing into a row of trees and coming to rest next to Bannial Flat Farm, two miles west of Whitby. Two of the Heinkel's crew had been mortally wounded during the combat, a third later had a leg amputated and only the aircraft's pilot, *Uffz* Hermann Wilms, escaped unhurt.

Although this action took place some twenty miles to the north of East Yorkshire, a brief account of the incident has been included in this chapter

40 Far left: *F/Lt Peter Townsend, destined to become a fighter 'ace' during the Battle of Britain. Townsend had East Yorkshire connections, having attended a gunnery course at RAF Catfoss before the war. In later years he was romantically linked to HRH Princess Margaret, much to the annoyance of the Establishment of the time.*

41 Left: *The emblem of KG 26 on a shot-down Heinkel He 111 showing why it was known as the Löwen (Lion) Geschwader.*

[6]*Hallowes in L1847, FT-J Townsend in L2116, FT-?*

42: *The wreck of He 111H-3 1H+FM of 4./KG 26 at a wintry Bannial Flat Farm, which obviously had a lucky escape.*

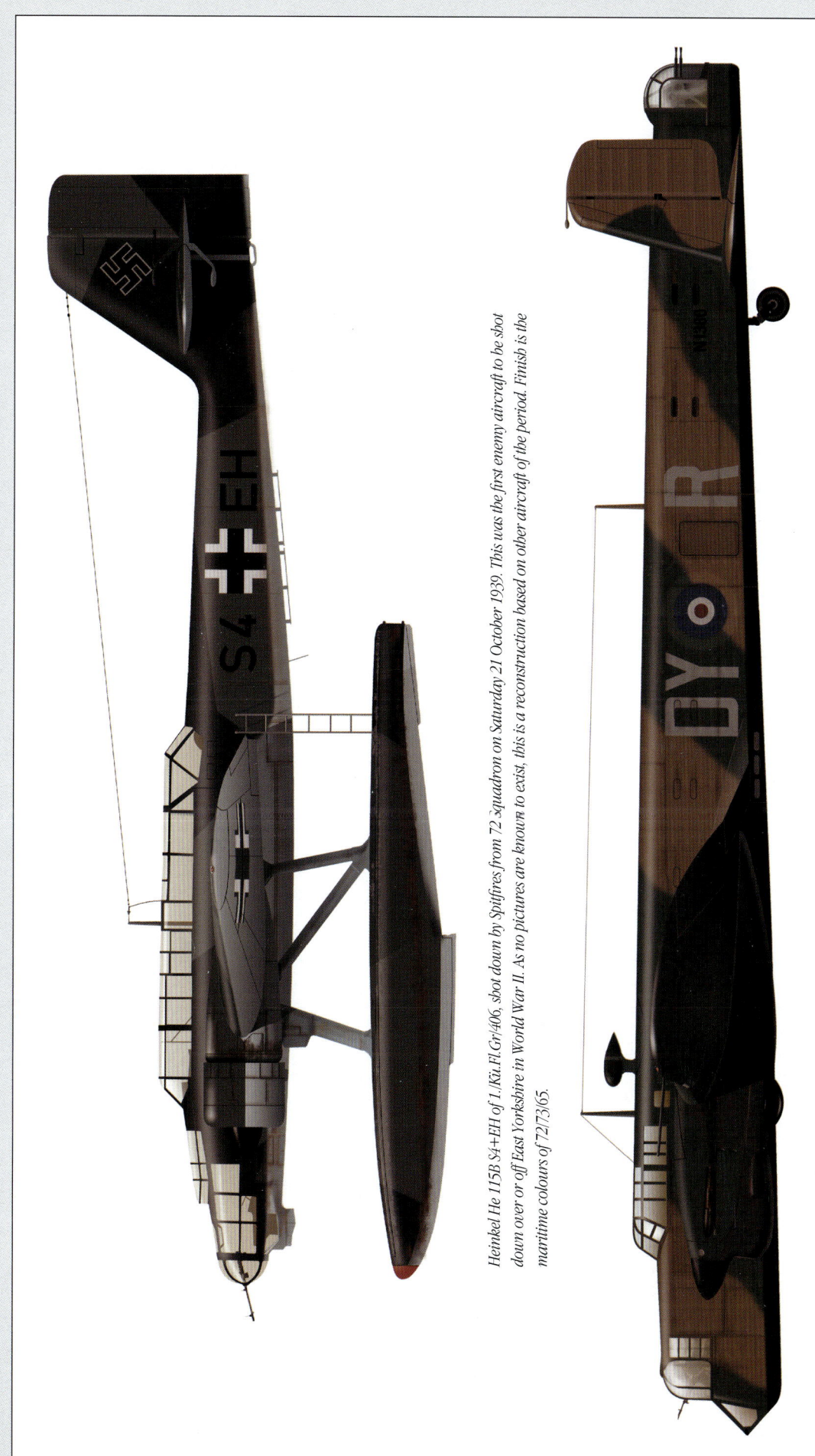

Heinkel He 115B S4+EH of 1./Kü.Fl.Gr/406, shot down by Spitfires from 72 Squadron on Saturday 21 October 1939. This was the first enemy aircraft to be shot down over or off East Yorkshire in World War II. As no pictures are known to exist, this is a reconstruction based on other aircraft of the period. Finish is the maritime colours of 72/73/65.

Armstrong Whitworth Whitley Mk V N1380, DY-R of 102 Squadron, based at Driffield. Piloted by S/L J.C. Macdonald, this was the first British aircraft to drop bombs on German soil in World War II, during a raid on Hornum seaplane base on 19-20 March 1940. The finish is the usual nondescript Dark Green/Dark Earth/Night of the period, with the original yellow outline to the fuselage roundel overpainted.

Avro Anson Mk I N5204, PG-N, of 608 Squadron flown by P/O A.D. Baird had the misfortune to be shot down in error by a Hurricane on 27 October 1939 while on convoy patrol. It came down in the sea near the Humber Lightship, three of the four crew being killed. It should have had its prewar squadron code letters changed to UL, but available pictures of squadron aircraft suggest that this was not done until some time after the outbreak of war. As a direct result of this incident all RAF fuselage markings were ordered changed to give better visibility. Finish is Dark Green/Dark Earth/Night undersides with white serials under the wings. Reconstruction.

Spitfire Mk I L1055, QJ-U, of 616 Sqn in early 1940 while based at RAF Leconfield. Used at night in June 1940, it is not known whether the anti-glare 'blinkers' were fitted at that time. Sombre finish is typical for the early part of 1940, with serial painted out, Dark Green/Dark Earth uppersides and Night/White and Aluminium undersurfaces. 30 inch diameter fuselage roundel and light grey code letters. *ILLUSTRATIONS NOT TO SAME SCALE.*

43 Far right: Pieces of shrapnel from the 250kg high-explosive bomb which detonated near Barf Farm, Hunmanby, on Thursday 6 June 1940.

Incident:
The first bombs to fall on Hull during World War II were a small number of HEs and IBs dropped at 23.13hrs on Wednesday 19 June 1940 (probably by KG 4) over East Hull. Properties in Victor Street, Buckingham Street and Chapman Street railway bridge were all slightly damaged. There were no casualties.

because 1H+FM was the first Luftwaffe aircraft to be brought down on English soil in World War II. Furthermore, the RAF pilot who led the attack, F/Lt Peter Townsend, had spent some time pre-war on a gunnery course at RAF Catfoss. It had been time well spent at that bleak East Yorkshire airfield and over the range at Skipsea.

As a thaw set in at last and spring approached, the 616 Sqn fighter pilots at RAF Leconfield were soon back in the air, but boredom and frustration quickly set in as a result of their daily routine of practice flights and convoy patrols, without any contact with enemy aircraft. It was towards the end of May before these pilots found themselves in combat with the Luftwaffe, but not over East Yorkshire or the North Sea but in the skies above the French coast and the English Channel.

On Monday 27 May 1940, S/Ldr Marcus Robinson led 616 Sqn south to RAF Rochford, near Southend in Essex, to provide cover during the evacuation of the BEF (British Expeditionary Force) from Dunkirk on the French coast. In their absence, the Spitfires of 74 'Tiger' Sqn flew into RAF Leconfield, led by F/Lt A.G. 'Sailor' Malan. 74 Sqn's brief stay at Leconfield, until 6 June, was uneventful, but a welcome break for the squadron's battle-weary pilots. In contrast, at RAF Rochford, 616 Sqn pilots were in action at last, destroying three German aircraft and damaging several others during their nine days at the Essex airfield.

When the elated pilots of 616 Sqn returned to RAF Leconfield, on Thursday 6 June, they heard that the first bombs had fallen on East Yorkshire. During the previous night, a single enemy bomber had dropped a stick of high explosive bombs near the village of Preston, four miles to the east of Hull. There was little damage and no injuries.

Then, during the evening of 6 June, another lone raider dropped its bomb load about one mile south-south-east of the author's home village of Hunmanby. The stick of HEs fell in a line between Vicarage Farm and the Hull to Scarborough LNER railway line. Again, there was only minor damage and no injuries, although one of the 250kg bombs exploded uncomfortably close to the Smithson family's Barf Farm. The Luftwaffe target on this occasion was most probably the searchlight unit at Graffitoe Farm, about half a mile east of Vicarage Farm, rather than the railway line. During the same night a cluster of incendiary bombs showered down and ignited on the cliff top between Barmston and Fraisthorpe. There was some damage to crops but nobody was hurt. On the following night four HEs exploded harmlessly near the village of Lund, six miles north-west of Beverley.

Later in June HEs fell at RAF Leconfield, on Flamborough Head, at Atwick, Saltend, Beeford, Burton Fleming, Stillingfleet, near Buckton Hall, Hull and in fields adjacent to Marton Road in Bridlington. The main targets, other than the Fighter Command station at Leconfield, appear to have been search-light units and port installations. There was an attempt to bomb RAF Driffield on Tuesday 18 June, but the Luftwaffe pilots were deceived by the bomber base's 'Q-Site' — a skilfully constructed decoy with lights laid out to resemble an airfield's flarepath — at Skerne, two miles south-east of Driffield.

The Luftwaffe had at last bombed East Yorkshire, although it had been a distinctly feeble effort so far. Little damage had been done by the German bombs and there had been no reports of any fatalities.

Meanwhile, the Whitley bombers of 77 and 102 Squadrons based at RAF Driffield were hitting back at the enemy, attacking targets in Germany, Italy and France. One typical raid, by eight 102 Sqn Whitleys to bomb a road bridge at Abbéville East in France, on Sunday 9 June 1940, warrants a special mention. Flying that night as second pilot to P/O F.H. Long in Whitley N1499/DY-M was one P/O G.L. Cheshire, destined to become Bomber Command's most highly decorated airman in World War Two, the legendary Leonard Cheshire. P/O Cheshire had joined the squadron four days earlier from 10 OTU (Operational Training Unit) at RAF Abingdon in Oxfordshire. Cheshire was most fortunate to be crewed with New Zealander Frank Long, a regular officer who had joined 102 before the war. During the next few weeks, the meticulous Long became Cheshire's mentor and a strong feeling of mutual respect rapidly grew between the older, more experienced Long and the young but confident and ambitious Cheshire. Frank Long quickly realised that Leonard Cheshire was an exceptionally talented pilot and had no reservations about handing over the controls to his second pilot for long legs of their bombing operations. At 2105 hours on Saturday 10 August, P/O Cheshire took off from RAF Driffield on yet another raid on an industrial target in Germany, only this time Leonard Cheshire was captain of his own aircraft.

Up to 25 June 1940, the Luftwaffe had been lucky, not losing a single bomber while operating over East Yorkshire. During the early hours of Wednesday 26 June, however, their luck ran out when a Heinkel He 111P-2 of 3./KG 4, the *General Wever* Geschwader, operating from Soesterberg in Holland, was intercepted and shot down by a 616 Sqn Spitfire piloted by P/O D.S. Smith. Scrambled from RAF Leconfield at 0115 hours, Donald Smith quickly located the Heinkel which had been illuminated by a coastal searchlight unit. After combat over Withernsea, Smith's attacks caused the He 111, 5J+BL, to crash into the sea a little before 0130 hours. *Lt* Helmut Furcht (pilot), *Hptm* Heinz Schröder, *Ofw* Martin Hartel and *Fw* Eugen Seitz were all killed in the crash. This had been the first air battle to take place over East Yorkshire in World War II[7].

"I attacked him from dead astern"

Three days later another 616 Sqn pilot was in combat with an enemy aircraft over the region. At about 0115 hours, P/O R. Marples sighted a Heinkel He 111 coned by searchlights between Catfoss and Withernsea:

> "Attacked him from dead astern and slightly below at approx. 250 yds. The first burst brought a burst of return fire from E/A (enemy aircraft) from bottom rear gun. I noticed by this time that I was overtaking very quickly so I throttled back and fired another burst, this time noticing rear gun was silent and also thick white plume of smoke issuing from E/A and also flames appeared to be coming from both engines. As I broke away to approach for a new attack the searchlights went out."

Roy Marples then lost the Heinkel in cloud and the badly damaged German bomber could only therefore be classified as 'unconfirmed'.

Two days later, during the morning of Monday 1 July, F/O R. Miller (Red One) of 616 Sqn was leading two of his squadron's trainee pilots, P/O R.A. Smith (Red Two) and P/O W.L.B. Walker (Red Three), through a series of 'battle climbs' over Leconfield when the section was vectored (given a heading to fly) towards a possible 'bandit' (enemy aircraft) in the vicinity of Hull. A Dornier Do 17Z was quickly located at 20,000 ft and at 1020 hours Robert Miller and Robert Smith both attacked in quick succession before the Dornier dived steeply and disappeared into cloud. William Walker also dived after the German bomber but discovered to his utter disbelief that his Spitfire's guns were unloaded, the aircraft having been used previously for cine-gun practice.

During the early afternoon of the same day, a Heinkel He 111H-4, 5J+EL, of 3./KG 4 took off from Soesterberg in Holland. On board were *Oblt zur See* Friedrich-Wilhelm Koch (captain/navigator/bomb aimer), *Ofw* Hermann Raisbach (pilot), *Fw* Alfred Weber (wireless operator/air gunner) and *Ofw* Rudolf Ernst (flight engineer/air gunner). Along with a He 111 from 1./KG3 and another from 2./KG3 their target was a chemical works at Middlesborough, but in the event of unsafe bombing conditions over Teesside (less than 5/10 cloud cover) they were to divert to their secondary target, oil storage tanks at Saltend on the north bank of the Humber, just east of Hull.

Landfall for Koch's Heinkel was Flamborough Head. After crossing the East Yorkshire coast just south of that prominent headland, Koch appears to have become rather indecisive as to whether he should go for their primary or secondary target. The KG 4 bomber flew south, then north, then east over East Yorkshire while Koch made up his mind. The He 111's approach had been detected by radar operators at RAF Staxton Wold and its subsequent manoeuvres monitored by Observer Corps posts across the region and, at 1631 hours, Yellow Section of 616 Sqn was scrambled at RAF Leconfield. The Spitfires of F/O R. Miller, F/O J.S. Bell and P/O J. Brewster were soon airborne and heading for a position about six miles north-west of Bridlington at Angels 15 (15,000 ft). Nothing was found, but as they were being vectored towards Withernsea Miller spotted a Heinkel He 111 just above cloud at 13,000 ft. Miller (Yellow One) closed in, opened fire and saw his bullets striking the enemy bomber's fuselage. Miller's Spitfire was fired at from both of the Heinkel's rear-firing gun positions, after which the Luftwaffe aircraft disappeared into cloud before Bell and Brewster could launch their attacks.

Raisbach used the cloud cover above the coast to shake off the pursuing fighters before turning onto a west-south-west heading, bringing his Heinkel in over Holderness and flying straight for the oil storage tanks at Saltend. The KG 4 aircrew may have lost the three Spitfires but as they settled into their bombing run the Royal Artillery gunners to the east of Hull were ready for their unwelcome visitor. The 3.7 inch heavy AA guns unleashed a deadly carpet of shell bursts and flying shrapnel unpleasantly close to the German plane. In fact, some of the shell fragments penetrated the extensive Perspex nose section of the Heinkel and smashed into the instrument panel in front of Raisbach.

Despite the worrying distraction of shrapnel crashing into his cockpit, the remarkably cool Raisbach calmly held a steady course at an altitude of just below 12,000 ft until Koch had released their twelve 50kg bombs across the oil storage tanks at Saltend. There was at least one direct hit and a large fire ensued.

---

[7] This was the first daylight bombing raid against the East Riding — and England. Not only that, very few victories were scored by the Spitfire at night — it was not well suited to the role on account of its narrow track undercarriage and lack of instrumentation. Several days later, two bodies were recovered from the sea by the destroyer HMS *Brazen* and buried at sea. (The ship was in turn sunk by the Luftwaffe on 20 July).

44 Far left: *F/O J.S. Bell of 616 Sqn at RAF Leconfield who, along with F/O R. Miller and P/O J. Brewster, shared in the shooting down of Oblt F-W Koch's Heinkel He 111 off the Humber on 1 July 1940. This was exactly one month after Bell had himself been shot down over the English Channel during the Dunkirk evacuation. John Bell (23) was killed on 30 August 1940 when he was shot down during combat with Messerschmitt Bf 109s over Kent.*

45 Left: *P/O A.D.J. Lovell who, in a 41 Sqn Spitfire, led the attack on the Junkers 88 which eventually crashed at Aldbrough on Monday 8 July 1940. Of the five RAF fighter pilots involved in combat with this enemy bomber, only Lovell and P/O Hugh Beazely survived the war. By an odd coincidence, Lovell and Eveline Cardwell's son, Norman, had earlier been pupils together at Ampleforth College.*

46 Above: *102 Sqn's Whitley V 'P-Peter' taking off from RAF Driffield on yet another 'Nickel' operation in September 1939.*

47 Right: *A key landfall point for raiding Luftwaffe bombers was Flamborough Head. (Simmons Aerofilms R965)*

48 Below: *A close-in view of an Heinkel He 111H-6, introduced at the beginning of 1941, making landfall over an unidentified coastline. It differed from earlier models primarily in having extra bomb-racks under the fuselage centre-secton.*

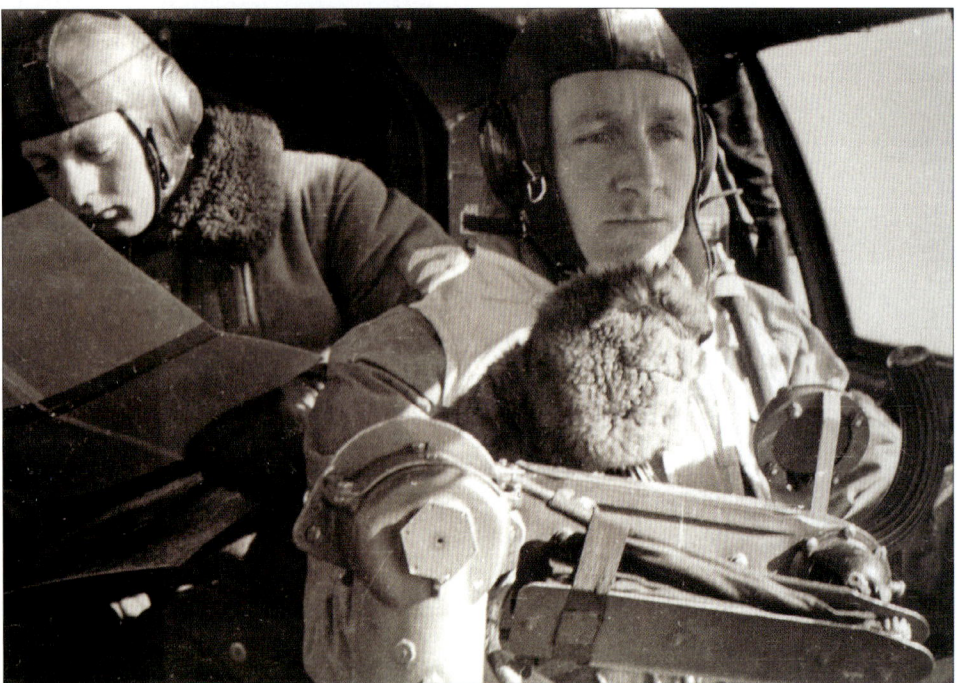

49 Far left: *In early 1940 there was still some chivalry. Oberstlt Hans Hefele of II./KG 26 thanks the skipper of the drifter Silver Line for rescuing his crew from the sea after they were shot down on 3 April 1940.*

50 Left: *The emblems of KG 4 'General Wever' (the device is a weaver's shuttle) and III./KG 30 'Adler - Eagle'.*

51: *The pilot Obfw Hermann Raisbach (right), with his flight engineer Obfw Rudolf Ernst, at the controls of Heinkel He 111H-4, 5J+EL, of 3./KG 4, in which they were shot down off Withernsea on 1 July 1940, as related opposite. (Goss/Rauchbach Archives)*

52: *Evidence of combat. The tattered remnants of the fabric patches which normally covered the gun apertures in the wing of a Spitfire I (of 19 Sqn) confirm that the guns have been fired. Armourers are busy reloading the four machine-guns in each wing prior to the next mission.*

Incident:

The fire which ensued at the Saltend oil storage tanks following the bombing on 1 July was fought by members of the Shell-Mex and BP company and local fire crews. Between them they earned five George Medals for bravery that day, awarded to: George Howe, George Sewell and William Sigsworth from the depot staff and Jack Owen and Clifford Turner of Hull Fire Service. These were some of the first awards (in October 1940) of a medal which was only instituted a month earlier.

53 Below: *A Sunderland I, L2163, DA-G, of 210 Sqn on patrol in 1940. It was an aircraft similar to this which spotted Koch and his crew in their dinghy and directed a rescue ship to them. The flying boat was well respected by the Luftwaffe opposition who named it the 'Flying Porcupine'. L2163 had a long career, eventually succumbing to the sea, when sunk at its moorings in a gale in 1943.*

It was now time for the Heinkel to make a swift exit from the target area and the menace of the AA guns; Koch ordered Raisbach to turn sharply to port and dive steeply. Levelling out at about 7,000 ft, Raisbach then headed eastwards for the mouth of the Humber and the homeward leg across the North Sea. Unfortunately for Koch and his crew, however, the intense AA fire to the east of Hull had been observed by Miller, Bell and Brewster, who decided to investigate.

Koch's He 111 was sighted flying out to sea at 7,000 ft and, at 1745 hours, combat commenced. Miller, Bell and Brewster dived in from astern in quick succession, their incendiary ammunition streaking into most parts of the enemy bomber. Miller (Yellow 1) led the attack, firing all his ammunition in three bursts between 300 yards and almost point-blank range and quickly silencing the Heinkel's rear-firing guns:

"Return fire had ceased before end of first burst."

Next in was Bell (Yellow 2) who fired three bursts between 250 and 25 yards:

"Bits flew off the machine and smoke issued from both engines, the port engine burst into flames."

Brewster (Yellow Three) completed the action, firing one long burst of 8 seconds at a range of between 220 and 50 yards after which he was forced to break off his attack:

"My windscreen was now covered in oil and it was impossible to distinguish the E/A in the smoke...I broke right...I then turned to the east at about 4,000 ft and saw the E/A below me diving down to the sea on fire."

F/O Robert Miller and F/O John Bell returned safely to Leconfield, but for F/O John Brewster it was a tricky landing at base, having to bring in his Spitfire by looking out of the cockpit's side windows due to the thick film of oil on his windscreen. Brewster's aircraft was also bent and dented in many places, the damage having been caused by flying debris from the enemy bomber.

Koch and his crew, however, were faced with far greater problems. Their Heinkel was doomed, and there would be no glorious return to Soesterberg, no celebratory glass of schnapps that night. With a smashed instrument panel, an engine out of action...then the other, damaged flaps and ailerons, there would have to be a ditching in the North Sea. To make the situation even more critical, the aircraft's undercarriage had dropped down which would make a sea landing extremely hazardous.

As soon as the German bomber's landing gear dipped into the waves the aircraft looped, throwing the four Luftwaffe men around the interior of their plane as the sea came pouring in. Although severely battered and bruised, and with Weber and Ernst injured with bullet wounds, all four succeeded in escaping from the sinking Heinkel and clambering into their rubber dinghy. Realising their perilous plight, drifting helplessly in the North Sea some 30 miles out from Spurn Head and with Weber seriously wounded in the head, eye and chest, distress flares were fired. These were spotted by the crew of a Short Sunderland flying boat and soon the German airmen were picked up by the Royal Navy sloop *Black Swan*. On board ship the prisoners were fed, re-clothed and Weber and Ernst received treatment for their injuries. During the following morning they were transferred to another Royal Navy ship which landed them at Harwich on the Essex coast around noon. For Friedrich-Wilhelm Koch, Hermann Raisbach, Rudolf Ernst and Alfred Weber their war was now over.

While Koch and his crew were heading for England and internment, the Luftwaffe lost another aircraft off the Yorkshire coast. At 0835 hours on 2 July the pilots of 611 Sqn's Red Section were scrambled at RAF Digby in Lincolnshire. F/Lt W.J. Leather (Red 1), P/O J.R.G. Sutton (Red 2) and P/O J.W. Lund (Red 3) were despatched to investigate a 'bogey' (unidentified aircraft) heading for the East Yorkshire coast in the vicinity of Withernsea.

31

Death of a Dornier 215

It was just past 0900 hours before the three Spitfire pilots sighted the aircraft under suspicion, which they identified as a Dornier Do 17Z. On seeing the approaching Spitfires, the Dornier's pilot put his aircraft into a tight 180 degrees turn in an attempt to escape eastwards across the North Sea. But it was no contest as, at 0915 hours, the three RAF fighters caught up with the Dornier and attacked in line astern. Soon, the enemy bomber had thick black smoke pouring from both engines and it dived steeply towards the sea.

Although none of the 611 Sqn pilots had seen the Dornier crash into the sea, the Luftwaffe later revealed that they had lost one aircraft that day off Northern England, only the victim had been a Dornier Do 215B-4, (G2+?H), not a Dornier Do 17Z. The Do 215B was a more advanced Dornier being operated out of France by 1.(F)/Aufkl.Gr 124, a special long-range reconnaissance unit, on behalf of the *Oberbefehlshaber der Luftwaffe* (Luftwaffe High Command). The four crew members: pilot *Fw* Helmuth Apitz, *Ofw* Heinz Friedrich (navigator), *Uffz* Walter Neige (radio operator) and *Gefr* Herbert Habel (flight engineer), were all listed as 'missing'.

Next day, Wednesday 3 July, it was the turn of three 616 Sqn Spitfires to go into action. Scrambled at 0900 hours, the fighters of the squadron's Green Section piloted by F/O G.E. Moberley, P/O H.S.L. Dundas and F/Sgt F.P. Burnard took off from RAF Leconfield to investigate a 'bogey' approaching the Holderness coast. Flying east-south-east at full throttle, a Dornier Do 17Z (probably of KG 3) was soon encountered at 4,500 ft, flying just below a layer of broken cloud. Moberley (Green 1) led the attack closely followed by Dundas (Green 2) and Bernard (Green 3). The Dornier's pilot attempted to shake off the Spitfires by climbing into the layer of cloud, but there were too many gaps in the cloud cover for him to evade his pursuers for long. All three Spitfires made successful attacks on the Dornier, which was sent crashing into the sea a few miles out from the Holderness coast. A rear-firing gunner in the German plane had fought back bravely and some of his bullets had struck Dundas' aircraft in the port wing, fortunately without inflicting any serious damage on the Spitfire.

Dundas and Bernard then pursued another Dornier which, although damaged, escaped into cloud. The Luftwaffe did not reveal any details relating to these two Dorniers or their crews, but it is likely that they were engaged in reconnaissance flights along the Yorkshire coast. The Luftwaffe bombers soon hit back with a number of sneak raids, each carried out by single aircraft. On Thursday 4 July, RAF Driffield was bombed for the first time when, at 2235 hours, a stick of HE bombs was dropped on the Bomber Command station causing some damage to accommodation blocks and slightly injuring a number of RAF personnel. Five minutes after the raid, Blue Section of 616 Sqn was scrambled at RAF Leconfield. The three Spitfire pilots soon located an unidentified aircraft flying out to sea but lost it in cloud without combat taking place.

Death of a gunner

Next, on Friday 5 July, an attempt was made by a lone German aircraft to bomb the important Chain Home radar station at Staxton Wold. At Manor Farm in Reighton, shortly before 1800 hours, the Bradshaw family watched in amazement as the enemy bomber flew inland just to the south of their village. Ted Bradshaw:

"There he was, as bold as brass, a Junkers 88 flying in from the sea in broad daylight. The plane wasn't very high and looked as though it had come in over Flamborough Head and was making a beeline for the RAF station at Staxton Wold."

The daring Luftwaffe intruder, thought to have been a KG 30 Ju 88 from Aalborg in Denmark, dropped four 250kg high explosive bombs which fell in a line between the radar base and Flixton village. The attack caused no serious damage but one soldier, in the Royal Artillery, engaged in the station's ground defences, was killed. The dead soldier, Gunner Edward H. Smethurst, was buried at Driffield five days after the raid.

Then, two nights later, another single German aircraft dropped a stick of HEs at Reighton Gap, hitting a bungalow called 'Redcote' and injuring three soldiers from the Royal Berkshire Regiment. All three casualties were rushed to Scarborough Hospital where one of them, a Lt Scott, later died. 'Redcote' was just one of the hundreds of holiday properties along the Yorkshire coast which had been requisitioned by the military and used as billets for service personnel.

Facts:
Two of the most popular songs of 1940 were Glenn Miller's In the Mood *and Anne Shelton's* A Nightingale Sang in Berkeley Square. *Walt Disney released his film* Fantasia. *For the house-hunter a small bungalow cost £250.*

54: *The headstone of the grave of Gunner Smethurst in Driffield Cemetery, the first serviceman to be killed during an air raid on East Yorkshire in World War II. This was the attack on Staxton Wold on 5 July 1940.*

55: A Dornier Do 215 of the type shot down by 611 Sqn on 2 July. It differed from the similar Do 17Z by virtue of its more powerful Daimler-Benz 601 in-line engines and more sophisticated navigation equipment. It was also fitted with an Rb 50/30 aerial cameras in the bulge under the cockpit.

56: A classic in-flight shot of a Hawker Hurricane 1, P3428, in early war-time finish. It was sent to 245 Sqn in Northern Ireland in September 1940, with whom it served (as DX-N) until June 1941 when it crashed. While never as glamorous as its stablemate, the Spitfire, it has to be said that it was the Hurricane that did most of the work of defeating the Luftwaffe in the Battle of Britain.

57: A common opponent for RAF fighters over East Yorkshire was the Junkers Ju 88A-4, here in service with 2. Staffel of I./KG 30, whose white shield and eagle badge is carried on the nose. It also has yellow under the engine cowlings and wing tips which indicate that it is operating in Northern Norway and over Northern Russia. The Ju 88 was an excellent aircraft; the Lufwaffe's jack-of-all-trades: as long-range fighter, night-fighter, dive-bomber, reconnaissance aircraft, torpedo-bomber, trainer, missile, it excelled as all of them.

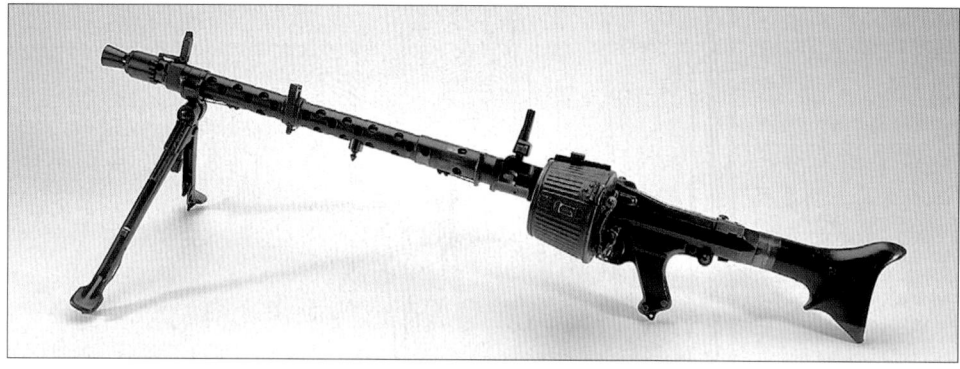

58 Above: Heinkel He 111 crewmen waiting for the start of the next mission. The tension is apparent in their faces. Note the bulky kapok-filled lifejackets worn by some of them.

59 Left: The standard defensive weapon on German bombers of the period was the 7.92mm calibre MG 15, seen here with a bipod for ground use. One was not much of an antidote to the eight guns of a Hurricane or Spitfire, but courageous gunners could, and sometimes did, prevail.

60: A closeup of the cockpit of an early-model Ju 88A of KG 30 at Aalborg. The various defensive MG 15 guns can be seen. In view of the long over-water flights between Denmark and Britain, the crew are wearing white or yellow covers over their flying helmets to assist in being spotted should they come down at sea.

"He dropped all his bombs at once"

The Luftwaffe bombers involved in these nuisance raids on East Yorkshire 4-7 July 1940 had all escaped but, on Monday 8 July, RAF fighter pilots gained some revenge in a morning air battle which took place between a point some seven miles off Scarborough and Skipsea. On this occasion, the aerial combat involved one Junkers Ju 88, two 41 Sqn Spitfires from RAF Catterick and three 249 Sqn Hurricanes, normally based at RAF Church Fenton but operating that day from RAF Leconfield.

First to attack, at 1130 hours, was F/O A.D.J. Lovell of 41 Sqn's Blue Section. Lovell had spotted a lone Ju 88 at 18,000 ft about seven miles out from Scarborough:

"I carried out an attack from slightly below but found the slipstream very upsetting so attacked from slightly above. After my second burst he dropped all his bombs at once. He was firing cannon from the top rear turret. After my fourth burst I saw large fragments come from the fuselage and tail and the cannon stopped. He then did a stalled turn and started gliding towards the land."

F/O Lovell's partner in this combat with the enemy, Sgt J.W. Allison, then made his attack as the Ju 88 headed south towards Flamborough Head, but after firing two short bursts, Allison lost his adversary in cloud.

With Lovell having used up all his ammunition and Allison having failed to make any further contact with the German bomber, it was now left to the Hurricane pilots of 249 Sqn's Green Section to finish the job. F/O D.G. Parnall, P/O H.J.S. Beazley and Sgt A.D.W. Main all attacked the severely damaged Ju 88 between Flamborough Head and Skipsea. With the pilot dead at his controls and their aircraft completely disabled, the three surviving Luftwaffe men had no option but to bale out as the crippled Ju 88 went into its final dive towards the village of Aldbrough.

At 1200 hours, Hornsea ARP informed Hornsea Police that *"…parachutist seen coming down a short time ago Aldbrough way."*

Minutes later, the ARP Sub-controller at Hornsea reported to ARP Beverley Control:

"Plane down in flames – reported to be German. 3 parachutists seen descending near Bewick. Troops and police on scene."

This information was subsequently passed on to ARP Regional Control in Leeds.

At 1300 hours, Inspector Etherington of the East Riding Constabulary compiled this report:

"At 1155 today a Ju 88 was brought down by 3 Spitfires. Fight appeared to take place off Skipsea. Plane crashed and burst into flames in a wheat-field between Aldbrough and Crossmere Hill.

4 occupants – one killed in the plane – other 3 baled out between Hatfield Wood and Aldbrough. One arrested by military and now in custody at Aldbrough P.S. He has needed medical treatment for cuts, abrasions and shock.

Remaining 2 airmen have been captured – 1 at Aldbrough and the other Burton Constable. Removed under armed guard to Infantry Training Centre, Beverley. Military guard over wreckage."

The capture of one of the German airmen was to bring both fame and a medal to one East Yorkshire woman. It was around midday, and farmer's wife Eveline Cardwell was alone at East Carlton Farm, one mile west of Aldbrough, when a drama unfolded which stayed fresh in Mrs Cardwell's mind for the rest of her life. This is what happened, in Mrs Cardwell's own words:

"I was sorting out Home Guard papers in the house when one of the farm men banged on the door and cried 'German parachutists are coming down!' He then disappeared. Well, at that time you'll remember we were all very het-up about invasion. I live in a very lonely place. The village is about a mile away and I was completely on my own.

I went into the garden and saw a plane going over. Something like a puff of smoke came out of the back of it, but I soon saw that it was a parachute, with an enormous pair of feet, coming straight into the paddock.

I went into the house to telephone the police, but the line was dead. So I went out again to find out what was happening and saw the German walking towards the house.

As soon as I got to the paddock I shouted 'Hi! Put your hands up.' He put them up. I asked him what he thought he was doing, but he didn't seem to understand English. I then said 'Give me this', pointing to his revolver. He gave it to me. After that, I took him to the road, as I thought the whole British Army might go by without knowing I was there with a German.

While I was waiting, he showed me how to blow up his Mae West (life jacket). Then a couple of soldiers came up on a motor-bike and sidecar. They asked me where his revolver was and I said 'Here it is'. I wished they had let me keep it. When an officer finally arrived, he asked 'Who got the prisoner?' They said 'The lady'.

The next day I filled in my monthly report[8], and to my husband's horror, I put at the end 'Captured, one German'. The next night I heard I'd been awarded a decoration."

Eveline Cardwell's photograph subsequently appeared in several national newspapers and Prime Minister Winston Churchill enthused over the propaganda value of her actions.

The enemy bomber which had crashed near Aldbrough was later identified as Junkers Ju 88A-1 (*Werk Nr* 3094), 5J+AT, of 9./KG 4, based at Soesterberg in Holland. Piloting the aircraft had been one of KG 4's most experienced officers, *Hptm* Kurt Rohloff, *Staffelkapitän* of 9./KG 4, who had died in

[8] *Eveline Cardwell was the WVS Centre Organiser for Central Holderness.*

his bomber. The three survivors who had parachuted to safety were *Unteroffiziers* Georg Abel, Artur Kuhnapfel and Heinz Oechler. It is not clear which of the three was captured by Mrs Cardwell.

This was the last air battle to take place over East Yorkshire prior to that most critical period in the war against Germany, the Battle of Britain.

61 Far left: *The British Empire Medal.*

62 Left: *Mrs Eveline Cardwell being presented with the BEM (British Empire Medal) by King George VI, accompanied by Queen Elizabeth at Hornsea on Thursday 1 August 1940. The location is outside the Marine Hotel on Marine Drive. Her citation read: 'With great pluck and presence of mind Mrs. Cardwell disarmed and took into custody an airman who had landed by parachute from an enemy aircraft damaged during an attack on North East England on Monday 8 July 1940.'*

63: *Mrs. Cardwell left the house at East Carlton Farm through a door on the right-hand side of the building. She went through a gate into the paddock and saw a German airman approaching her from across the paddock.*

64: *Prime Minister Winston Churchill pictured at the firing ranges at Rolston during a morale-boosting visit to the Hornsea district on 31 July 1940. Churchill, ever the old warhorse, happily posed with an American Thompson submachine gun (the famous 'Tommy' gun of American gangsters of the '30s). Nazi propaganda seized upon the image and attempted to portray him as a gangster on leaflets scattered over Britain. In fact the effect was to simply confirm to the British people that they, and their Prime Minister, were prepared to fight to the last.*

65: *Some of the local lads, not at all overawed by their august visitors, cheerfully 'man the barricades' in an unidentified East Yorkshire village in July-August 1940. Churchill is clearly not at all displeased.*

66: *In June 1940, despite the determination of the British people, the odds were still stacked in favour of the enemy. This is the scene at Nieuport near Dunkirk after the evacuation. The French destroyer* Bourrasque, *which sank after hitting a mine with the loss of 150 lives, lies beached off the embarkation beaches with her bows broken off. Wrecked British Morris trucks sit abandoned on the sand.*

67 Right: *The great fear of the time was a landing in Britain by German parachutists, a new element in warfare. This dummy shows the uniform and equipment of a typical* Fallschirmjäger.

68 Far right: *A barrage balloon is raised over Queen's Gardens in central Hull. The Dock Offices, now the Hull Maritime Museum, can be seen in the background. Behind that the dome of the City Hall can be just made out.*

> *"What General Weygand called the Battle of France is over. I expect that the Battle of Britain is about to begin. Let us therefore brace ourselves to our duty, and so bear ourselves that, if the British Commonwealth and its Empire lasts for a thousand years, men will still say, 'This was their finest hour'."*
>
> From the speech by Winston Churchill to the House of Commons on 18 June 1940.

69 Far left: While the Germans busied themselves humiliating the French by dismantling the First World War Memorial at Compiegne, the British prepared themselves for new battles.

70 Left: Men of the East Yorkshire Regiment being inspected by King George VI after their return from Dunkirk.

From the Führer's Speech

On July 19, the Führer and Chancellor Adolf Hitler addressed the German Reichstag with a speech in which he gave the German nation an account of the military operations carried out up to the present. The Führer described the German Army's wonderful achievements in Norway and on the Western Front, which in every case led to the complete rout of the enemy within a few weeks. He then dealt generally with Germany's position after ten months of the war, and stated that it was singularly languorable in view of the coming final battle with England. The German people, he said, were united as never before in their history, and would follow their leaders to the end. As far as food supplies were concerned, the war could last for any length of time. Since wide areas in Europe had by now been occupied, Germany would be able to draw on inexhaustible resources of raw materials. From now on, time would work for Germany. Germany commanded the strongest forces the world had ever seen, and was firmly resolved, side by side with allied Italy, to throw them into an attack against Britain, if this should prove necessary. In spite of Germany's overwhelming superiority and her unique strategic advantages — as opposed to the utter isolation of Britain —, the Führer once more upheld the policy of an understanding with Britain, which he has followed all these years, and again appealed to reason and common sense before starting out on a battle which, in its consequences for England, is beyond imagination.

The Führer said:

"Ever since the commencement of the National Socialist régime, two points were prominent in the programme of its foreign policy:

1. The achievement of a real understanding and friendship with Italy, and
2. the achievement of the same relationship with England.

You are aware, Gentlemen, that these ideals inspired me twenty years ago to the same extent as they did later. I have expressed and defended these ideals in print and in speeches on innumerable occasions, as long as I was only a member of the Opposition in the democratic Republic. As soon as the German nation entrusted me with its leadership, I immediately attempted to realize in practical form this, the oldest of the ideals of National-Socialist foreign policy.

Even today I still regret that, in spite of all my efforts, I have not succeeded in achieving that friendship with England which, as I believe, would have been a blessing for both peoples. I was not successful in spite of determined and honest efforts."

Later in his speech, the Führer said:

"In my speech on October 6, I prophesied correctly the further development of this war.

I assured you, Gentlemen, that never for one moment did I doubt in our victory.

As long as one does not insist on regarding defeat as the visible sign and guarantee of ultimate victory, I would appear to have been justified by the course which events have taken so far.

Although I was convinced of the course they would take, I nevertheless at the time held out my hand in an endeavour to reach an understanding with France and Britain.

You will remember the answer which I received. All my arguments as to the folly of continuing the struggle, and pointing to the certainty that at best there was nothing to gain, but all to lose, were either received with derision, or completely ignored. I told you at the time that on account of my peace proposals I expected even to be branded as a coward who did not want to fight on, because he could not. That is exactly what did happen.

I believe, however, that the French — of course not so much the guilty statesmen as the people — are beginning to think very differently about that 6th of October. Indescribable misery has overtaken that great country and people since that day.

I have no desire to dwell on the sufferings brought on the soldiers in this war.

Even greater is the misery caused by the unscrupulousness of those who drove millions from their homes without reason, merely in the hope of obstructing German military operations — an assumption which it is truly difficult to understand. As it turned out, the evacuation proved disastrous for Allied operations, though far more terrible for the unfortunate evacuees.

Neither in this world nor in the next can answer, Churchill and Reynaud answer for the suffering they have caused by their counsels and decrees to millions of people.

All this, as I said once before, need never have happened, for even in October I asked nothing, from either France or Britain, but peace.

But the men behind the armaments industries wanted to go on with the war at all costs, and now they have got it.

I am too much of a soldier myself, not to understand the misery caused by such a development.

From Britain I now hear only a single cry — the cry not of the people but of the politicians — that the war must go on.

I do not know whether these politicians already have a correct idea of what the continuation of this struggle will be like.

They do, it is true, declare that they will carry on with the war and that, even if Great Britain should perish, they would carry on from Canada.

I can hardly believe that they mean by this that the people of Britain are to go to Canada; presumably only those gentlemen interested in the continuation of their war will go there. The people, I am afraid, will have to remain in Britain.

And the people in London will certainly regard the war with other eyes than their so-called leaders in Canada.

Believe me, Gentlemen, I feel a deep disgust for this type of unscrupulous politician who wrecks whole nations and states. It almost causes me pain to think that I should have been selected by Fate to deal the final blow to the structure which these men have already set tottering.

It never has been my intention to wage wars, but rather to build up a state with a new social order and the finest possible standard of culture. Every year that this war drags on is keeping me away from this work.

And the causes of this are nothing but ridiculous nonentities, as it were, Nature's political misfits, unless their corruptibility labels them as something worse.

Only a few days ago, Mr. Churchill reiterated his declaration that he wants war. Some six weeks ago he began to wage war in a field where he apparently considers himself particularly strong, namely, air raids on the civil population, although so-called military objectives. Since the bombardment of Freiburg, these objectives are open towns, market places and villages, dwelling-houses, hospitals, schools, kindergardens and whatever else may come along.

Until now I have ordered hardly any reprisals, but that does not mean that this is, or will be, my only reply.

I know full well that our answer, which will come one day, will bring upon the people unending suffering and misery.

Of course not upon Mr. Churchill, for he, no doubt, will already be in Canada, where the money and the children of those principally interested in the war have already been sent. For millions of other people, however, great suffering will begin.

Mr. Churchill ought perhaps for once to believe me, when I prophesy that a great empire will be destroyed — an empire which it was never my intention to destroy or even to harm.

I do, however, realize that this struggle, if it continues, can end only with the complete annihilation of one or the other of the two adversaries. Mr. Churchill may believe that this will be Germany. I know that it will be Britain.

In this hour I feel it to be my duty before my own conscience to appeal once more to reason and common sense, in Great Britain as much as elsewhere. I consider myself in a position to make this appeal since I am not the vanquished begging favours, but the victor speaking in the name of reason.

I can see no reason why this war must go on.

I am grieved to think of the sacrifices which it will claim. I should like to avert them, also from my own people.

I know that millions of German men, young and old alike, are burning with the desire at last to settle accounts with the enemy, who for the second time has declared war upon us for no reason whatever. But I also know that at home there are many women and mothers, who, ready as they are to sacrifice all they have in life, are yet bound to it by their very heart strings.

Possibly Mr. Churchill will again brush aside this statement of mine by saying that it is merely born of fear and of doubt in our final victory. In that case I shall have relieved my conscience in regard to the things to come."

72 Above: *A Whitley Mk V of 77 Sqn at Driffield. In the evening of 27-28 March 1940 N1357/KN-H had the misfortune to be shot down by a Dutch Fokker G.1 fighter when it inadvertently intruded into Dutch airspace while returning from a reconnaissance mission. The aircraft crashed in the docks area of Rotterdam, one member of the crew being killed. The rest of the crew were briefly interned before being returned to this country.*

71 Left: *More hubris from Hitler in a speech in the Reichstag on 19 July 1940, his 'last appeal to reason'. By that date any promise from Herr Hitler had proven to be worthless. This air-dropped propaganda leaflet was picked up in Filey in August 1940.*

INTO THE BATTLE OF BRITAIN
Coastal attacks and the Poles at Leconfield

On 17 June 1940, Marshall Pétain, the new French Prime Minister broadcast to the French people, telling them:

"Il faut cesser la lutte". ("We must give up the fight").

Next day, Britain's Prime Minister, Winston Churchill told a packed House of Commons:

"What General Weygand called the Battle of France is over. I expect the Battle of Britain is about to begin."

The Battle of Britain did not, however, officially begin until Wednesday 10 July 1940, with the conflict lasting until Thursday 31 October 1940. Within that period, the most savage and spectacular air battles the world had ever seen took place over the south of England. The primary objective of the Luftwaffe was to destroy the airfields and aircraft of the Royal Air Force in preparation for a massive military operation code-named *Seelöwe* (Sea Lion), the invasion of Britain.

The aerial combat over southern counties has been excellently researched and documented over the years, but what happened in and over East Yorkshire and adjacent coastal waters during that memorable summer of 1940 has received less attention.

On Thursday 11 July 1940, the first civilian deaths to result from a German air raid on East Yorkshire occurred when Bridlington was attacked. Air raid warnings had sounded across the town shortly before 1100 hours, and at 1105 hours a lone Luftwaffe KG 30 Junkers Ju 88 roared in from the North Sea to drop a stick of high explosive bombs between the railway station and Hilderthorpe Road.

Bridlington railway station was damaged while in a nearby siding a number of ammunition trucks were set alight. Railway staff toiled valiantly to bring a dangerous situation under control and three railway workers, including Mr E.V. Barker, a ticket collector at the station, were subsequently awarded the George Medal. Five civilians were killed by the bomb which exploded on Hilderthorpe Road. They were Charles and Gertrude Wainwright who ran a gents outfitters at 83 Hilderthorpe Road, Mabel Potter at 85 Hilderthorpe Road, Clara Hildrew and Agnes Annie Nicholson who was in the area at the time but whose home was on South Back Lane. A soldier, Gunner P. Rogers of the Royal Artillery, was also killed.

Exactly one week later, on Thursday 18 July, there was an attack by a single enemy aircraft in the Skipsea area. At around 0700 hours a Ju 88 flew in from Bridlington Bay and dropped two HEs, one failing to explode as it hit open ground and the other falling harmlessly into the sea. The Luftwaffe bomber then machine gunned Skipsea as it swung south; there were no casualties in Skipsea and little damage had been inflicted by the ricocheting bullets. Minutes later, the same aircraft fired at a cottage in Bewholme, four miles south of Skipsea. The residents, a Mr. and Mrs. Wiles, had a lucky escape as bullets crashed through their roof and thudded into the bed which they had vacated only minutes earlier. Later, the couple told how they had seen the firing coming from the rear of the departing enemy plane.

Then, on Monday 22 July, there was a second sneak raid on the Skipsea area. On this occasion, at 0154 hours, a German aircraft dropped several bombs

39

which fell harmlessly between Skipsea and Ulrome. There was one unexploded bomb which was of considerable interest to the bomb disposal squad which later dealt with it. In a follow-up ARP Report it was noted that the UXB was "...*a new type of bomb containing petrol, paraffin and other oils.*"

There was then a lull in enemy activity over East Yorkshire, during which Prime Minister Winston Churchill made a surprise visit to the Hornsea district on Wednesday 31 July 1940. There he met Army personnel and local units of the Home Guard. A photograph of Britain's war leader posing with a Tommy gun was subsequently turned into a propaganda leaflet by the Nazis; thousands of these leaflets were then dropped over several parts of Britain.

Although Luftwaffe bombers were seldom heard over East Yorkshire during the last week in July and the early part of August 1940, the more reassuring sound of RAF aircraft operating against enemy targets on the continent was much in evidence. Bomber Command aircrews had serious air battles of their own to contend with on these operations which could last up to eight hours or more. Apart from the considerable threat posed by enemy flak and night fighters RAF bombers were often struggling home with almost empty fuel tanks.

Many a Hampden, Wellington or Whitley was forced to ditch in the North Sea as tanks ran dry. RNLI lifeboats, RAF Air Sea Rescue launches and fishing boats did a tremendous job in rescuing downed aircrew.

The arduous and hazardous nature of early bombing operations over Germany is well illustrated by the experience of one 77 Sqn Whitley crew from RAF Driffield. On the night of 3/4 August 1940, P/O I.M.R. Brownlie was at the controls of Whitley N1474 as it lifted off from Driffield at 2105 hours, one of seven squadron aircraft heading for an oil storage plant at Mannheim. The raid was carried out successfully, but on the return leg the Whitley crews were informed of thick fog in the Driffield circuit and instructed to divert to other airfields. Approaching Flamborough Head with fuel tanks virtually empty, P/O Brownlie knew that he had no chance of reaching any RAF airfield and so opted for a forced landing in a large field at Head Farm, a few hundred yards from Flamborough Lighthouse. The Whitley was damaged in the landing but the five crew members escaped unhurt. Brownlie's aircraft had touched down at 0555 hours after a flight which had lasted almost nine hours.

Five days later, a Vickers Wellington, R3293/HD-Y, of 38 Sqn based at RAF Marham in Norfolk, force-landed at Filey, 120 miles from base. Piloted by Sgt Lupton, the aircraft was returning from a raid on Hamburg and had been lost for some considerable time before running out of fuel and belly-landing in a field alongside Muston Road, now the site of Filey School.

Returning to Fighter Command, the air defences of East Yorkshire were to be strengthened by the formation of a second fighter squadron at RAF Leconfield. On 13 July 1940, 302 'City of Poznan' (Polish) Squadron came into existence, the first Polish squadron to be formed in Britain during World War II. The squadron was equipped with Hurricane Is. Initially, 302 Sqn was jointly commanded by Squadron Leader Mieczyslaw Mümler, a Pole, and Squadron Leader W.A.J. (Jack) Satchell of the RAF.

At Leconfield there was more than a little tension between the Polish pilots and their RAF instructors. This was not simply because of language difficulties, but due to the fact that most of the Poles

Incident:
1/2 August 1940: While sailing in convoy along the east coast, the Hull-based steamship Highlander, *1,216 tons, was attacked by two Heinkel He 111s from KG 26. In a bizarre event, both were shot down, the second by means of the Holman Projector, a compressed air-powered grenade launcher, which blew off a wing. This crashed onto the vessel, which entered port at Leith with the wreckage still on board. There were no survivors from either aircraft.*

73: *Devastation along Hilderthorpe Road in Bridlington following the air raid by a single Ju 88 of KG 30 on 11 July 1940. The first civilian casualties in East Yorkshire occured here when five people were killed. (ERYC I&LS)*

74: *Burnt out railway wagons at Bridlibgton station, 11 July 1940.*

[9] *John Dundas was a leading ace in the Battle of britain, with 12 kills and 2 'probables' to his credit. He was to gain immortal fame, although at the cost of his own life, on 28 November 1940 when he shot down the then leading Luftwaffe fighter ace, Major Helmut Wick (56 victories), Kommodore of JG 2. Moments after this event Dundas was shot down and killed by Wick's wingman, but too late, the Luftwaffe's top 'experte' had gone.*

were already very experienced in aerial combat, having participated in many fierce air battles over Poland and France. Having to take advice on tactics from far less experienced RAF officers really grated with the Polish pilots. The latter were ruthless and bloodthirsty in their outlook; all they wanted to do was take off in their Hurricanes, shoot down enemy aircraft and kill German airmen. This was perfectly understandable considering what destruction and atrocities the Polish airmen had witnessed as the airmen and soldiers of the Third Reich had ravaged their homeland.

Their spirits were lifted temporarily on Wednesday 7 August when they received a visit from General Wladislaw Sikorski, Commander-in-Chief of the Poles in Britain. The proud pilots of 302 Sqn put on an immaculate fly-past in his honour, but P/O Stanislaw Skalski, Poland's top-scoring fighter pilot in the air battles over his own country, was so dissatisfied with the monotonous training flights and absence of combat that he was soon demanding a transfer to an operational squadron. On 27 August Skalski got what he requested when he was posted to 501 Sqn at RAF Gravesend in Kent.

Although fully operational, the Spitfire pilots of 616 Sqn at RAF Leconfield were similarly frustrated with the lack of action. Daily, they were hearing on the radio and reading in their newspapers of the fierce air battles taking place over the southern counties. None was more fed up with the situation than

than P/O Hugh 'Cocky' Dundas, whose brother John[9] was a pilot in 609 Sqn based at RAF Middle Wallop near Southampton and in the thick of the action.

Apart from regular convoy patrols off the Yorkshire coast, the 616 Sqn pilots were also involved in dog-fight tactics and night-flying practice. It was during such training flights that the squadron lost two pilots in early August 1940 and had a number of their Spitfires damaged, some beyond repair. First, on Sunday 4 August, Sgt J.P. Walsh was killed when his Spitfire went into an uncontrollable spin during dog-fight manoeuvres and crashed near base. Then, on Wednesday 7 August, P/O R.A. Smith lost his life in a night-flying accident when his Spitfire dived into the ground just three miles from Leconfield. During the same night, Sgt T.E. Westmoreland wrote off his Spitfire in a landing accident but escaped unhurt.

Monday 12 August was a sad day for 616 Sqn as the whole squadron attended the funeral of P/O Russell A. Smith at St. Catherine's Church in Leconfield. All flying duties were suspended for the day.

The following day should have been *'Adler Tag'* (Eagle Day) for the Luftwaffe, the first day of a massive air assault by German aircraft on the airfields, aircraft and airmen of the RAF. On account of overcast conditions and poor visibility over the north of England, however, Luftwaffe activity was confined to attacks on airfields in the south. Savage air battles raged over southern counties and 47 enemy aircraft were

75: *This No 38 Sqn Vickers Wellington Ic, R3293/HD-Y, which had to make an emergency landing in a field adjacent to Muston Road at Filey on 9 August after running out of fuel when returning from a raid on Germany. This location is now part of Filey School's playing fields. The light patch below the fin is probably the torn fabric covering where the fire extinguisher has been removed.*

41

shot down. The day was a quiet one at RAF Leconfield, as was the next, apart from one uneventful patrol off Flamborough Head.

Eight miles up the A164, life was far from quiet for the Bomber Command aircrew and groundcrew at RAF Driffield. From there, the two resident Whitley squadrons were now carrying out regular raids against enemy targets in France, Germany and Italy. For example, on the night of 14/15 August 1940, nine Whitleys of 102 Sqn were detailed to attack the Caproni aircraft factory in the Italian city of Milan, flying south to refuel at Harwell before overflying France and the Alps en route to their target. During the same night, twelve Whitleys of 77 Sqn were despatched to bomb the Bordeaux oil refinery in France.

As these Whitleys headed for Italy or France, two new recruits arrived at RAF Driffield to join 102 Sqn. They were Sgt A. Sleath (pilot) and P/O R.C. Rivaz (air gunner), excited at the prospect of shortly taking part in bombing raids against enemy targets on the European mainland. The two newcomers could never have anticipated that within the next twenty-four hours they would be on the receiving end of German bombs.

76 Below: *Two Spitfire Is of 616 Sqn in the early phase of the Battle of Britain. Thanks to an administrative oversight 616 and 92 Squadrons shared the same 'QJ' code letters until mid-1941.*

Facts:
154 Polish pilots served with the RAF during the Battle of Britain. From first entering combat in August until 31 October 1940, they shot down 203 enemy aircraft; 7.5% of the total German losses.

77 Left: *P/O Tom Murray (left) and P/O Lionel 'Buck' Casson of No 616 Sqn, patiently waiting for the 'scramble' call out at RAF Leconfield in early August 1940. Both pilots survived the war.*

78: *A poor quality, but extremely rare picture of a Hurricane I, WX-U, P3923, flown by P/O Franciszek Jastrzebski of 302 Sqn, shortly after the unit was formed. Despite being the first Polish squadron to be formed in the RAF, and the first to see action, it is not well documented.*

79: One of 5./KG 30's Junkers Ju 88A-4s, 4D+FN, in Norway in mid-1940. It was aircraft from this unit which provided much of the force attacking East Yorkshire in 1940. Note how the eagle emblem on the nose is on a red background, indicating both Staffel and Gruppe.

80: Luftwaffe armourers loading the external bomb racks of a Ju 88A with 250kg bombs. The rear of the underfuselage gondola has been swung down to give access to the cockpit (note the ladder). In action it could be manned by a gunner lying prone on a mattress, which gave it the grim name of the 'death bed', as it was usually the first position to be hit by attacking enemy fighters.

81 Below: Spitfire Is of 616 Sqn in late summer 1940. Y-QJ/X4329, the nearest is in 'B' Scheme camouflage. QJ-P behind is X4388 in 'A' Scheme camouflage. Note the different code letter positions.

THE 'EAGLES' ATTACK
Target — RAF Driffield

82 Above: A Junkers Ju 88A of KG 30 is fuelled up prior to the next mission. It has already been loaded up with bombs. The picture was probably taken in 1941-42 when the unit was involved in operations over the Arctic Ocean and Northern Norway as a yellow fuselage band can just be made out.

This is an account of the only major daylight raid on a Yorkshire target during World War Two, the surprise attack on RAF Driffield on Thursday 15 August 1940. It is a story which has never been fully or accurately told. What follows is an analysis of what happened that day, based primarily on RAF records – Operations Record Book entries, Combat Reports and Air Intelligence documents, Luftwaffe loss details as recorded by I and III/KG 30, ARP and Police messages and reports, plus a number of eye-witness accounts.

The story starts at Aalborg, a Luftwaffe bomber base located on low, flat land in the north of German-occupied Denmark. As the Junkers Ju 88 aircrews of KG 30, the *Adler* (Eagle) Geschwader, awoke on 15 August they were confident that there would be no bombing operations against the British that day. Rain was pouring down from a thick, dark grey blanket of cloud, forming extensive pools of water at their airfield. Yet, they could hear the familiar sound of Jumo engines being run and, on looking out across the airfield, could see groundcrew working on their bombers.

This unexpected activity at Aalborg was the result of early morning flights by Luftwaffe reconnaissance aircraft, which had revealed improving weather conditions over the British Isles. German meteorological officers advised that a high pressure system was moving in over Britain and that within a few hours there would be ideal bombing conditions over KG 30's allocated target for the day — RAF Bomber Command's No 4 Group base at Driffield in East Yorkshire.

Approximately 475 miles to the south-west of Aalborg, at RAF Driffield, 77 Sqn and 102 Sqn groundcrews were also hard at work, servicing the Whitley bombers which had returned during the early hours from operations over France and Italy. Meanwhile, the exhausted bomber crews would be enjoying several hours of uninterrupted sleep — or so they hoped.

Eight miles down the A164 at RAF Leconfield there were six new arrivals when, at 0715 hours, S/Ldr M.W.S. Robinson led in the six Hurricanes of 73 Sqn's 'A' Flight, moved forward to Leconfield from the Sector HQ airfield at Church Fenton in West Yorkshire. A number of important convoys were scheduled to pass along the Yorkshire coast that day and the Hurricanes would be available to assist the Spitfires of 616 Sqn in carrying out patrols off Flamborough Head and the Holderness coast. Several such patrols were carried out during the morning of 15 August, but there was no sign of the Luftwaffe.

Back at Aalborg, however, there was action of a different kind. In mid-morning, bomber after bomber

44

Facts:

On Monday 1 July 1940, the Royal Navy had 55 capital ships and about 1,100 small craft dispersed in harbours around Britain. Three cruisers and seven destroyers were in the Humber on that day. An aircraft carrier, three cruisers and 30 destroyers were at sea on escort duties.

83 Below: *A Blenheim IF fighter of 248 Sqn, WR-E/ L1336, in late 1939. Aircraft very similar to this served with 219 Sqn and took part in the action against KG 30 on 15 August 1940. Note the gun pack under the fuselage containing four .303 inch calibre Browning machine-guns.*

took off from the KG 30 airfield, climbing ponderously towards a still grey sky. As the 50 Ju 88s flew south-west over the fields and farms of the Danish countryside, they slowly closed up to form a menacing air armada. Soon, the bomber force was out over the North Sea; oxygen masks were donned as the aircraft flew higher and higher until they had reached their selected cruising altitude of 18,000 ft. They were now well on track for the Yorkshire coast, with landfall expected to be in the vicinity of Flamborough Head.

Unknown to the German bomber crews, their approach had been detected by the radar operators at RAF Staxton Wold. Their cathode-ray tube displays revealed a large, unidentified force approaching the Yorkshire coast from the north-east. Messages were swiftly telephoned to Fighter Command HQ at Stanmore in Middlesex and to 12 Group HQ at Watnall near Nottingham "*...20+ hostile*", soon amended to "*...30+ hostile*". A major raid on Yorkshire was becoming increasingly imminent, but what would be the Luftwaffe's target? Would it be RAF airfields at Driffield, Leconfield or Church Fenton, the city of Hull, the coastal towns of Bridlington or Scarborough, or perhaps the convoy code-named 'ARENA' sailing north from Hull?

In 12 Group HQ, Group Commander Trafford Leigh-Mallory and his senior officers studied the worsening situation at the plotting table in their Operations Room and prepared for action.

Lunch was coming towards an end at RAF Leconfield, East Yorkshire's only fighter station in 1940, when at 1300 hours the call came:

"*616 Squadron scramble, 616 Squadron scramble, all aircraft.*"

Desserts were hastily abandoned as the excited pilots rushed to their battle-ready Spitfires. Two minutes later a similar call summonsed 73 Squadron's 'A' Flight into action with the flight's six Hurricanes.

The Spitfires and Hurricanes roared off from Leconfield's grass runway, heading for the coast at Hornsea before being vectored towards Flamborough Head. At approximately 1315 hours another 616 Sqn Spitfire took off piloted by F/O G.E. Moberley:

"*I was virtually on 24 hours leave but hearing the squadron ordered to scramble I seized the last available aircraft and took off about 15 minutes after the squadron. From conversations on the R/T (radio-telephone) I decided to make for Flamborough at 20,000 ft.*"

According to 616 Sqn's Operations Record Book "*...contact was made about 10 miles out to sea at 15,000 ft...they were in a poor formation flying abreast with several stragglers.*" The RAF fighter pilots estimated that there were 50 Junkers Ju 88s.

By now, air raid sirens were sounding across much of East Yorkshire. In Hunmanby, the hurried arrival of a soldier at the author's front door in Station Road resulted in my mother, grandmother and myself being rushed across the road to take shelter in a trench behind the REME (Royal Electrical and Mechanical Engineers) unit's garage. The soldiers had been informed that a major raid on the area was very imminent. During the next hour we heard the faint sound of distant machine gun fire but all we saw was one lone Hurricane fighter hurtling overhead in the direction of Filey Bay.

Once the size of the incoming hostile force had been established, back-up for the Spitfires and Hurricanes of 12 Group was provided by 13 Group of Fighter Command. Twelve Blenheims of 219 Sqn, normally based at RAF Catterick but on this day operating from RAF Leeming, were scrambled to join the battle. Although twelve Blenheims did take off, from 1310 hours, one was forced to return to base because of mechanical problems, a massive disappointment for pilot Sgt Grubb (Blue 3) and his air gunner. Few books on the Battle of Britain have ac knowledged 219 Squadron's involvement in the air battles of 15 August 1940, but their Blenheims were definitely up there, very scattered, but with their greater range enabling them to operate up to 150 miles out over the North Sea.

The Junkers Ju 88 aircrews of KG 30 were shocked at the sight of so many Spitfires and Hurricanes suddenly appearing from the British mainland. German intelligence had led them to believe that most of the RAF's fighters in the North of England had been diverted to defend key airfields in southern counties. Fortunately, Fighter Command Commander-in-Chief Sir Hugh Dowding had implemented the wise policy of rotating fighter squadrons between northern and southern counties and never leaving the north without effective fighter cover.

As the Spitfires and Hurricanes took up attacking positions, the large Luftwaffe formation split, with fewer than half of the original force of 50 aircraft maintaining a heading for RAF Driffield. Some of the German pilots chose to jettison their bombs into the sea and attempt a hasty exit away from the Yorkshire coast. This is what happened in the case of the first chosen target of 73 Sqn's Sgt A.L. McNay (Red 3):

"I selected one and fired a burst at about 800 yards. He turned out of formation. I closed to about 400 yards and fired another burst. He jettisoned his bombs into the sea."

As McNay moved in for the kill, he was distracted when the panel blew off his port machine guns and the enemy bomber managed to escape eastwards.

Not so fortunate was the crew of another Ju 88 off Flamborough Head. Their aircraft was quickly doomed as 616 Sqn pilots Sgt R. Marples (Blue 3) and then F/Lt D. Gillam (Blue 1) swept in to deliver blistering attacks on the KG 30 bomber. The initial damage was done by Marples's accurate fire but it was Gillam's devastating onslaught which finished off the enemy plane:

"I kept up a continuous fire down to 6,000 ft. The enemy dropped its bombs, part of the tail came off and it turned on its back…the engines were burning and the fuselage was on fire. It crashed into the sea."

The combined efforts of two other 616 Sqn pilots, F/Lt R. Hellyer and P/O D.S. Smith, led to the destruction of another Ju 88 a few miles east of Flamborough Head. P/O Smith:

"At 1315 hours on 15/8/40 I was Red Two, 616 Sqn, and was in line behind F/Lt Hellyer (Red One).

We sighted formation of E/A at 18,000 ft E of Flamborough. We dived astern of one Ju 88 and F/Lt Hellyer fired all his rounds at it in a prolonged astern attack. I took up the attack and, as it turned left, fired a number of rounds at it using about a 20 degrees deflection. At about 6,000 ft the E/A dived steeply into the sea and was immediately submerged. The attack was at a range of about 100 yds all the time."

Another Ju 88 fell into the sea some ten miles off Flamborough Head as a 616 Sqn Spitfire, piloted by P/O H.S.L. Dundas (Green 1), raked the bomber with a lethal cone of machine gun fire that silenced the enemy aircraft's gunners and caused both engines to burst into flames. Hugh Dundas then pursued and attacked another Ju 88 which was flying very low out to sea, but his ammunition ran out before he could notch up his second 'kill' of the day.

The Hurricane pilots of 73 Sqn were also heavily involved in combat. Six miles off Flamborough Head, S/Ldr M.W.S. Robinson (Yellow 1) attacked and damaged two enemy bombers. Almost simultaneously, Sgt J.J. Griffin (Red 2) attacked and shot down a Ju 88 six miles from the coast. John Griffin:

"I attacked a Junkers 88 from the rear at a range of approx. 300 yds and closed in to 200 yds as the e/a tried to dive away. The aft gunner returned my fire for a short while and then ceased. I continued to dive after the e/a and as it tried ineffective evasive action fired first into the starboard engine and believe I succeeded in hitting the pilot. The aircraft stalled at about 1,000 ft and with parts falling from the engine and fuselage dived into the sea."

Although the bulk of the combat was taking place off Flamborough Head, interceptions were also taking place over Filey Bay and Bridlington Bay. F/Lt R.E. Lovett (Red 1) of 73 Sqn pursued one Ju 88 across Filey Bay and *"…gave him long bursts using all my ammunition. E/A went down in a steep dive and I lost E/A 5 miles west of Filey entering cloud."*

Another 73 Sqn pilot, P/O P.E.G. Carter (Yellow 3), had two confrontations with enemy bombers off Flamborough Head into Bridlington Bay. The first aircraft was badly damaged and when Peter Carter attacked a second one:

"…I saw him cartwheel into the sea about 4 miles from the coast and 6 miles south of Flamborough Head."

All the initial combat had taken place between approximately 1310 and 1320 hours, and during the fierce air battles off Flamborough Head two of the inbound Ju 88s had slipped away from the action to release their bomb loads over Scarborough and Bridlington. One flew across Scarborough's South Bay before turning inland over the northern tip of Oliver's Mount. What happened next was witnessed at close hand by two local lads.

Sixteen-years old Robert Blake of Seamer Moor Road was cycling up Queen Margaret's Road towards Filey Road at about 1315 hours when he was suddenly

Facts:
The initiative to invade Norway and Denmark, where KG 30 was based, came not from Adolf Hitler, but from Grossadmiral Erich Raeder, *Commander in Chief of the Kriegsmarine — the German Navy — because he was concerned to protect the supply of iron ore from Norway and Sweden, which provided 54% of the steel used in the construction of German ships and armaments.*

84/85 Left: *P/O R. Marples (far left) and F/Lt. D.E. Gillam, whose collective efforts resulted in No 616 Squadron's first 'kill', on 15 August 1940. Denys Gillam DSO, DFC, survived the war but Roy Marples DFC (24) was killed in a mid-air collision over Sussex on 26 April 1944.*

86 Above: *The only resident bomber squadrons based in East Yorkshire during the early months of World War Two were No 102 Sqn (Code DY) and No 77 Sqn (Code KN) at RAF Driffield. Both units flew the Armstrong Whitworth Whitley V, which had a crew of five. Those above are from 102 sqn, the nearest machine being N1421, 'C', which was shot down by flak near Oslo on 29 April 1940, four of the crew surviving to become POWs.*

87 Right: *Target area for a lone Ju 88, which escaped from the Spitfires and Hurricanes off Flamborough Head and headed for Scarborough. Crossing the photograph from top (north) to bottom (south) are the Scarborough to Hull/York railway lines. Just above centre on the left are engine sheds and to their left is Seamer Road. To the right (east) of the railway lines is Scarborough Gasworks, hit by high explosivse bombs on 15 August 1940. (Robin J. Lidster)*

47

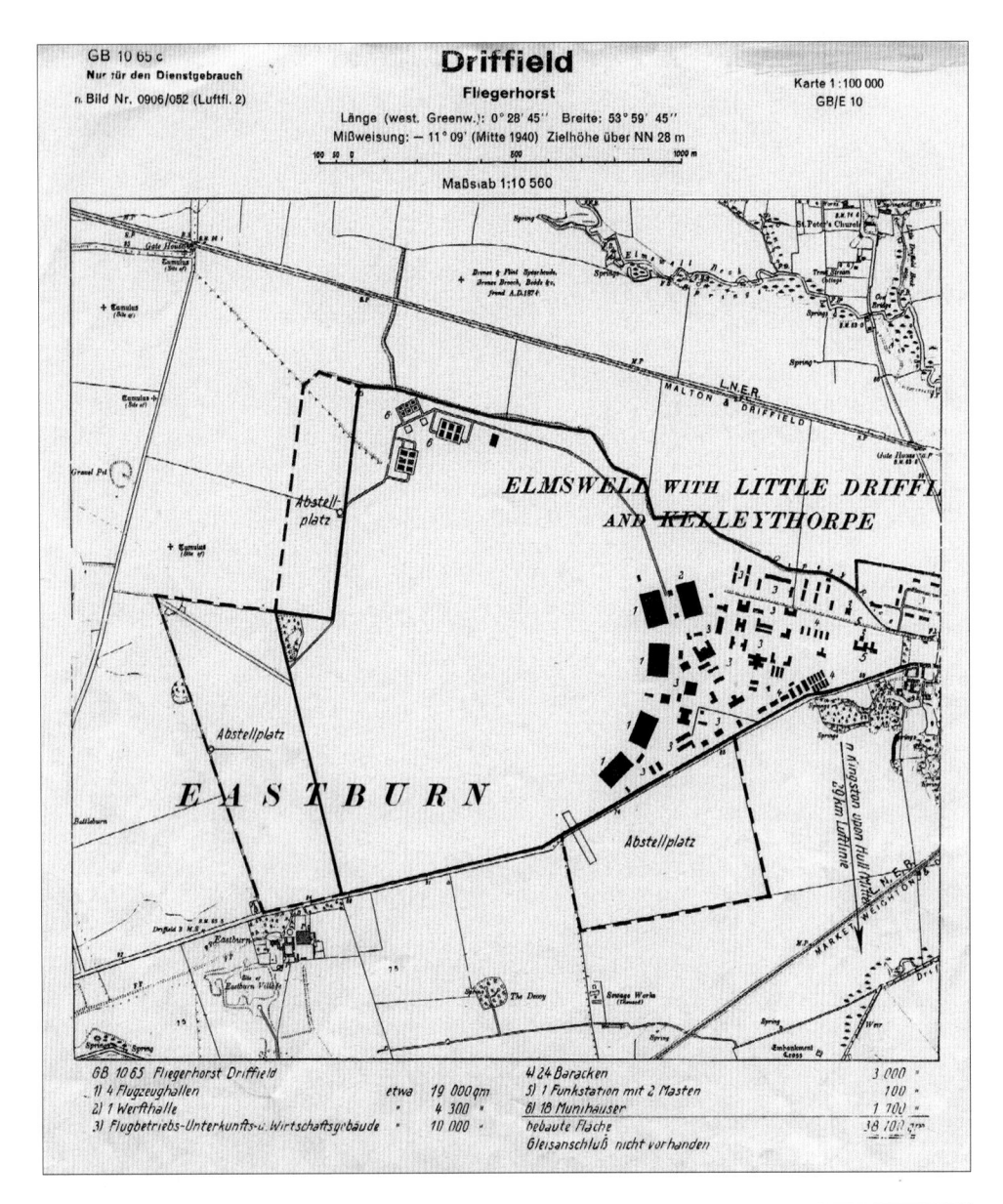

88: A Luftwaffe briefing map of RAF Driffield, used along with air reconnaissance photographs in preparation for air raids on the airfield in 1940. German intelligence officers have meticulously superimposed airfield details on a British 6 inches to 1 mile Ordnance Survey map.
Key:
1: 4 hangars
2. Repair shop hangar
3. Workshops, living quarters, storage buildings
4. 24 huts
5. 1 radio station with 2 masts
6. 18 munition sheds (bomb dumps)
'Abstellplatz' — dispersal areas for aircraft.

89: This is part of another Luftwaffe briefing document used in connection with the raids on RAF Driffield; it gives landmarks in relation to Driffield airfield. It is clear from the note next to Skipsea that the Germans were well aware that 'Skipsea airfield' was a dummy. It was a decoy airfield (an RAF Type 'K') with artificial buildings and fake Whitleys. The reference to a landing strip at Dotterell dates from several years before World War II when two banner-towing biplanes had operated from there in connection with advertising for Cadbury's chocolate. Obviously German intelligence or Nazi sympathisers had been doing their homework well before September 1939.

startled by the disturbing sound of machine gun fire. As he looked up, a dark-coloured German aircraft loomed overhead, the black and white Luftwaffe crosses clearly visible on the underside of its wings. Robert froze with fear as the enemy bomber turned sharply to the left, taking it over the gasworks off Seamer Road where it released four bombs. As three of the HEs exploded, Robert took cover behind a tree as bricks, other debris and shrapnel were sent flying over a wide area.

At the other side of Seamer Road, twelve-years old Leslie Wiffen of 27 Milton Avenue was enjoying the warm sunny weather in the field behind his street, when he saw an aeroplane flying towards him over Oliver's Mount. Initially, Leslie thought that it was a RAF Blenheim but quickly realised his mistake as the aircraft opened up with its forward-firing machine gun. Leslie thought that he was the target and his stomach 'turned over' as the German bomber dived down towards Seamer Road. Although frightened,

[10] Pre-war RAF Fighter Command had adopted rigid attack patterns numbered 1 to 6, chosen according to aircraft numbers and weather conditions. Combat experience soon led to modifications in line with the Luftwaffe's more flexible battle-tested tactics.

[11] This was probably when the Ju 88's navigator, Uffz W. Evers, jettisoned the cockpit roof in case the crew had to bale out and maps, papers and other loose items blew out of the cockpit.

90: *The cockpit of a Junkers Ju 88A showing the excellent view for the crew, despite the heavy canopy framing. German cockpits of the period were models of order and ergonomic thought, with ease of crew operation a priority. By contrast British aircraft tended to have instrumentation wherever the structural designers could find space for them; one of the most notorious examples being the propeller pitch controls in the Blenheim being behind the pilot's seat! note the Revi reflector gunsight on the left for the pilot.*

Leslie nevertheless watched the drama unfold just a few hundred yards away. He clearly saw the enemy aircraft drop four bombs as it roared over the gasworks, heard three loud explosions, saw a huge black cloud rise above the gasworks and bricks flying through the air. Leslie reckoned that the Ju 88 was no more than 250 ft above the valley floor as it sped south, overflying the Scarborough to Hull/York railway lines as it headed towards Seamer before banking left and heading out to sea.

The other breakaway Ju 88 released its four HEs over Bridlington, the bombs falling on the Byas Avenue-St. Alban Road part of town. Immediately after three of the four bombs had exploded, the following dramatic message was sent from the ARP Sub-Controller in the town to the ARP Regional Control Centre in Leeds:

"Bombs dropped 1320. Aerial battle proceeding over Bridlington now."

Shortly after the bombs fell on Bridlington, 616 Sqn's Sgt J. Hopewell (Green 3) located a Ju 88 flying at 8000 ft just off Flamborough Head:

"I immediately manoeuvred my aircraft into a suitable No.1 position[10] and then gave him a short burst at approximately 400 yards. The E/A started to climb, turning into a northerly direction. I immediately positioned and delivered a quarter attack from starboard at 300 yards, giving two or three second bursts. The ammunition seemed to penetrate mainplanes and cockpit…immediately the E/A started to evade me by turning west and following him I fired some more ammunition into his tail and engines… I noticed parts of the a/c disintegrating.[11] The E/A then pushed his nose down and made for land, finally coming down in an estimated position 3 miles NNW of Bridlington…it was noticeable that the enemy did not attempt to lower his undercarriage."

"The eagles are going to attack the lion"

Despite the valiant efforts of the Spitfire and Hurricane pilots, a formation of Ju 88s flew on towards RAF Driffield. Captaining one of the leading KG 30 bombers was Oblt Rudolf Kratz of KG 30's Stab (Staff) Flight:

"Our target, an English airfield…we know its layout accurately from aerial photographs taken during reconnaissance flights…every hangar, every barracks…The coast. The initial aiming point. No time for thinking…there lay England, the lion's den. But the eagles are going to attack the lion in his lair and wound him grievously."

Soon the menacing sound of enemy aero engines would be heard above the roar of tractor engines and the chatter of binders on farms close to the flight path of the Ju 88s. Horace Howard was a Speeton farmworker, harvesting on Henry Watson's Southfield Farm. Work had just resumed after a lunch break when:

"…I heard a loud droning noise…there they were…at least fifteen German bombers flying in from the sea just this side of Flamborough Head. They were in a kind of V-formation. I didn't see any RAF fighters but a few minutes later could hear the sound of machine gun fire."

Some sixteen miles south-west of Speeton, more harvesting was underway at Tibthorpe, a small village about two miles west of RAF Driffield. In a field of oats, one quarter of a mile north of the Tibthorpe crossroads, young J.W.H. 'Dick' Bradshaw was driving a tractor which was pulling a binder being operated by his father. Work was temporarily suspended when a message was brought to Bradshaw senior, ARP Head Warden for the district. The message stated 'Air Raid Warning Red', which meant that an air raid was likely in the area within the next ten minutes. Bradshaw junior then saw and identified the approaching aircraft as Junkers 88s:

"There were probably about fifteen of them. They circled to the west, then turned east and attacked the aerodrome."

The raid on RAF Driffield was also seen, and heard, by Nafferton youngster John Rudd:

"Ken Appleby, Eric Atkinson and myself were looking for pigeon eggs in the warehouse at Nafferton station when we heard the sound of many aircraft overhead. We rushed outside just in time to see the first bomber come out of a bank of cloud and dive earthwards over RAF Driffield, followed by loud explosions. Several more aircraft followed. Ack Ack (heavy anti-aircraft guns) and Pom-Pom (light anti-aircraft guns) were firing and all hell seemed to break loose. We, of course, ran home; had there been a record for 300 yards for nine-year olds we would easily have broken it!"

Most of the Ju 88s came in diagonally across the airfield to dive bomb the hangars and buildings in the south-east corner of the Bomber Command base.

Others targeted the Whitleys, which were dispersed around the perimeter of the airfield, or flew in low to strafe RAF Driffield with cannon and machine gun fire in a daring and spectacular attack.

Several RAF personnel recorded their impressions of what it was like to be caught in the middle of the bombing at RAF Driffield. In the ante-room of the Officer's Mess, at about 1320 hours, P/O Leonard Cheshire was chatting to his second pilot, P/O Desmond Coutts, while his new rear gunner, P/O Dick Rivaz, was writing a letter. Rivaz later told the story of what happened next:

"The air raid siren had sounded, and I looked out of the window and saw people running to the shelters… While the siren was still going there came an unearthly screaming noise. All other sounds were promptly drowned by the largest explosion I had ever heard…and the windows of the ante-room were blown in with a din like rifle shots. The next thing I remember was lying on my face in a passage…covered in dust and choking and surrounded by broken glass and rubble. I got to my feet and saw that the Mess a few feet behind me was a complete ruin. I could hear the whine of diving aeroplanes and the scream of falling bombs while all the time the ground shook with explosions. I was frightened, really frightened…more frightened than I had ever been before.

I went to the hangars to see what damage had been done there. They had been badly knocked about and one was on fire; the fire party was at work with their hoses amid a great din of crackling and sizzling.

On my way to Sick Quarters I saw a party of men digging furiously around a shelter that had received a direct hit; the ambulance was there… and the orderlies were lifting a man, with his tunic, face and hair covered with earth, onto a stretcher. Someone put a cigarette between his lips and lit it for him. Sweat was pouring off his face and caking the earth…and I noticed that his legs were in an unnatural, twisted position. Someone was digging around another pair of legs; the body was still buried and the legs were obviously broken. I saw two other men crushed, with faces nearly the colour of their tunics; they were both dead."

Incident:
On 15 August a Junkers 88 bomber (4D+?M of KG 30) crashed and blew up in a field farmed by the Hyde family of Lodge Farm, Fraisthorpe. One of their men had a most unpleasant shock when he picked up an airman's glove near the wreckage and found that there was still a hand inside it.

91: *Armourers and a fitter frantically prepare a Hurricane of an unidentified squadron for the next mission during the Battle of Britain period. Note the cover giving access to the gun breeches and ammunition bays lying on the ground. The muzzles for the four Browning machine-guns were totally recessed within each wing.*

92: *A typical harvest scene in East Yorkshire during the glorious summer of 1940 showing Jack Megginson (without hat) of Manor House, Fraisthorpe, with wagoner George Brockless. As an air battle developed over the district during the early afternoon of 15 August Jack Megginson and some of his farm workers had to abandon their stooking and dive for cover under a small stone bridge, which took a cart track over a muddy dyke. Back at Manor House, Jack's wife Irene and her mother-in-law Nellie sought shelter in a dark, windowless passage; there was so much noise from explosions and gunfire that they thought that the Germans were invading East Yorkshire. (Irene Megginson)*

93: *Supermarine Spitfire Is of No 616 (South Yorkshire) Sqn at dispersal, RAF Leconfield in 1940. The Squadron's QJ code can be seen on the fuselage of each aircraft.*

94: *No 616 Sqn's QJ-W, which was regularly flown by F/Lt. Denys Gillam during the first year of the war. The Sky colour 'fighter band' on the rear fuselage indicates that this picture was taken after 12 December 1940.*

51

P/O I.M.R. Brownlie, a 77 Sqn pilot, had been on the previous night's operation to bomb an oil refinery in France and was still in bed when the German bombers struck:

"I was asleep in my room on the first floor of the west wing of the Officers' Mess. My room was at the north end of the wing.

I was awakened by the noise of the air raid siren and soon realised that this was not another practice when the sound of exploding bombs came nearer. I got out of bed and went to the back of the bedroom door to put on my dressing gown. As I reached for the dressing gown the last bomb of the stick exploded on the south end of the west wing. The door blew open pinning me against the wall; the ceiling came down crushing my bed to the floor and visibility was instantly zero with dust.

I was unhurt, protected by the angle of the door and the wall. When the dust cleared I tried to get my shoes but they were trapped under the bed. As bombs were still going off and the need for shelter was obvious I got out of the room in bare feet, not really worried about broken glass and rough debris. The main staircase had collapsed but I got down and out to a nearby shelter via an intact service staircase. By then the raid was over."

Some of the departing low-flying Ju 88s despatched parting shots into streets and at farms as they raced for the coast. Not far from Driffield town centre, young Bill Milner had a graphic glimpse of one such incident:

"At that time I was eight-years old and lived with my family at Bridge Street, close to the parish church. On the day of the air raid, my sister and I were watching the frenzied activity of planes overhead in a blue cloudless sky and listening to the dull noise of exploding bombs and staccato gunfire. Suddenly a low-flying bomber appeared over the church tower heading due east above Bridge Street, directly towards us. When we could clearly see the pilot in the glazed cockpit my sister asked, 'Is that one of ours?'

95: *A group of 616 Sqn Spitfire pilots at RAF Leconfield during the Battle of Britain. Back row, l-r: P/O R. Marples, P/O H.S.L. Dundas, P/O H.K. Laycock, F/Lt D.E. Gillam, P/O T.B. Murray, P/O L.H. Casson, Sgt P.T. Wareing. Front row, l-r: Sgt T.E. Westmoreland, Sgt J. Hopewell, F/Sgt F.P. Burnard. All except Laycock (posted to 79 Sqn), Wareing and Burnard saw action during the daylight raid on RAF Driffield on 15 August. That day Jim Hopewell shot down the Ju 88 which force-landed near Bridlington reservoir.*

96: *A Hurricane of 73 Squadron during the winter of 1940-41. The dark spinner backplate gives an interesting effect.*

52

97: *This head-on view of a captured Junkers Ju 88A-1 dive-bomber clearly shows the shorter wingspan of the early variants. The later and improved Ju 88A-4 which saw much action over East Yorkshire had its winspan increased by 1.83m.*

The rat-a-tat of machine gun fire answered her question. We slammed the door, dashed into the closet under the stairs, and clutched each other in absolute stark terror and listened to the zings as bullets smashed into the side brick wall of the house."

There were other instances of machine-gun fire from departing enemy aircraft at Buckton, Nafferton, Hornsea and Skipsea between 1330 and 1400 hours. Near Buckton Hall, farmworker Ernest Shepherdson was hit in the face by a ricocheting bullet and taken to hospital in Bridlington. A gardener at 'White Stacks' on Rolston Road in Hornsea was similarly injured. Electricity cables and telephone wires were brought down in and around Skipsea but there were no casualties in the village.

"The vicar's wife dispensed coffee to the Luftwaffe"

Departing KG 30 aircrews felt confident that once they were clear of the target area they would have a safe flight back to Aalborg. For some, however, there would be no return to their Danish base as a few Spitfire and Hurricane pilots still had some ammunition left and were on the look out for enemy aircraft. Others would experience several tense minutes as 219 Sqn Blenheims pursued them out to sea.

To the south-east of Driffield, Sgt Alexander McNay (Red 3) of 73 Sqn shot down a brace of homeward-bound Ju 88s. McNay's first victim was using the ploy of 'hedge-hopping' in an attempt to avoid detection by RAF fighters. So low was the enemy bomber that it broke some telephone lines near Hornsea. Eventually, bullets from McNay's Hurricane sent the Junkers crashing into the sea about ten miles east of Hornsea. It had been an exhilarating chase for McNay, with combat taking place at about 50 ft over land and as low as 5 ft above the sea.

Sgt McNay's second 'kill' involved a close-range chase over the East Yorkshire countryside near Hornsea before the Ju 88, with an engine on fire and its pilot injured, belly-landed just north of Barmston.

The final moments of this particular enemy bomber were witnessed by a group of Army officers who had just finished lunch in their caravan near the coast at Barmston. One of them was Capt G.C. Griffiths, a Medical Officer based at Sledmere House — the HQ of 6th Brigade Field Ambulance, and a lunchtime guest of Capt. A.H. Williams, Company Commander of the 1st Battalion, the Royal Welch Fusiliers. The officers had heard the sound of bombing coming from the direction of Driffield followed by the sight of damaged German aircraft heading for the coast, including one which banked round the church tower in Barmston at a very low altitude. Capt Griffiths later described what happened next:

"Another Ju 88 banked round the church tower with its port engine on fire, circling north across the road and disappearing as it landed in the DLI (Durham Light Infantry) sector with the sound of machine gun fire. The watching figures were galvanised into action, and reached the scene by means of a hurried jeep ride. The plane looked very new, only the port engine and the adjacent wing along which flames were spreading with black, oily smoke, an exception. The heat of the burning engine was matched by the mood of the workmen working on the coastal fortifications who had come under fire from the rear gunners as the plane crash-landed in a field near the coast. The crew was being marched out at bayonet point by some of the DLI who kept them moving, and ensured that the workmen were kept at bay.

The Company Commander, having confirmed the bomb racks were empty, climbed into the cockpit to salvage equipment. The heat was terrific, although the flames hadn't yet reached the cockpit, but he managed to get a satchel containing the log and a lot of papers, including a map showing the North Sea and part of the Scandinavian sector. An aerial camera was retrieved by dint of smashing the glass front of the cockpit with a rifle butt. Amongst the other equipment salvaged was a collapsible boat. The satchel was sent to Battalion HQ and the DLI took the rest…

The pilot was first in line of the crew as they moved slowly from the plane with their hands up, but the pilot's progress was particularly slow and he attempted to point down to his right thigh where it was subsequently found he had a neat row of bullet holes. A splint was applied but morphine was refused, presumably as the pilot considered it a security risk. Meanwhile, the cockpit blew up and the sound of exploding ammunition accompanied the departure of the MO and the two wounded members of the crew to the First Aid Post in the village street, near the church, where the vicar's wife dispensed coffee to the Luftwaffe from a Coronation mug!"

53

Army personnel in the area had also witnessed the demise of another of the KG 30 bombers:

"A crescendo of sound pinpointed a black arrow of smoke northwards as another Ju 88 plunged earthwards in the DLI sector some distance away, the impact travelling more as a solid vibration than a noise."

There would be no prisoners from the particular Junkers 88 which had been attacked by Sgt D.S. Scott (Yellow 2) of 73 Sqn. One of the enemy bomber's crew had baled out during Scott's attack but his parachute had wrapped itself around the aircraft's tail; he went down with the plane. Scott then…

"…followed down and saw E/A blow up on ground. A flash and then black smoke. Then I saw pieces of E/A spread over the ground, scars on the ground and what appeared to be two craters. Also an open parachute nearby."

Meanwhile, two 616 Sqn pilots, Sgt G.E. Moberley and Sgt T.F. Westmoreland dived their Spitfires in pursuit of a brace of Ju 88s fleeing eastwards across Bridlington Bay. Both pilots claimed a success but Westmoreland did not see his target crash into the sea.

By now the Spitfire and Hurricane pilots were having to break off from combat as they expended their ammunition and were running dangerously low on fuel, but the 219 Sqn Blenheims continued to harass the homeward-bound German bombers, although the Junkers Ju 88 proved to be a faster and more manoeuvrable aircraft than its British twin-engined opponent.

Sgt F. Nightingale and his air gunner, Sgt G.W. Benn, experienced a few dramatic moments when they caught up with one escaping Ju 88 before it had reached the Yorkshire coast:

"Attacked one Ju 88…a quarter attack developing into a stern chase. Starboard engine of E/A belched black smoke. After third burst, appeared a glow in the cockpit; the front gunner was observed trying to beat out the flames with his hands. Followed E/A down to 2000 ft and forced to break off attack on account of being fired at by first a Blenheim and then three Spitfires."

A World War Two example of 'friendly fire.'

Two other Blenheim pilots, P/O K.W. Worsdell and Sgt A.J. Hodgkinson, attacked Ju 88s *"near Flamborough Head"* and *"off Flamborough Head to 50 miles out."* Strikes were seen on the enemy aircraft but the latter outpaced the Blenheims as they fled out to sea.

Apart from chasing Junkers Ju 88s, F/O T.P. Harnett, P/O G.M. Head, P/O D.M. Lake, P/O W.G. Lambie and P/O J.G. Topham all reported making contact with Heinkel He 111s, while Harnett, Head, and F/Lt Goddard also mentioned Dornier Do 17s in their Combat Reports. As these pilots had become involved in combat more than 100 miles out from the Yorkshire Coast, it is highly likely that they had encountered German bombers which had carried out a major raid on Tyneside and Wearside. From Stavanger in Norway, 63 Heinkel He 111s of KG 26 escorted by 21 Messerschmitt Bf 110s of ZG 76 had participated in this attack on the North East. As, however, no Do 17s were in action over the North of England that day, one must assume that some Blenheim pilots must have mistaken the Bf 110s for Dorniers, both aircraft having two engines and a similar twin-fin tail feature.

The 219 Sqn Blenheim crews had shown great courage and tonacity in pursuing enemy bombers so far out over the North Sea. This was exemplified by the actions of Sgt O.A. Dupee (pilot) and Sgt T.H. Banister (air gunner). Off the Yorkshire coast, they had been in combat with a German bomber and had

Incident:
14 August. Whitley Mk V P5044 of 77 Sqn was returning from a mission against oil refineries in Bordeaux when it became lost in cloud. While descending to ascertain their position, the aircraft hit balloon barrage cables near Eastleigh, Hants, and crashed, killing F/O W.A. Stenhouse and his crew.

98: *One of No 219 Sqn's most successful pilots during World War II was J.G. Topham. P/O Topham, flying a Bristol Blenheim, claimed a Ju 88 'probable' during the 15 August attack against RAF Driffield and another Ju 88 'probable' that night after a combat off Flamborough Head, both in association with his air gunner Sgt T.R. Marshall. Topham is seen here, second left, front row, after he had switched to flying the Bristol Beaufighter and had been promoted to the rank of Flight Lieutenant. Second right back row is Sgt H.W.W. Berridge, who was Topham's AI operator. Both Johnny Topham DSO, DFC and Horace Berridge DSO, DFC survived the war. (219 Sqn Association via Bill Norman)*

54

This almost brand new Junkers Ju 88A-5 4D+KL of 3./KG 30 was shot down at Bernston by Sgt Alexander McNay of 73 Sqn on 15 August 1940 after it had attacked RAF Driffield. I Gruppe of KG 30 was unusual in that it carried the Gruppe emblem on the aircraft nose and also a Staffel badge, the background colour of which may have varied according to the staffel, on the engine cowlings. The photo of the cowling emblem of this aircraft is not good enough to be certain of the colour, but it could have been yellow. 4D+KL is in the standard 70/71/65 camouflage finish with the aircraft letter 'K' and spinner tips in yellow.

Hurricane Mk I P3310, TP-G, of 73 Squadron as flown by Sgt Alexander McNay when he shot down the Ju 88 4D+KL of 3./KG 30 seen above on 15 August 1940. The aircraft wears typical Battle of Britain period markings, with a slightly non-standard fuselage roundel, probably as a result of in the field modifications. Note that 'G' carries the night-flying 'blinkers' indicating the dual role envisaged for many RAF fighter aircraft at that time. Finish is Dark Green/Dark Earth and a version of the new 'Sky' underside colour.

ILLUSTRATIONS NOT TO SAME SCALE.

55

been on the receiving end of a spirited response from the enemy machine's dorsal gunner. Machine gun bullets had smashed through the glazing of the Blenheim's cockpit, hitting Sgt Dupee in one arm.

The relevant entry in 219 Sqn's Operations Record Book read:

"Sgt Dupee was wounded in the right arm by the enemy's return fire. Sgt Banister, his Air Gunner, assisted in bringing the machine back over the coast and making a good landing at Driffield with the wheels retracted. Both these airmen were recommended for and have since received the Distinguished Flying Medal."

By 1400 hours, all 616 Sqn Spitfires and 73 Sqn Hurricanes had returned safely to RAF Leconfield, but it would be another hour before all 219 Squadron Blenheims, with the exception Sgt Dupee's aircraft, were back at base.

Soon, the RAF, ARP and Police were compiling their reports on the afternoon's events, while captured Luftwaffe airmen were being interrogated.

During the evening of 15 August, 73 Sqn pilots P/O Donald Scott and Sgt John Griffin drove over to the East Yorkshire coast to inspect the Ju 88s shot down by Scott and McNay. A number of 'trophies' were recovered from the enemy bombers and taken back to RAF Church Fenton.

Oblt Rudolf Kratz, on board one of the attacking Junkers Ju 88's, had boasted that *"...the eagles are going to attack the lion in his lair and wound him grievously."* Well, the lion had roared from his lair, fought back, and given the attacking eagles quite a mauling.

Footnote:

This major raid on RAF Driffield would never have taken place at all if only a certain Bomber Command operation, two days earlier, had resulted in a succesful outcome.

At 0840 hours on 13 August, twelve Bristol Blenheim Mk. IVs of 82 Sqn had taken off from RAF airfields at Bodney and Watton in Norfolk. Their objective had been to attack and inflict serious damage on KG 30's base at Aalborg in north-east Denmark. One of their number had turned back with a technical problem, but the remaining eleven had flown on across Denmark. Not one of the eleven Blenheims returned to England. Hit first by German flak and then attacked by Messerschmitt Bf 109s, all eleven 82 Sqn aircraft were shot down and their pilots and gunners either killed or taken prisoner.

The Aalborg raid on 13 August 1940 had been a disaster for 82 Sqn, but the failed operation was also bad news for RAF Driffield. With the Luftwaffe airfield and aircraft at Aalborg unharmed, KG 30 was able to launch its attack on RAF Driffield on 15 August with a full complement of bombers.

99 Above: *A 250kg high explosive bomb demolished this bungalow at No 16 St Alban Road in Bridlington. Miraculously, a woman in the building survived the explosion and was brought out from the wreckage by an ARP Rescue Party. (ERYC L&IS)*

100 Far left: *F/O P.E.G. Carter of 73 Sqn shot down a Ju 88 during combat over Bridlington Bay on 15 August. Peter Carter (21) later moved to 302 (Polish) Sqn and was killed on 18 August 1940 when he baled out of his Hurricane at too low an altitude over Kempton Park Racecourse in Surrey.*

101 Left: *219 Sqn Blenheim pilot Sgt Fred Nightingale and his air gunner, Sgt. George Benn, were chasing a Ju 88 towards the East Yorkshire coast when they were fired at by four RAF aircraft. However no harm was done and they were able to return to base. Nightingale (26) was later killed in a Beaufighter crash on 17 December 1940. Benn survived the war.*

102: *This No 77 Squadron Whitley was totally destroyed when a 250kg high explosive bomb crashed through the hangar roof. 77 Squadron aircraft destroyed in the bombing were:*
KN-M/N1353
N1501
N1506
P5056

103: *Oblt Werner Bachmann's Junkers Ju 88 A-4, 4D+DR of 7./KG 30 lies in a field of oats three miles north-north-west of Bridlington. Note the white spinners, the staffel colour.*

104: *Whitley DY-B of 102 Sqn. was damaged beyond repair. Other 102 squadron aircraft destroyed in the raid were:*
N1378
N1413
N1420/DY-L
P4945/DY-L
P5022

AFTER THE BATTLE
The cost

The damage done by the raiders at RAF Driffield had been considerable, but the situation would have been far worse if all fifty of the Aalborg-based bombers had got through to attack the airfield. There have been exaggerated claims that all of the Ju 88s reached their target and that they dropped 169 bombs on RAF Driffield, but an Air Ministry document – Summary 393/Item 459 – clearly states that:

"Driffield aerodrome was bombed at 1330 hours by 17 enemy aircraft which dropped 32 HE bombs…"

This statement confirms a point made in the previous chapter, namely that only about half of the Ju 88s carried HE bombs; the rest of the enemy raiders were used in a strafing capacity, although it is possible that these low-flying aircraft also dropped batches of small fragmentation bombs as they criss-crossed the airfield.

The 'Diving Eagles' had been very accurate with their bombing which had left four of RAF Driffield's five hangers badly damaged; No 5 hangar was completely destroyed and never rebuilt during World War II. Blocks of buildings at the airfield, including the Officers' Mess, Sergeants' Mess and a barrack block had also suffered serious damage, and several wooden huts used by the army had been burnt out.

Also, the Guard Room had been wrecked, an air raid shelter hit, and a water main fractured. Ten Whitley bombers, five each from 77 Sqn and 102 Sqn, had been destroyed and others damaged. Apart from the destruction and damage done by the bombing, more harm had been done by the low-flying Ju 88s which had strafed aircraft, buildings, shelters and gun emplacements with machine gun and cannon fire[12].

Sadly, there had been thirteen fatalities at RAF Driffield, twelve service personnel and one civilian.

One of the fatalities, LAC Kenneth Eric New of 77 Sqn, was from Eighth Avenue in nearby Bridlington. ACW Marguerite Hudson was a driver at the bomber base and was the first WAAF to be killed by enemy action in World War Two. The five soldiers killed had all been involved in the airfield's ground defences. The one civilian to die, Frank Ibbitson, was a local man and a former postman, who lived on George Street in Driffield.

During the following day the death toll rose to fourteen when LAC Bertrand Ash of 102 Sqn died from injuries received during the air raid. Ash had been sheltering behind a steel hangar door with his friend John Grimstone, a radio mechanic at the base. Grimstone escaped unscathed but Ash, upon seeing a panic-stricken horse, abandoned while still attached to the shafts of a cart, had rushed out to rescue the distressed animal. As he ran from the hangar a 250kg HE bomb exploded in the vicinity of the horse and cart, blasting out a deadly shower of shrapnel, some of which ripped into Ash's body inflicting dreadful

105 Above: *Another view of Bachmann's bomber. Behind the hedge in the distance is the A165 Bridlington (to the left) to Scarborough road. Just out of the photograph to the right is Bridlington Reservoir. This is the Ju 88 shot down by Sgt. Jim Hopewell of No 616 Sqn. (ERYC L&IS)*

[12] *The Ju 88A-1 and A-5 could both be fitted with an MG 15 machine-gun firing through the nose glazing, as well as a similar weapon fixed to fire through the pilot's windscreen. Some were fitted with a 20mm MG FF cannon, but not usually as early as this date. The fighter Ju 88C, fitted with four machine-guns in the nose, was, however, just entering service and could well have been used in the strafing role.*

wounds upon the young 102 Sqn Leading Aircraftman.

There had also been several injuries; fourteen service personnel and two civilians had been detained in hospital. Two RAF officers hospitalised, P/O Timoney (pilot) and P/O Saltzgeber (navigator) of 77 Sqn, had been on the previous night's operation to bomb an oil refinery in France. P/O Saltzgeber, a Canadian of German parentage, had been enjoying a relaxing bath when the raiders struck.

Driffield town, however, had remained virtually untouched during the raid on the neighbouring airfield. There had been a little superficial damage to buildings, caused by machine gun fire from departing Ju 88s, but no casualties. The only serious damage to civilian property in the Driffield district occurred at Kelleythorpe where, across the A163 from RAF Driffield, four HEs had hit the farmhouse and outbuildings. Again, there were no casualties. West along the A163, Eastburn Farm had a lucky escape as one stick of bombs fell on three Whitleys dispersed across the road. The blast from the bombs caused some minor damage at the farm and flying shrapnel killed or injured a number of farm animals. A farm worker at Eastburn had a lucky escape as shrapnel from one exploding bomb rattled into the tractor under which he was sheltering.

Away from Driffield, there had been instances of serious damage to property, two fatalities and a number of civilian injuries. Another farm to be hit was Home Farm at the eastern end of Burton Agnes alongside the A166 Driffield to Bridlington road. Here, three HEs had severely damaged farm buildings and a threshing machine and a pony and two cows had been killed. Nearby houses had suffered only minor damage but no person had been killed or seriously injured, although a number of local people had been badly shocked by the exploding bombs. Fires started among stacks at the farm had spread to an adjacent ammunition dump and also to several Army vehicles. AFS trailer pumps had been sent from Bridlington, but at first the military would not allow the AFS crews to tackle the blaze as munitions were involved and there was one unexploded bomb.

At Bridlington, there had been considerable damage to housing where three HEs had detonated in the Byas Avenue-St Alban Road area; a fourth HE had buried itself in the ground at the corner of St Alban Road and St Cuthbert's Road but failed to explode. With regard to casualties, one person had been killed and three people taken to hospital, while two others had been treated for minor injuries at a nearby First Aid Post. At 16 St Alban Road, a Miss P. Machon had been lucky to survive as the blast from one of the bombs had caused her bungalow to collapse around her. Miss Machon had been rescued from the ruins of her home by ARP Rescue Party Leader Tom Alderson. We shall hear more about the work of Mr Alderson later.

North along the coast at Scarborough, where another breakaway Junkers 88 had dropped four 250kg HE bombs, there had been some damage at the town's gasworks and at the LNER engine sheds close to Seamer Road. Again, one of the four bombs had failed to explode. Six workmen in the vicinity had been injured and four of them detained in Scarborough Hospital. Later that afternoon, twelve-years old Leslie Wiffen, who had watched the bombing from behind Milton Avenue, was saddened to learn that the one fatality in this instance had been his young friend Ernest Gates (8) of 18 Quarry Mount. Ernest's body had been discovered at Purnell's Wood behind the gasworks.

Following combat with the KG 30 bombers on 15 August 1940, the 616 Sqn Operations Record Book noted:

"Eight Ju 88s confirmed, four unconfirmed, two damaged."

The 73 Sqn ORB stated:

"7 E/A confirmed losses, 3 E/A unconfirmed, 2 damaged." while 219 Sqn's ORB recorded:

"…two aircraft were believed to be destroyed."

So, according to the respective ORB's at least fifteen KG 30 aircraft had been destroyed during the air battles on 15 August. This was an exaggeration, but is understandable considering the chaos in the air as aircraft dived, wheeled and climbed in the skies above Flamborough Head, the East Yorkshire countryside, and adjacent coastal waters. It is highly probable that two or more pilots had made the same claim and there were definitely cases where pilots had not seen their claims actually crash.

The widely accepted RAF conclusion was that seven KG 30 Junkers Ju 88s had been shot down on 15 August – three on land and four in the North Sea – and that three other Ju 88s had later crash-landed on the continent with combat damage, two in Holland and one at KG 30's Aalborg base in Denmark. According to official KG 30 loss details for 15 August, however, six KG 30 aircraft had been lost on their operation to RAF Driffield, not seven. What is definite is that three KG 30 Junkers Ju 88s were brought down in East Yorkshire on that day. These aircraft were 4D+DR of 7./KG 30, 4D+KL of 3./KG 30, and 4D+?M of 4./KG 30. The uncertainty about the individual letter of the third of these planes stems from the fact that this particular bomber had blown up and disintegrated after diving into the ground, thus making complete identification out of the question.

What is in dispute in relation to the above aircraft is the crash locations of the three Ju 88s which came down on land and what happened to their crews. It is in this area that the author must take issue with the facts as presented in other respected publications for all contain a number of inaccuracies relating to the three German bombers shot down over East Yorkshire on 15 August 1940.

All state that Junkers Ju 88 4D+DR of 7./KG 30

Facts:
On August 10 1940, the RAF had 749 single-engined serviceable fighters, with 372 in storage. The Luftwaffe had 805, plus 224 twin-engined fighters, 261 dive-bombers and 998 bombers. By 17 September the RAF still had 723 single-engined fighters and 225 more in storage. On the same date the Luftwaffe now had 276 single-engined fighters, 230 twin-engined fighters, 343 dive-bombers and 750 bombers.

106: Some of the damage at RAF Driffield after the daylight raid on 15 August 1940. This is the wrecked Officers' Mess; now quite literally 'a mess'.

107: This is the air raid shelter which received a direct hit resulting in several deaths.

108: The burnt out remains of Junkers Ju 88A-5 4D+KL of 3./KG 30, which was belly-landed between Hamilton Hill Farm and the cliff top at Barmston by Uffz Ludwig von Lorenz without injury to himself or his crew. It was brought down by a No 73 Sqn Hurricane piloted by Sgt Alexander McNay. (Hull Daily Mail)

109: This view of Oblt Bachmann's Ju 88 clearly shows the white aircraft letter 'D' identifying it as from the 7th Staffel of KG 30.

110 Right: 4D+DR was used as a convenient platform for numerous propaganda photos of the time. Note the white shield behind KG 30's diving eagle.

111 Far right: Oblt Werner Bachmann, the pilot of 4D+DR pictured here at KG 30's Aalborg base in Denmark just days before the bomber was shot down over East Yorkshire on 15 August 1940.

112 Right: An engine plate from one of the Ju 88s brought down over East Yorkshire, believed to be from the one shot down near Ottringham on 20 August.

113 Far right: Uffz Werner Evers (navigator/bomb aimer) on the left, with Flgr Robert Walther (flight engineer/air gunner) of the crew of 4D+DR, captured at the crash site near Bridlington Reservoir. (Goss/Rauchbach Archives)

114: The memorial plaque dedicated to those who died in the attack on RAF Driffield on 19 August 1940. It is located just inside the main gate of the former bomber base.

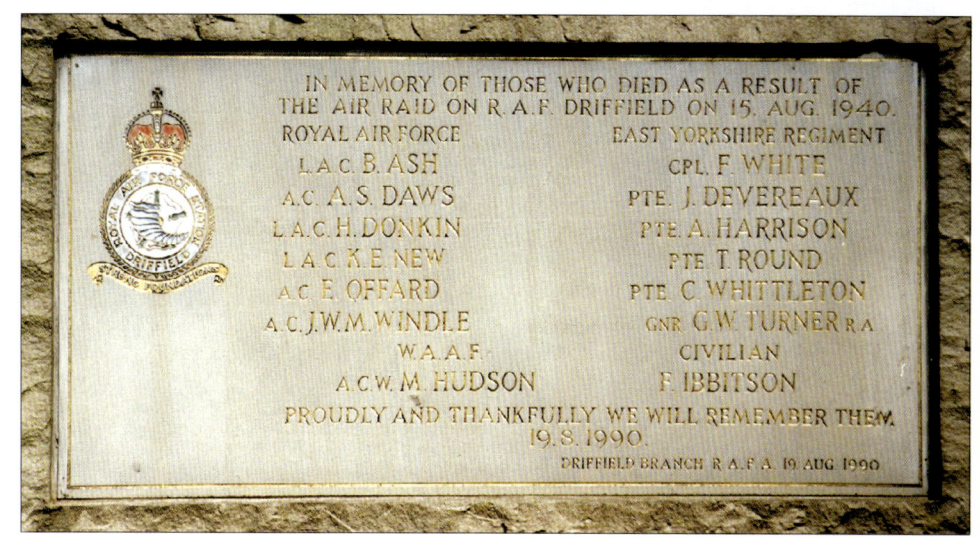

61

came down 'near Hornby'. This statement is disproven when one studies photographs of the crashed bomber, ARP/Police messages relating to the incident, the Combat Report of Sgt James Hopewell of 616 Sqn, the relevant Ordnance Survey map and considers a number of eye-witness reports.

Some of the accompanying photographs of this particular Junkers 88 clearly show the individual aircraft letter 'D' painted in white, the colour of 7 Staffel. A police message gives the location of the downed bomber as "...*near Bridlington Reservoir on Scarborough Road*". This is in line with Sgt Hopewell's Combat Report which states "...*estimated position 3 miles NNW of Bridlington*". An examination of a local Ordnance Survey map reveals that there is no such place as 'Hornby' anywhere near the crash site.

A number of civilians, schoolboys at the time, have also confirmed the crash location of 'D-Dora'. News had quickly spread that there was a German aircraft down at the top of White Hill, the long climb out of Bridlington to the north of the town. One of the first civilians to arrive on the scene was 14-years old Alan Staveley, a Speeton lad. At the time of the raid on RAF Driffield, Alan was working for local farmer Norman Marshall in a field opposite the Dotterel Inn at Reighton. He had been given the tedious job of walking up and down rows of turnips pulling out troublesome weeds. What promised to be a most boring afternoon for Alan was suddenly brightened by the arrival of his pal Gordon Hayward with some startling news:

"Hey Al, there's a German plane come down at Brid Reservoir. Are you coming?"

Alan did not hesitate. He grabbed his bicycle from behind a hedge and off the pair went, speeding downhill from the Dotterel, passing under the railway bridge at the bottom of the hill and then pedalling furiously uphill to the reservoir. Alan picks up the story:

"*We rode off the road onto the grass verge near the reservoir. Over the hedge, lying on its belly with its nose pointing towards the Brid-Scarborough Road, was a Junkers Ju 88. But then we got one hell of a shock; leaning against the reservoir railings were three German airmen, still wearing their flying helmets, with a fourth lying on the ground in front of them. We thought that he was probably dead. We dare not go any closer, thinking that they might shoot at us*".

Another schoolboy to head for the crash site was Bill Skelton who shortly after the 'All Clear' had sounded, had cycled up White Hill from his home at 36 Nelson Street in Bridlington. Bill, whose father was a coastguard in the town, gave his version of events in a letter to the author:

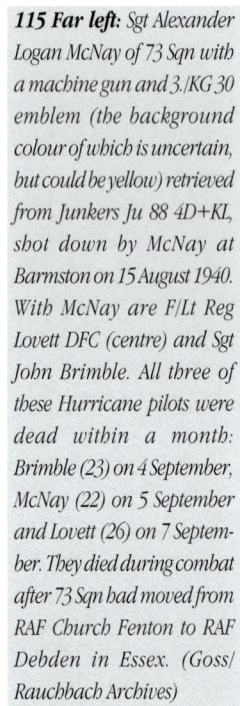

115 Far left: Sgt Alexander Logan McNay of 73 Sqn with a machine gun and 3./KG 30 emblem (the background colour of which is uncertain, but could be yellow) retrieved from Junkers Ju 88 4D+KL, shot down by McNay at Barmston on 15 August 1940. With McNay are F/Lt Reg Lovett DFC (centre) and Sgt John Brimble. All three of these Hurricane pilots were dead within a month: Brimble (23) on 4 September, McNay (22) on 5 September and Lovett (26) on 7 September. They died during combat after 73 Sqn had moved from RAF Church Fenton to RAF Debden in Essex. (Goss/Rauchbach Archives)

116 Left: F/Lt. Reg Lovett DFC, seen centre with two other 73 Sqn pilots: P/O Donald Scott who shot down the Junkers 88 which which crashed at Auburn on 15 August and P/O Robert Rutter. They are pictured here enjoying a quiet pint in the Ship Inn at Selby shortly before their squadron moved south to RAF Debden. Scott and Rutter survived the war but Lovett was dead just days after this photograph was taken. (Goss/Rauchbach Archives)

117: This is another of I./KG 30's Ju 88s, crash-landed in Denmark. Although not confirmed, this is believed to show one of the attackers which was damaged during the 15 August attack on RAF Driffield and was written off when it returned to base.

62

> *"I can recall being at the top of the hill on the Scarborough road about three miles from the centre of Brid. I was accompanied by one or two of my cronies, all with our bicycles. I'll never know how we got the information about the downed aircraft, but the 'jungle telegraph' was very efficient during the war with the Police, Observer Corps, Air Raid Wardens and Coastguard all keeping each other and the public up-to-date, contrary to edicts. As we arrived at the point where the road to Scarborough turns northwest, on the east side and between 100 and 200 yards from the carriageway was an aircraft and a man in flying gear was being escorted from the machine. The aircraft was lying with no visible damage, the undercarriage was up and from its position looked as though it had landed from the east".*

Bridlington School pupil Brian Colley of St Johns Street became very popular with his friends following his father's involvement with Junkers 88 4D+DR:

"My father was James Colley, a member of the East Riding Constabulary stationed in Bridlington and was on duty when the raid developed. Immediately after the raid was over, he was transported to White Hill to 'Watch Over' the Ju 88 which was there until the arrival of Army/Royal Air Force guards. Some two hours later when he returned to our house he produced a piece of bloodstained German Air Force uniform and half a dozen rounds of ammunition from the plane".

On a personal note, the author also has a clear recollection of this particular Junkers 88, having been taken by his parents 'to see what a German bomber looked like'. The aircraft was painted a very dark colour with a large swastika on its tail; it appeared to be virtually undamaged, apart from bent propellers, and had belly-landed in a field of oats.

Finally, who were the four German airmen on board Ju 88 4D+DR and what happened to them? The Ju 88's crew was as follows: *Oblt* Werner Bachmann (pilot), *Uffz* Werner Evers (observer), *Fw* Georg Henneske (wireless operator) and *Flgr* Robert Walther (flight engineer/airgunner). Their one casualty was Henneske, shot in the head during combat with Sgt Jim Hopewell's Spitfire. Bachmann and Evers also feared the worst for Walther, who had been lying in the belly of the plane when Bachmann carried out a textbook wheels-up landing, but after Bachmann and Evers had removed Henneske's limp body from above Walther's position, out crawled the shocked, shaken, but otherwise unhurt flight engineer.

Soon, Bachmann, Evers and Walther were surrounded by British soldiers. After handing over their pistols, the three Luftwaffe men were transported under armed escort to Hunmanby Hall, the nearest Army base with secure guard room accommodation. They were then interrogated by a RAF Intelligence Officer before being transferred to prisoner-of-war camps.

The conveyance of the three Germans to Hunmanby was witnessed by a young Reighton man. Ted Bradshaw was working in one of his father Ben's fields near the Dotterel to Hunmanby/ Reighton to Grindale crossroads when an Army lorry drove past:

"The tarpaulin was thrown back and I had a good view of three German airmen sitting there. A couple of our soldiers carrying rifles were in there with them. It gave us something to talk about at tea-time!"

But what of the mortally wounded *Bordfunker* (wireless operator), Georg Henneske? Bachmann and Evers both thought that their comrade had been killed in the cockpit during combat, hit by bullets from Jim Hopewell's Spitfire. Alan Staveley also thought that Henneske was dead when he saw him lying on the ground near Bridlington Reservoir. Yet entry 11749 in the 'Bridlington Register of Burials, No 12' states that Georg Henneske (25) died *"...at Sledmere House"* on 15 August 1940 and that he was buried in Bridlington Cemetery, grave 230 West Section, four days later. This piece of information suggests that Henneske must have been taken to Sledmere House, the HQ of 6 Brigade Field Ambulance and not to Hunmanby with the other three crew members as recorded in a police message.

The second Luftwaffe bomber to come down in East Yorkshire on 15 August 1940 was Junkers Ju 88 4D+KL. In some Battle of Britain books the crash location of this 3./KG 30 aircraft is given as 'Hamilton Hill Farm, Barnstown'. Hamilton Hill Farm is confirmed in ARP/Police reports, but for 'Barnstown' one should read 'Barmston'.

At Barmston, the four captured crew members of Ju 88 4D+KL were *Uffz* Ludwig von Lorentz (pilot), *Uffz* Heinrich Kenski (observer), *Ogefr* Heinrich Trumann (wireless operator) and *Gefr* Johann Gobel (air gunner). Later, under interrogation, they revealed that they had bombed RAF Driffield before being attacked by a Hurricane.

What of the third Junkers 88 to crash in East Yorkshire on 15 August 1940? When the author read in all of the leading Battle of Britain books that Junkers Ju 88 4D+?M had crashed 'at' or 'near Hunmanby' it was apparent that something was wrong. At the time of KG 30's raid on RAF Driffield, the author's father was an auxiliary fireman in Hunmanby. If a German aircraft had crashed in the Hunmanby area on 15 August then the family would certainly have known about it.

Eventually, in the County Archives at Beverley, the author discovered ARP/Police messages which give the crash location of this Junkers 88 as *"...at Auburn on cliff top"*. As many East Yorkshire folk will know, Auburn was actually one of the many 'lost villages' along the Holderness coast, lost to the destructive power of marine erosion. All that remains

118: *Hunmanby Hall, where a number of Luftwaffe airmen were interrogated after their capture on 15 August 1940.*

119: *Junkers Ju 88 4D+KL burning fiercely shortly after it crash-landed between Hamilton Hill Farm and the cliff top at Barmston. The crew were quickly captured by men of the Durham Light Infantry. Despite the poor quality of the picture, the yellow individual aircraft letter 'K' can be clearly seen.*

120: *RAF Intelligence officers trying to glean something of value from the wreckage of Junkers Ju 88 4D+?M, which dived into a field and blew up just north of Auburn Farm, three miles south of Bridlington. This is the bomber shot down by P/O Donald Scott in a 73 Sqn Hurricane. (ERYC L&IS)*

121: Confirmation of the crash locations of the three Junkers 88s which came down on 15 August 1940. This is the first police message.

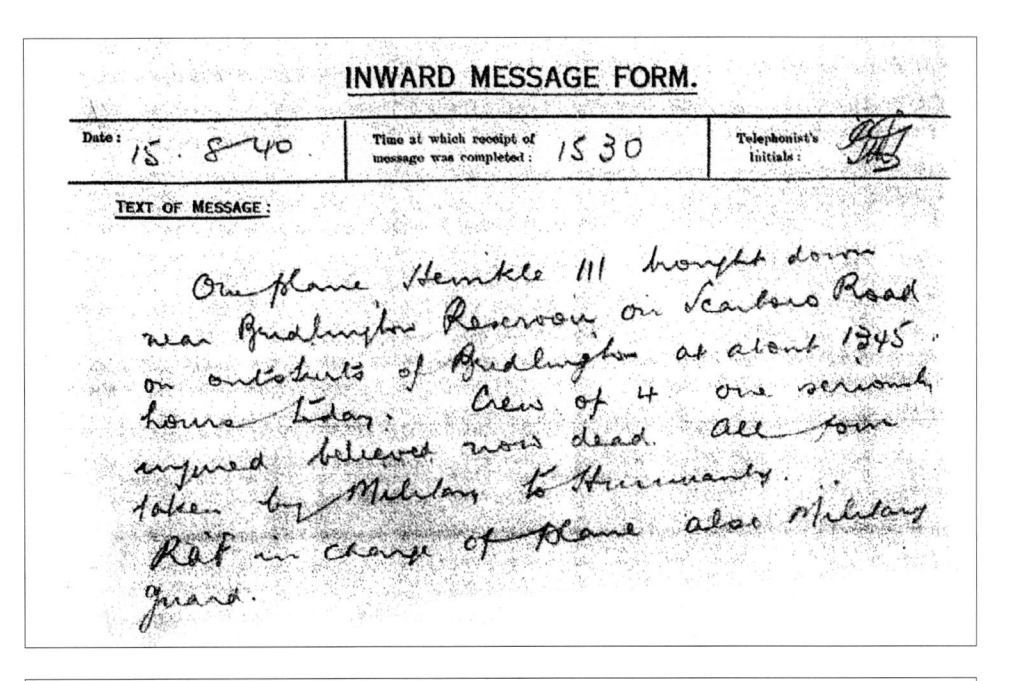

122: While this is the ARP message which correctly identifies the aircraft type.

now is a farm, Auburn Farm, which is in the parish of Fraisthorpe. Irene Megginson, who was living at Manor House in Fraisthorpe during the summer of 1940, told the author how this German bomber had crashed into a field to the south of Auburn Farm between Fraisthorpe village and the cliff top.

There were no prisoners from this 4./KG 30 aircraft, which had dived at a steep angle into a field and exploded. Initially, only one body was found, that of wireless operator *Uffz* Severin Kursch, who had baled out during Hurricane pilot Sgt Douglas Scott's fierce attack, but whose parachute had become entangled around the bomber's tail unit. Kursch's last few moments alive must have been horrific as his diving, out of control Ju 88 dragged him to a violent death on a quiet East Yorkshire cliff top. A second airman's body was later recovered, that of observer *Fw* Robert Pohl. All that was found of the other two crew members, *Fw* Rudolf Bihr (pilot) and *Uffz* Arnulf Neumeyer (air gunner) was a scattering of body parts.

Pohl and Kursch were buried at Bridlington Cemetery, Graves 248 and 239 West Section respectively, on Monday 19 August 1940. The shattered remains of Bihr and Neumeyer were placed in a single grave, Grave 257 West Section, on the same day. At some later date, the coffins containing the bodies of the five German airmen killed in combat over East Yorkshire on 15 August 1940 were transferred to the *Deutschen Soldatenfriedhof* (German War Cemetery) at Cannock Chase in Staffordshire.

Eight more Luftwaffe airmen lost their lives during the 15 August raid on RAF Driffield but they have no known graves, their bombers having been shot down over the North Sea. Their aircraft were both 7./KG 30 Ju 88s, piloted by *Fw* Bernard Gutow and *Lt* Wolf-Dietrich Riede.

It is thought that a sixth KG 30 Ju 88 was lost on the same operation but details are sketchy, the relevant page of III/KG 30 loss details having been fire-damaged during an attempt to destroy Luftwaffe records towards the end of the war. What is certain is that three other KG 30 Ju 88's crash-landed on the continent when returning from the Driffield raid, two in Holland and one at KG 30's Aalborg base. All three had battle damage and one was a write-off.

It is perfectly understandable why the leading books on the Battle of Britain all state that Ju 88 4D+DR came down 'near Hornby' and that 4D+?M crashed 'at' or 'near Hunmanby'. The answer lies in the following extract from the Appendix to Air Intelligence Report AI 1(k) No 267/1940, which was compiled after the initial interrogation of captured German airmen and early reports from RAF officers who had visited the crash sites of the three Ju 88s:

11	15/8/40 Nr Hornby	Ju 88	7./KG 30 4D+DR
12	15/8/40 Near Bridlington	Ju 88	3./KG 30 4D+KL
13	15/8/40 Nr Hunmanby	Ju 88	4./KG 30 4D+-M

But, there is a note at the beginning of this report which says "*...the statements made have not as yet been verified*". One can only assume that Hunmanby entered the equation because some of

123: Heinkel He 111s of KG 26 also took part in the major raid on the north-east on 15 August. This one is shown a few months later, probably in about December, when the II Gruppe moved to Sicily to begin operations in the Mediterranean and North Africa.

the captured German airmen were interrogated at Hunmanby Hall. It is more difficult to explain the appearance of 'Hornby' in the AI report, unless in all the excitement and confusion as messages were flashed to and fro 'Hunmanby' became 'Hornby'. However, the accompanying copies of ARP/Police messages recorded on 15 August 1940 confirm conclusively where the three Junkers 88s in question came down in East Yorkshire.

The air battles over East Yorkshire and adjacent coastal waters between the Hurricanes, Spitfires and Blenheims of the RAF and the Junkers 88s of the Luftwaffe had been a one-sided contest. At least six KG 30 bombers had been destroyed and three others badly damaged, while at least thirteen German airmen had lost their lives and another seven made prisoners-of-war. This was in stark contrast to one rather bent, but repairable, 219 Sqn Blenheim and its slightly injured pilot.

Following the failure of the unescorted major daylight raid on RAF Driffield, Lt Werner Baumbach[13] of 5./KG 30, destined to become one of the Luftwaffe's finest pilots and most highly decorated officers, commented:

"Without fighter cover, bombers, even when flying in dense formations, were easy meat for British fighters. And the fighters of the Royal Air Force are good".

But even the presence of a fighter escort did not guarantee success for the Luftwaffe bombers. As the 50 Junkers 88s of KG 30 were approaching the East Yorkshire coast on 15 August, to the north an even larger Luftwaffe force, consisting of 63 Heinkel 111s of KG 26 with an escort of 21 Messerschmitt 110s of KG 76, was heading towards the Northumberland coast. All these aircraft had taken off from Stavanger in Norway with the intention of attacking the airfields of 13 Group Fighter Command. Despite the strong German fighter presence, the enemy force was given a severe mauling by the Spitfires of 72 Sqn and the Hurricanes of 79, 605 and 607 Squadrons. The 13 Group airfields were left unscathed as the Heinkel 111s were forced to release their bombs over the North Sea or the coastal towns and cities of Wearside and Tyneside. Eight Heinkel 111s and seven Messerschmitt 110s were shot down and several others severely damaged. Never again would the bombers of Luftflotte 5 launch a major daylight raid on targets in the North of England.

Apart from the 21 German aircraft destroyed in the North, another 53 Luftwaffe planes were shot down in the South. This had been the heaviest day's fighting in the Battle of Britain so far, and with German losses for the day totalling 74 aircraft it was appropriate that the Luftwaffe should refer to Thursday 15 August 1940 as 'Schwarze Donnerstag' — 'Black Thursday'.

[13]*Later commander of KG 200, the Luftwaffe's most secret unit, involved in agent-dropping and special operations and the development of unorthodox weapons.*

124: The second police message concerning the locations of the crashes of Ju 88s 4D+?M and 4D+KL.

125 Above: *The ruins of Foley's Cafe and Restaurant, next to Woolworth's on Prince Street in Bridlington, after it had been completely wrecked by a 250kg high explosive bomb in the early hours of Friday 23 August 1940. Four civilians were killed in the explosion and a fifth rescued from the cellar. (ERYC L&IS)*

Incident:
On the night of 16-17 August 1940 a Blenheim of 29 Sqn, flown by P/O Rhodes and Sgt Gregory, shot down Junkers Ju 88C-2 4D+GZ, Werk Nr 0245, of 4./NJG 2 which was engaged in minelaying off Spurn Head. Fw Gustav Schramm (pilot), Gefr Hans Roth (radio operator) and Ofw Fritz Zenkel (flight engineer / airgunner) were all posted as 'missing'.

HIT AND RUN RAIDS
Bridlington bombed and Spitfire funds

After 'Black Thursday', the Luftwaffe resorted to surprise attacks, often carried out by a single bomber. This tactic made detection by radar more difficult and interception by RAF fighters less likely.

The first of a succession of such raids occurred on Monday 19 August 1940 when the Luftwaffe made a return to RAF Driffield. At 2255 hours, a lone KG 30 Junkers 88 from Aalborg dive-bombed the station's No 1 Hangar, the one hangar to have escaped serious damage during the daylight attack four days earlier. Although only one of the bomber's 250kg HEs hit the hangar, the building was soon in flames. Driffield's AFS was called in to assist the station's own firefighting unit, but it was not until 0134 hours the following morning before the fire was finally extinguished. One AFS fireman was injured during the firefighting operation, but there were no other casualties at the bomber base on this occasion.

As the hangar fire was being tackled at RAF Driffield, another KG 30 Ju 88 attacked Bridlington. It was early on Tuesday 20 August when a 250kg high explosive bomb scored a direct hit on the town's main post office on Quay Road. The GPO building, which also housed Bridlington's telephone exchange, was wrecked and Alfred William Anderson, a telephonist, was killed. After the raid, 11 people trapped in the collapsed building were brought out alive by ARP Rescue Party Detachment Leader Tom Alderson and his brave team. Considerable damage was also done by the three HEs which fell in the surrounding area, but there were no other fatalities.

A little under three hours later, Filey was bombed for the first time in World War Two. At 'Tile Cottage' on West Avenue, Mrs Clay and her daughters Mary and Rachael had all gone to bed at the sound of the 'All Clear' following an air raid warning earlier in the night. Also, the ARP wardens who used the garage and an outhouse as an ARP Post and gone off duty, while Mrs Clay's husband Percival was still on duty at Filey Police Station. Although it was now well past midnight, Mrs Clay was still awake and listening to the sound of aero engines, circling Filey and quite low. Suddenly, there was a very loud explosion and all the windows in the house were shattered. The Clay's then ventured downstairs and found that a bomb had made a deep crater in their garden. In a local ARP report the bomb is recorded as having exploded at 0321 hours.

67

Within minutes, help was at hand for the Clay family. First to arrive on the scene was Mr Waller who had rushed from the nearest First Aid Post; he was relieved to find that Mrs Clay and her girls were unhurt. Mr Waller was quickly followed by a Mr Harland and a Mr Whitfield, plus a sergeant major who was billeted at the Crescent Hotel. These willing helpers checked out the state of 'Tile Cottage' and found that the only serious damage was to windows – every pane of glass had been blown out by the exploding bomb. In view of the vulnerable state of the house, Mr Harland, a special constable, agreed to stay at the scene and guard the property, while the Clays stayed overnight with their friend Mrs Burgess at 'Deepdene'.

Over the next few days, the Clay family made the most of the large crater in their garden, inviting people to come and view the crater in return for a contribution to the town's Comforts Fund, a fund to raise money to purchase little extras for men serving in the armed forces.

The explosion had scattered Mr Clay's new potatoes far and wide across the neighbourhood and, surprisingly, this led to a complaint from one Filey woman. A Miss Sullivan made it known that she was "…*very annoyed about the whole affair*" as some of Mr Clay's potatoes had come down her chimney.

A few of the Few

At RAF Leconfield, 302 City of Poznan (Polish) Sqn had at last become operational, on 15 August, and there was great excitement at the fighter airfield when, during the evening of Tuesday 20 August, the squadron registered its first 'kill'. S/Ldr W.A.J. 'Jack' Satchell, joint CO of 302 Sqn, was leading Green Section (P/O S.J. Chalupa in WX-T/V7417 and F/Lt William Riley in WX-M/R4095) in his Hurricane WX-L /P3817 on a routine patrol over the Holderness coast when, at 1900 hours, the call came to orbit Hull at Angels 5 (5,000 ft). While heading south towards Hull, Satchell spotted a lone Junkers 88 overflying East Yorkshire at about 3,000 ft. As the Hurricanes dived in pursuit of the enemy bomber, its pilot swung his aircraft into a tight climbing turn and disappeared into cloud. But, with only 5/10 cloud cover the Ju 88 could not hide for long as it twisted and turned and slid from cloud to cloud. Satchell (Green 1) was able to get in three bursts of well-directed machine gun fire in an astern attack. P/O S.J. Chalupa (Green 2), followed with a brief tail-chase before the German bomber again entered cloud. After the Green Section pilots had returned to base, at 1935 hours, it was confirmed that their Ju 88 had crashed approximately six miles south-west of Withernsea.

According to ARP and Police messages and reports, Junkers Ju 88A-1, *Werk Nr* 7069, 4D+IS, of 8./KG 30 crash-landed in a field of wheat to the south of the railway crossing on the A1033 Hull to Withernsea road, one mile east of Ottringham and not far from Westlands Plantations. The Ottringham ARP warden reported to ARP Control Beverley:

"*German bomber now on fire, blazing fiercely. One man injured, two alright.*"

Inspector Nicholls of the East Riding Constabulary reported:

"*Injured airman removed to hospital* (Patrington Military Hospital). *Remainder of crew captured by the Cameron Highlanders*".

Police later revealed that a fourth German airman had been discovered in a ditch; he had serious head injuries and appeared to have fallen or jumped from the Ju 88 as it came in for a wheels-up landing. Both critically injured men, *Uffz* Werner Kruczinski (wireless operator) and *Uffz* Willi Rautenberg (air gunner) were treated at Patrington before being transferred to Hull Royal Infirmary, where they both died within two days of the crash. More fortunate were *Uffz* Franz-Georg Wolff (pilot) and *Fw* Hugo Keller (observer); they were only slightly injured and were soon able to be interrogated by F/O J. Robinson, RAF Intelligence Officer at RAF Leconfield. During interrogation, Wolff and Keller revealed that it had been S/Ldr Satchell's third burst of gunfire which had set their cockpit on fire and made it impossible for them to continue to their target, RAF Thornaby in North Yorkshire. This 8./KG 30 crew was operating out of Aalborg in Denmark and five days prior to their crash had returned unscathed from the ill-fated raid on RAF Driffield. This was the first ever victory to be credited to a Polish squadron in the RAF in World War II.

> "*The gratitude of every home in our Island, in our Empire, and indeed throughout the world, except in the abodes of the guilty, goes out to the British airmen, who, undaunted by odds, unwearied in their constant challenge and mortal danger, are turning the tide of war by their prowess and by their devotion. Never in the field of human conflict was so much owed by so many to so few.*"
>
> From the speech by Winston Churchill to the House of Commons on the afternoon of Tuesday 20 August 1940, broadcast later that day.

Between 21-28 August 1940 there was considerable Luftwaffe activity over East Yorkshire. First to be attacked was Bridlington when, at 1540 hours on Wednesday 21 August, a lone bomber dropped four 250kg HEs on the town. The target was Bridlington harbour, but the worst damage in the raid was at the Britannia Hotel on Prince Street which received a direct hit. Half of the hotel was destroyed and two people in the building, Esther Shaw of Oxford Street in the town and a soldier, were killed in the explosion. It was

126: *Searching the wreckage of Ju 88 4D+IS which crashed near Ottringham during the evening of Tuesday 20 August 1940. The incident was reported in the* Hull Daily Mail *to have been the work of a Polish airman in a Spitfire, but it was an Englishman co-commanding a Polish squadron who shot down this aircraft — flying a Hurricane.*

127 Below: *In the background to this picture of 4D+IS is Westlands Plantation, between Ottringham and Patrington. The propeller spinner seems to be yellow.*

128 Right: *On 24 September 1940, a new British medal, the George Cross, was instituted. It was to be the supreme civilian award for acts of great courage in circumstances of extreme danger.*

129 Far right: *The very first recipient of the new medal was Thomas Hopper Alderson of Bridlington, seen here after the investiture at Buckingham Palace on 20 May 1941. He received the award for his heroic work as an ARP Rescue Party Detachment Leader following air raids on Bridlington in August 1940.*

Tuesday 20 August 1940 was a cloudy, rainy day. At 19.10 in the evening, Junkers Ju 88A-1, 4D+IS, Red 'I', Werk Nr 7169, of 8./KG 30, was shot down at Ottringham by six Hurricane fighters from Green Section of 302 Squadron, based at Leconfield. The Luftwaffe aircraft, based at Aalborg in Denmark, was returning to base having attacked the RAF airfield at Thornaby. This was the first victory over an enemy aircraft by a Polish squadron in the RAF. The Hurricanes were led by the joint CO of the squadron, Sqn Ldr W.A.J. Satchell (it then being the practice for the Polish squadrons to be led by a Polish and RAF CO until they were fully integrated into the RAF, all other personnel being Polish). Aircraft which participated, and their pilots, were: WX-L/P3812, S/Ldr Jack Satchell (British); WX-N/ M R4095, Flt Lt William Riley (British); WX-T/P3934, P/O Stanislaw J. Chalupa; WX-U/P3923, P/O Franciszek Jastrzebski; WX-X/P3930, Sgt Edward Paterek; WX-Y/P3924, F/Lt Stefan Wapniarek. The print depicts S/Ldr Satchell hitting the Ju 88 in the cockpit area, while P/O Chalupa banks away.*

70

130: *The Britannia Hotel in Bridlington after it had been hit by a 250kg high explosive bomb during the afternoon of Wednesday 21 August 1940. The poster next to the window tells us that, despite the war and the danger of air raids, a popular local band led by Ceres Harper was still playing for dancing at the Spa Royal Hall in the town. (ERYC L&IS)*

Incident:
Wednesday 21 August 1940. Sgt Stanislaw Chalupa of 302 Sqn, who had assisted in the destruction of the Ju 88 which crashed at Ottringham the day previously, had to force land his Hurricane WX-U, P3923, with engine trouble after combat with Ju 88s off Bridlington. He was unhurt and the aircraft was repairable.

*Larger size prints of this illustration suitable for framing are available either from the publisher or direct from:
Aeroprints
113 East End Road
East Finchley
London
N2 0SU
Tel: 0208 444 4510
or visit their website at:
www.aeroprints.co.uk
where a wide variety of aviation prints can be seen.*

a miracle that only two people died in the raid as so many were shopping in the vicinity at the time. One woman who had a lucky escape was Nellie Megginson from Fraisthorpe; she was in Woolworth's, across the road from the Britannia, and was sheltering behind a counter when the bomb exploded sending lethal shards of glass flying through the store.

As Bridlington was being bombed, Blue Section of 302 (Polish) Sqn was scrambled at RAF Leconfield and ordered to patrol Bridlington at Angels 12 (12,000 ft), while Green Section was also sent up to patrol the Driffield area at cloud base. Two Junkers 88s were sighted, one over the sea to the east of Bridlington and the other east of Driffield. A tail-chase ensued and combat took place at around 12,000 ft. Both enemy bombers were damaged but managed to escape into cloud. Luftwaffe sources later revealed that two of their Aalborg-based Ju 88s, one from 7./KG 30 and the other from 8./KG 30, had made it back to base with visible signs of combat and had been further damaged in heavy landings.

Then, at 0250 hours on Friday 23 August, Bridlington was raided again when a KG 30 Junkers 88 roared in from the North Sea to drop four HEs over the harbour area. One of the bombs struck the pleasure boat *Royal Sovereign*, a second landed in the harbour but failed to explode, while the other two hit property not far from the waterfront. One of them exploded on Foley's Cafe and Restaurant, which was completely wrecked, and also badly damaged the F.W. Woolworth Store next door. Four civilians died in the cafe; they were James and Dorothy Watson who ran the cafe, their daughter Evelyn Parkin and waitress Betty Spear from Cardigan Road. A fifth civilian, Evelyn Parkin's husband Walter, was rescued from the wreckage and eventually recovered from his serious injuries. All five were brought out from the cellar by an ARP Rescue Party, led once again by the intrepid Tom Alderson. The fourth bomb hit the Cock and Lion Inn, causing considerable damage but not resulting in any casualties.

This had been a daring low-level attack on Bridlington, but the raiding enemy bomber, identified as a Junkers 88, was able to fly in and out unchallenged, the Hurricanes of 302 (Polish) Sqn having been grounded by low cloud and poor visibility in the Leconfield area.

The busiest night across East Yorkshire during the summer of 1940 occurred on 24/25 August when bombs were dropped on the region between 2215 and 0345 hours. Using small numbers of aircraft and staggered bombing times ensured that air raid sirens were being frequently activated throughout the night. On this occasion, the raiding bombers were not KG 30 Junkers 88s from Aalborg, but Ju 88s of KG 4 flying from Schipol in Holland. The first bombs to fall that night exploded harmlessly on farmland near Bridlington and on Carr Naze at Filey, late on Sunday 24 August. Early the following morning, more HEs fell at RAF Driffield, Rotsea Farm near Hutton Cranswick, Hedon, Meaux, Hall Farm at Sewerby, Hull, Skipsea, Newbald, Cottingham, Londesborough and High Barn Farm near Weaverthorpe.

Luckily, little serious damage was done and there were few casualties. The one exception was at Hull, where two bombers dropped eight HEs which landed on Carlton Street, Eastbourne Street, Rustenburg Street and Morrill Street. Six civilians died in these streets, the first civilian deaths to result from an air raid on Hull in World War Two. Elsewhere in East Yorkshire, the raid on RAF Driffield was the only one of any significance. Twelve HEs were dropped on the bomber base in three separate attacks at 0107 hours, 0218 hours and 0238 hours. The Sergeants' Mess, already damaged in the 15 August raid, was reduced to rubble, electricity and water supplies were disrupted and one Whitley bomber was slightly damaged, but there were no serious injuries.

After this, the third air raid on RAF Driffield in ten days, the decision was made to move out the two resident bomber squadrons for major reconstruction work to start at the airfield. On Monday 26 August, all 102 Sqn personnel transferred to RAF Leeming with RAF Topcliffe being used for the dispersal of their Whitleys. Two days later, all personnel and aircraft of 77 Sqn were also on the move; groundcrew and aircrew would be based at RAF Linton-on-Ouse, their aircraft at RAF Tholthorpe. It was the spring of 1941 before bombers returned to RAF Driffield.

Most of the bombs dropped on rural East Yorkshire during the night of 24/25 August appear to have been directed at searchlight units. Such attacks continued well into September 1940. In one such raid, the searchlight battery on Paull Road at Hedon was hit, resulting in a number of searchlights and accommodation huts being destroyed and two soldiers injured.

October 1940, the last month in the Battle of Britain, saw two minor air raids on Hull, attacks on the airfields at Driffield and Leconfield and the machine-gunning of the centre of Beverley. At Hull, a single aircraft dropped four 50kg HEs at 2020 hours on Sunday 13 October. Several houses were damaged and two people were killed. Then, at 0140 hours on Tuesday 22 October, two 1,000kg parachute mines caused extensive damage to residential property, especially on Silverdale Road, Sutton Road, Maybury Road and Bellfield Avenue. No fatalities were recorded in this latest raid on Hull.

The last 'tip-and-run' raids of any note occurred during the early evening of Sunday 27 October. First to be attacked, at 1800 hours, was RAF Driffield when three 8./KG 30 Junkers 88s from Schipol flew in low to drop 12 HEs and machine gun the aerodrome. There were no casualties and little damage was done to airfield buildings, but road traffic past the RAF station was disrupted when one bomb blew a deep crater in the A163 Driffield to Market Weighton Road. This raid came as something of a surprise as all aircraft had left RAF Driffield before the end of August. Furthermore, the accompanying Luftwaffe briefing photograph shows a total absence of aircraft in the airfield's dispersal areas (*Abstellplatz*).

Aircraft may have left RAF Driffield but the station's anti-aircraft guns were still there. Their crews put up a fierce bombardment and claimed to have damaged all three of the raiding Ju 88s, yet the KG 30 aircraft survived and returned safely to Schipol.

Meanwhile, 12 miles to the south of Driffield, streets near the centre of Beverley were machine-

Incident:
24-25 August. While in pursuit of an enemy aircraft Sgt Maurice Leng of 73 Squadron (then based at Church Fenton) in Hurricane I P3758 was shot down by British AA fire at 0125hrs. Leng baled out safely, landing in the centre of Beverley where he was arrested by the Home Guard. His aircraft crashed a mile outside the town. He was not amused.

Incident:

27-28 August. The Lodge and the Maternity Hospital on Hedon Road in Hull were destroyed by HE bombs. There were no casualties.

132: *A schoolboy pauses to look at the ruins of Bridlington Post Office on Quay Road, wrecked by high explosive bombs on Tuesday 20 August 1940. It was a miracle that only one person, a male telephonist, was killed in the building. (ERYC L&IS)*

133: Oblt *Friedrich-Franz Podbielski's Junkers Ju 88, 5J+ER, under guard after it crashlanded at Duggleby on 27 October 1940*

131 Left: *A Luftwaffe reconnaissance photograph of RAF Driffield, taken on 7 September 1940. Dispersal areas for aircraft (Abstellplatz) and gun positions (Flak and MG Stellung) are clearly marked. Bomb damage in the built-up south-east corner of the airfield plus a scattering of bomb craters, the result of August 1940 air raids, can be seen. This photograph was used in the briefing of the three KG 30 bomber crews involved in the attack on RAF Driffield on 27 October 1940.*

Facts:

The most successful fighter pilot in the RAF during the Battle of Britain was a Yorkshireman: James Henry 'Ginger' Lacey of Wetherby. Then a sergeant, he shot down 25 German aircraft, including an He 111 which had bombed Buckingham Palace, and five 'probables' by the end of October 1940.

gunned at 1810 hours and three people were injured near North Bar. Minutes later, an enemy aircraft bombed nearby RAF Leconfield; one HE damaged a hangar, two others exploded harmlessly on tarmac, while a fourth did not detonate until the following day. One airman, a 303 (Polish) Sqn pilot, was wounded in the raid. This had also been a surprise attack which had caught the RAF unprepared. The raiding bomber, a Junkers 88 was most probably the one which had earlier machine-gunned Beverley. It escaped eastwards before the Hurricane pilots could be scrambled at RAF Leconfield.

But elsewhere there was a notable success for airfield anti-aircraft guns when a Junkers 88 of KG 30 had to make a forced landing on the Yorkshire Wolds at Duggleby. Initially, it was thought that this was one of the Ju 88s hit by AA fire at RAF Driffield, but the pilot of the downed bomber revealed during interrogation that his had been one of three 7./KG 30 aircraft which had attacked RAF Linton-on-Ouse in North Yorkshire. The pilot in question, *Oblt* Friedrich-Franz Podbielski who was the *Staffelkapitän* of 7./KG 30, had led the *kette* (trio) of Ju 88s across the North Sea from Schipol to Flamborough Head before flying low along the Yorkshire coast to Scarborough and then heading inland to the RAF bomber base at Linton.

III./KG 30 records confirm that Podbielski's target had been the airfield at Linton-on-Ouse, not Driffield, in their entry with regards to the loss of Ju 88 A-5 5J+JR, Werk Nr 6129:

"*Der Angriffe erfolgte auf Flugplatz Linton-on Ouse*". (outcome of the attack on Linton-on-Ouse airfield).

The three 7/KG 30 bombers had attacked their target airfield from the north-west before heading for the East Yorkshire coast in the vicinity of Flamborough Head. Podbielski's aircraft, however, had been hit in the starboard engine by an AA shell. As the damaged

73

engine stopped and the port one lost power, the Ju 88 quickly lost height and Podbielski had no option but to execute a wheels-up landing on farmland at Duggleby. *Oblt* Friedrich-Franz Podbielski, *Fw* Heinz Heir (observer) and *Ofw* Karl von Kidrowski (wireless operator) all survived the heavy landing, but *Uffz* Oskar Piontek (air gunner) was found critically injured, trapped under the aircraft's tail. Piontek was rushed to hospital in Driffield where he died that night. Oskar Piontek was buried at Driffield Cemetery on Thursday 31 October, but his body was later transferred to the German Military Cemetery at Cannock Chase in Staffordshire.

Some readers may be wondering why the KG 30 Junkers 88 which came down at Duggleby on 27 October bore the '5J' code of KG 4 and not the usual '4D' code of KG 30. The reason for this is that earlier in October the aircraft of III./KG 4 had been transferred to III./KG 30.

Although the Battle of Britain officially ended on 31 October 1940, there was no sudden end to Luftwaffe activity over East Yorkshire. In fact, on the very next day there were at least four occasions when air raid sirens in the region sent people scuttling to their shelters, or other places of refuge, after RAF Staxton Wold detected small numbers of inbound 'hostiles'. First, shortly before 0700 hours, a single raider dropped twelve 50kg HEs on Hull. There was some damage to houses and the railway system was disrupted by a number of direct hits; one person was killed and another seven seriously injured in the raid. Then, during the early evening, bombs fell at Bridlington and Hunmanby. In Bridlington, shortly before 1800 hours, several HEs exploded on Blenheim Road, Carlton Road and Quay Road, causing considerable damage to housing and seriously injuring two civilians. Then, at 1830 hours, twelve 50kg HEs were dropped at Hunmanby, fortunately falling in fields to the west and north-west of the village. There were no casualties in the parish and the only real damage was to the village's electricity supply, one of the bombs having severed an overhead cable. It was several hours before power was restored by the Buckrose

134: This is how the local Filey News *publicised Junkers Ju 88 3Z+DK which was displayed in Filey on 16 November 1940, to raise money for the local Spitfire Fund.*

135: Junkers Ju 88 3Z+DK which was displayed in Filey on 16 November 1940, to raise money for the local Spitfire Fund. This picture, however, was not taken in Filey.

Spitfire Mk I RN-N of 72 Squadron in use as a part-time nightfighter in May 1940. The overpainted serial is in the K99?? series. The personal emblem appears to be a kiwi. Finish is Dark Green/Dark Earth in type 'A' pattern with Night/White undersurfaces divided on the centreline. Light grey code letters and non-standard fuselage roundel. Note the 'blinkers' intended to prevent the pilot being blinded by exhaust glare.

Junkers Ju 88A-5, 5J+ER, Werk Nr 6129, of 7./KG 30. Flown by of Oblt Friedrich-Franz Podbielski, the aircraft still wears the code of KG 4, from which it had been recently transferred. After attacking RAF Linton-on-Ouse, it crashlanded at Duggleby on 27 October 1940 after being damaged by flak. Finish is standard 70/71/65, with the fuselage cross darkened by the application of temporary black paint. The aircraft still carries the bat emblem of 7./KG 4 on the nose.

ILLUSTRATIONS NOT TO SAME SCALE

Light and Power Company. Finally on 1 November, between 2235 and 2245 hours several HEs fell harmlessly on farmland near Kelk, Bainton and Huggate.

After the Battle of Britain, 'Spitfire Funds', devised to encourage British people from all walks of life to contribute to the cost of new fighter aircraft, continued through November 1940. Across Britain, virtually every district had a Spitfire Fund and there were many such funds in East Yorkshire. For example, in Filey the highlight of the town's Spitfire Fund activities was the exhibition of a downed Junkers Ju 88 bomber. On Saturday 16 November, this aircraft was put on display in a small car park at the junction of Station Road and Station Avenue, where a public garden is now located. There was an admission charge for local people to have a close-up view of an enemy bomber, including the opportunity to ascend a small flight of steps and look inside the cockpit. Photographs of the Ju 88 were also on sale to raise extra money for the district Spitfire Fund; the photograph included in this chapter is the one purchased by the author's father when the family visited the display. Contrary to some local opinion, this was not one of the KG 30 Junkers 88s shot down during the 15 August raid on RAF Driffield, nor was the photograph taken in Filey. The aircraft in the photograph is 2./KG 77's Junkers Ju 88 A-1, (*Werk Nr* 2142) 3Z+DK, which was shot down on Monday 30 September, during a raid on London, by a 501 Sqn Hurricane piloted by Sgt Paul Farnes. After combat over Surrey, the Ju 88's pilot, *Oblt* Friedrich Oeser, had to make a forced landing on Gatwick Racecourse.

After Air Intelligence officers had completed their meticulous inspection of the KG 77 Junkers 88, it was loaded onto a 'Queen Mary', a long low transporter vehicle, and taken on tour of Britain, greatly boosting district Spitfire Funds along the way.

Throughout the remainder of the year, there were a few minor raids on Hull and Bridlington, but little damage was done and there were no fatalities. As Christmas 1940 approached, there had still not been a major air raid on Hull, but the people of the city braced themselves for what they regarded as the inevitable — massive air raids, hundreds of bombs whistling down on their city, and high levels of death and destruction, which had already been experienced in other British cities, notably London, Liverpool, Birmingham and Coventry.

Incident:
1420 hrs 6 October. Spitfire I R6683 flown by Sgt F.F. Vinyard from 64 Sqn at Leconfield crashed into the sea off Flamborough Head through reasons unknown. Pilot 'missing'.

136: Part of the salvage effort in Hull: mountains of metal railings, fences and gates.

137: An Heinkel He 111 of 9./KG 26 having temporary black camouflage paint applied by the 'blackmen' (as Luftwaffe groundcrew were known on account of their black overalls) in an ominous precursor to the night Blitz on Britain.

138 Above: *A Junkers Ju 88A-4 of Stab 2./KGr 106, probably in early 1941, being loaded with an 1,800kg 'Satan' bomb. Only a few Luftwaffe crews were qualified to carry and drop it. Such a weapon as this could devastate an entire street, as happened to Scarborough Street in Hull on 19 May 1942, although KGr 106's primary task was anti-shipping raids. The temporary black camouflage over the fuselage cross combined with the light blue undersides shows that the Luftwaffe was already being stretched, with units being called upon to carry out day and night missions in the same aircraft.*

NIGHT BATTLES 1941
The Blitz on Hull

After the Battle of Britain, there were three significant changes in Luftwaffe tactics; from day to night bombing, from 'tip-and-run' attacks by small numbers of aircraft to major raids involving large numbers of bombers and the targeting of ports and industrial towns and cities rather than RAF airfields. This was hardly surprising as the Luftwaffe's attempts to destroy the fighter arm of the Royal Air Force had been successfully thwarted by the close liaison between the Chain Home radar stations and the RAF fighter squadrons.

Duels in the dark

Taking on the German bombers at night, however, was a totally different proposition. Even on clear, moonlit nights our night fighter pilots had great difficulty in locating incoming enemy aircraft and successful interceptions during the hours of darkness over East Yorkshire were few and far between. In fact, following the shooting down of a Heinkel over the Holderness coast on 26 June 1940, the next 'kill' recorded by RAF night fighter pilots over the region did not materialise until 8 May 1941. By then, the long-expected major air raids on Hull had already begun, with a series of ferocious attacks in March 1941 by large formations of Luftwaffe bombers. These were followed by further terrifying raids in April, May and July of that year. British defence chiefs had to come up with new and more effective methods of challenging enemy bombers at night if Hull was to be saved from further death and destruction on a massive scale.

Fortunately, from the spring of 1942, new and more powerful RAF night fighters equipped with the latest in radar technology were provided for the squadrons patrolling the region. Also, British scientists engaged in radio research developed a number of devices designed to confuse the raiding Luftwaffe bomber crews.

Despite these welcome innovations, however, German bombers were still able to penetrate our night defences and inflict serious harm, such as on the city of York at the end of April 1942. Luftwaffe aerial onslaughts on East Yorkshire were clearly far from over.

The winter of 1941 was exceptionally severe, with fierce blizzards raging across the region. At RAF Staxton Wold, the radar station was completely cut off for a period in January, while elsewhere in East Yorkshire RAF bombers and fighters were grounded. Conditions were also atrocious for the crews manning searchlights and anti-aircraft guns along the Holderness coast and at Spurn Head, so exposed to the bitter winds and driving snow coming in from the North Sea. But the German bombers kept on flying, their deadly loads of high explosive and incendiary bombs, plus the even deadlier parachute mines, bringing the war ever closer to communities

77

across East Yorkshire, not just to Hull and Bridlington, but to rural districts as well. Hunmanby, Brantingham, Walkington, Patrington, Willerby, Bishop Burton, South Frodingham and Little Weighton were just a few of the region's villages to receive 'calling cards' from the Luftwaffe during the winter of 1941.

The long expected heavy air raids on Hull, however, did not start until the spring of 1941 when, on the nights of 13/14 March, 14/15 March, 18/19 March and 31 March, hundreds of high explosive bombs, thousands of incendiary bombs, plus a scattering of parachute mines rained down on the city. There was widespread damage and destruction to docks, industries, the railway system, shops, schools and residential areas. Furthermore, approximately 200 people were killed and another 250 seriously injured during the March air raids.

By far the worst of these attacks was the one on the night of 18/19 March. During that night, ten different Geschwader, contributing a grand total of more than 350 Junkers Ju88s and Heinkel He 111s, homed in on Hull in a series of waves which meant that most of East Yorkshire was on 'Red Alert' from 2010 until 0048 hours as the enemy bombers swept in at regular intervals between Spurn Head and Filey. As scores of LC 50 parachute flares began to float slowly and eerily down to illuminate the blacked-out city, and as the sound of aero engines overhead intensified, the people of Hull knew that they were in for a very rough night, but they could never have anticipated the sheer ferocity of the attack and the terror and destruction associated with it. In the course of this air raid, 316 tonnes of HEs and more than 77,000 IBs fell on Hull. There were huge fires and explosions in the dock area; factories, shops, schools and churches were blasted or gutted, while 700 houses were destroyed and more than 90 people killed. To make matters worse, the city's infrastructure was seriously undermined as electricity, gas and water supplies were disrupted and deep bomb craters were left in roads and railway tracks. Finally, there was the added problem of some 30 unexploded bombs across the city. This had been Hull's heaviest and most devastating raid of the war so far.

Outside Hull, two children and their parents were killed when a parachute mine exploded close to a farmhouse at Hutton Cranswick. In Beverley, several people were seriously injured when two parachute mines were dropped on the town. Within an eight-mile radius of Hornsea, several HEs and IBs fell harmlessly on farmland. However, the heaviest and most destructive bombing during the night of 18/19 March away from Hull occurred to the north of the region, at Scarborough. As the first bombs of the night began to fall on Hull, at approximately 2010 hours, a mixture of HEs and IBs fell on the North Yorkshire town. The reason for this attack was that several of the Junkers 88s and Heinkel 111s bound for Hull, when confronted with mist, cloud and a very heavy AA barrage to the east of the city, opted instead to head for their 'soft' secondary target, Scarborough. There, 21 people were killed and 19 others seriously injured. At 120 North Marine Road, just below the entrance to Scarborough Cricket Ground, a Mr and Mrs Siddle and their four children were all killed when a high explosive bomb hit their home. Elsewhere in the town, four women and three children lost their lives when the bombing wrecked Nos 63, 65, 69 and 71 Commercial Street. There was also widespread severe damage to businesses, schools, churches and theatres in the town during the air raids of 18/19 March 1941, Scarborough's worst night of the war.

Despite the large numbers of Luftwaffe bombers wheeling around over East Yorkshire during the March Blitz, it was a barren month of the region's defences. RAF night fighters were scrambled and heavy anti-aircraft guns fired between 1000 and 2500 rounds during each major air raid, yet not one enemy aircraft was shot down.

In April 1941, the air raids on the region were of

Incident:
18-19 March. Hull was attacked by 378 bombers. 268 HEs and 77,068 IBs were dropped causing 700 fires. Sisson's paint works was virtually destroyed. 91 people were killed.

Incident:
19 March. Stabsfw Schied in He 111P G1+BT of KG 55, dropped five 250kg HEs and eight B2 IBs on Hull from an altitude between 5,200-2,700 metres.

139: *Another He 111 of KG 26 shows off its temporary black undersides, contrasting with the RLM 65 blue-grey colour of the SC 1800 bomb in front of it. Such a load had to be carried externally on the He 111, which normally carried its bomb load in vertical racks inside the fuselage. The crewman gives an idea of the massive size of the bomb, which was the largest used by the Luftwaffe. Note the letter 'D' applied to the wing leading edges, meant to assist groundcrews to find their charge in semi-darkness.*

140: Hull burns in May 1941.

141: During every major air raid on Hull, the city's firemen were in the front line. As bombs fell, they bravely continued to fight the fires. It was particularly hazardous for the men on the turntable ladders, but no firemen could ever feel safe from the blast and flying shrapnel as a high explosive bomb or parachute mine exploded. As one Hull fireman put it after the two major air raids in May 1941 "…it was a living nightmare out there."

142: This appears to be some kind of Hull warehouse, shortly after a bomb has left a smoking crater in front. Hull once had many fine buildings, dating from Georgian times and earlier, but the bombing destroyed most of these and some of the best public buildings. Planners and architects in the early 1960s did for many of the survivors.

It was a Saturday night

A few minutes after the red warning was signalled through, the sound of 'planes was heard, arriving over their target area to drop their deadly load of mines into the river.

The docks had a system of warnings, received from some headquarters, integrating the radar (when it came into operation) and observer services. The yellow warning signified that enemy aircraft were leaving the German or occupied coast; the purple warning meant that they were heading your way; the red warning was to say 'the 'planes are in your vicinity'. Incidentally, on the purple signal, all the lights went off in the dock area, then on came the hurricane lamps and candles were lit. My father was outside, trying to spot the aircraft flying high up in the moonlit night.

Suddenly he saw a parachute mine floating down towards the river, but a little too close for comfort. He was trying to find out the approximate position that it would land, which he judged would be just off the jetty opposite him, on the other side of our shelter. Without warning, there was a shattering explosion behind him, which blew him several yards from the effect of the blast. Unseen by him, another mine had landed on number one quay and had gone off, demolishing a crane. This was only a hundred yards from the side of our house, but luckily was partly shielded by a hydraulic tower. Inside the house, my mother, sister and myself were reposing in the large cupboard under the stairs (a haven we used until the raids became too heavy, then we would dash across to the shelter).

The blast had blown out windows, the ceilings were down, showing the wooden laths and even two heavy fireplaces were blown out of the walls. After the front door was forced, dad and the berthingman, Mr Fulstowe, accompanied us to the shelter, over broken glass and plaster.

The next day, being Sunday and Mo and I not being at work or school, dad sent us out with mum at tide time, so that a minesweeper could attempt to blow up the mine, the one that he saw floating down the previous night.

On returning from our long walk, we learnt that although the vessel had made many sweeps up and down, it had been unable to produce any result and had finally given up and returned to base.

We all carried on clearing up the mess from the 'real' mine and the railway company workmen started reglazing our windows, firstly in the rooms that we mainly lived in. These same men had also painted all the woodwork outside and had but finished about two weeks previously.

The next two days passed quietly enough and my father was teased by his colleagues who took full advantage of the mine episode.

'Seen any parachute mines today Jack?' I heard one say. 'They can say what they like, I saw the bloody thing', grumbled my old man.

The Wednesday following, I attended school as usual and came home for lunch, which on that particular day I remember, was stew. Dad was in the garden, on the river side, sewing vegetable seeds; Mum in the scullery and Mo and me in the kitchen eating. I was facing the window which overlooked the river.

Suddenly my heart froze as a terrific rumbling and intense rending explosion smashed into the noon day silence. Through the window I saw a huge column of light brown mud with a piece of barge hull, shooting up into the air, hundreds of feet and blotting out the sunshine.

We heard ma cry out, 'Your father!' Her subject of concern however, dashed into the house through the back door, just as the first of the tons of mud started to land. Within seconds, the house was pitch black inside as the mud, this thick brown stinking Humber mud, covered all the windows. We all ran through the hall and opened the front door. A fantastic sight met our eyes: everywhere one looked the ground was swimming in about a foot of thick mud. The smell was terrible and all the buildings looked as if they were some giant fairyland scene, coated with chocolate. 'Now who said that there wasn't a damned mine there!' — dad was struggling into a pair of gumboots. As he was leaving the house to enter the scene of sudden activity, two gatemen came across to meet him.

'It was a lighter[14] that sat on her sir,' one of them shouted. Both of these men were covered in mud also, because they had been having their lunch in the lock-head office, and on hearing the explosion had rushed outside, just in time to catch the intense rain of muck coming down, only to dive back inside, too late. Standing at the front door, I just caught the sound of a man's voice shouting for help, this man soon to be hauled to safety as many willing hands succeeded in getting him out of the water below the jetty.

Although a notice had been placed, to be clearly seen from the river, this lighter had moored onto the jetty, to await its call to enter the dock.

Three men had been on board, one below and two on deck. The man below and the man forward had been killed, the helmsman who had been on the stern was the one who was rescued. Another clean up job, this time outside, as the mud dried and cracked, and we eventually saw our new coat of cream paint again, but poor old dad's seedbed was a write-off.

John Cottrell-Smith's diary

John Cottrell-Smith was a boy at the outbreak of World War II. In September 1939 his father became assistant dockmaster at Alexandra Dock in Hull where the family lived, until bombed out, in a house among the dock buildings. He was therefore in a unique position to see and record the effects of the German bombing upon the city from firsthand experience. He has kindly allowed the use of extracts from his notes and diary in this book.

[14]*The Hull lighters* Monarch *and* Brakelu *were both destroyed at 1202hrs on Wednesday 26 February 1941 by a mine dropped on Sunday 23rd. 13 people were killed and 27 seriously injured.*

143: An Heinkel He 115 of the kind used for nocturnal minelaying missions over the Humber estuary and east coast of Yorkshire. This one is having a torpedo training round loaded into its bomb-bay. The type carried out the role of torpedo-bomber with some success against the Arctic convoys to Russia.

An Immingham tale

During WWII I was an Experimental Assistant in the Admiralty Signal Establishment at Portsmouth, the organization responsible for development of the Royal Navy's radar systems. In the course of this work I had a variety of interesting tasks and the following account describes one which took place at Immingham on the River Number. I was a member of a small team and twenty years-old at the time.

Despite the threat of enemy attack merchant ships steadfastly carried coal and other vital cargoes between UK ports throughout the War. Especially vulnerable were those which sailed along the East Coast where they came within range of German aircraft and were exposed to attack by fast E-boats and lurking U-boats. In the early stages of the War losses were high but as our defensive capability grew the enemy found it increasingly hazardous to make these attacks during daylight. Aided by radar our fighters, motor-torpedo-boats and destroyers became a force to be reckoned with causing the Germans to seek other ways of attacking our coastal shipping. They turned their attention to sowing mines at night in the navigation channels leading to the principal ports. Although the enemy now had little direct contact with their quarry some sinkings still took place but a much-increased burden was placed on our already over-stretched mine-sweeping forces which spent hours clearing the fairways of mines before the merchantmen could proceed. The port of Kingston-upon-Hull, which lies several miles up the River Number, had been particularly vulnerable to this form of attack and it was often late in the day before freighters could move towards the North Sea and head for their destinations. Even so, enemy submarines and E-boats sometimes lay in wait for our ships and attacked them in the deepening gloom or as they were silhouetted against the sunset.

The aircraft used for these mine-laying operations were the large Heinkel He115 seaplanes which could carry both ordinary and magnetic mines. At night, and under reasonable conditions, their crews could spot where they could alight, release their charges and then fly away. From the mine-sweepers' viewpoint it was difficult to know how many mine-laying aircraft had been operating, how many mines they had laid and where they had laid them. And so, as soon as dawn broke, the minesweepers set out to clear a great expanse of water of uncharted mines - mines which presented the minesweepers themselves with a real hazard. It would obviously be helpful if they knew where to look and also have some idea of how many mines there might be. Consideration of this problem suggested that radar might be used to detect and track the mine-laying aircraft and indicate where they had been active. However, there was a supply problem; all current production of radar equipment was already earmarked and unavailable for this purpose. Fortunately it was recalled that quite recently an early Type 287 radar system had been taken out of a warship, believed to be the battleship HMS Rodney, *and it lay in store at Portsmouth. It was likely to be in working order and, if so, might be useful in the current situation. But where should it be located to give good surveillance of the lower reaches of the Humber? By happy chance a roofed-in water tower, unused* for many years, stood close to the southern shore in the Immingham area and it seemed possible that the radar might be installed in the brick-built tank which stood on concrete legs about thirty feet above ground. Another consideration was that although the ranges involved in the proposed task were well within the equipment's normal capability both the outgoing and return signals would have to pass through a brick structure and become adversely affected. There was little time to explore this aspect but, since the brickwork was dry, expert opinion thought it worth the risk.

Next, from time to time the Luftwaffe sent reconnaissance aircraft which probably took photographs of the area and the enemy would probably be quick to spot if any activity took place in the vicinity of the old tower. It was therefore arranged that all deliveries would made at night, no vehicle was to be seen there by day and the whole site would remain undisturbed. The radar's aerial array, which gave a good directional beam, consisted of a line of horizontal dipoles mounted in a parabolic reflector which was roughly twenty feet long and six feet high. The whole assembly could be swung with precision over a wide arc. After several days and nights of hard work the system was installed and we got it up and running. To our relief good indications came from known targets in the area so a team of skilled naval radar operators took over and used a minesweeper to establish good range and bearing accuracy.

On recent nights Luftwaffe minelayers had been active in the area and we hoped they would pay a visit that evening. We were not disappointed and, as the Heinkels arrived one by one, they were tracked by the operators who relayed range and bearing information to a couple of navigation officers who marked out the minelayers' tracks on an Admiralty Chart. It was well past two in the morning when this long-drawn-out activity ceased and we travelled the short distance back to the local naval base, HMS Beaver II, where our beds awaited us and we fell asleep. Early next morning I was woken by a positive thump. The minesweepers, each armed with a copy of the marked-up Admiralty chart, had gone out at daylight to sweep the areas where the mines had been sown. I had heard the first one to be located being blown up. The minesweepers' procedure was to explode the mine if possible so that no hazard remained — a short burst of machine-gun fire was often effective. Soon afterwards another mine went up, at which point a Wren arrived at my door with a cup of tea. After we had exchanged 'Good mornings' she re-marked that it was unusually early to hear explosions — they usually took place later in the morning or during the afternoon! I made no comment. In a short while I made my way to the wardroom and, as did my colleagues, had a good breakfast. In the meantime a couple more explosions occurred and there was a general air of satisfaction about the place.

At this point the local Commander came in looking very cheerful indeed. He said that at this rate he could get the ships down river by mid-morning. He thanked us profusely for our help in bringing this about and, in a fit of enthusiasm, went on to suggest that we could choose what would be on the menu for dinner that evening! At that stage of the War food was tightly rationed, meat was very scarce and the long summer days were a long way off. Quite jokingly one of my colleagues said "How about liver and bacon?" to which another said "With lots of onions", a vegetable which was in extremely short supply at the time. Continuing in this jocular fashion I added "With strawberries and cream to follow!" Laughter all round. We spent the day resting after discussing how we might improve on last night's work but came to the conclusion that everything had turned out very well. We looked forward to a repeat performance tonight. Eventually it was dinner-time so we trooped into the wardroom and sat down. Imagine our surprise when stewards placed plates of liver and bacon before us and, when we had finished these and made many jokes about strawberries and cream to come, that was exactly what turned up!

The Commander had certainly gone to some lengths to meet our light-hearted suggestions. In talking to him afterwards it was revealed that the meat was obtained from a 'black-marketeer' whom his Chief Steward knew and that the strawberries, quite out-of-season, had been located at a well-known high-class grocery store in London. A dispatch-rider had gone to fetch them!

No mine-layers turned up that night so we returned to Portsmouth next day. It was later reported to us that the Germans made several more visits to the Immingham area but after a while they gave up, evidently realizing that they were now laying mines to little purpose. It was thought that they transferred their activities to Russian waters where the chances of radar detection were much lower.

Royston Powell

Incident:
'Reports on Enemy Action', classified as 'Most Secret', were issued daily by the Air Ministry War Room. Report No 131, dated 3 April 1941, noted that on 2 April 1941 at 1315 hours an enemy aircraft dropped twenty-two 50kg bombs at RAF Catfoss. Twelve fell on the aerodrome damaging six Blenheims. One Wellington was set on fire by machine-gun fire, but there were no casualties.

144: This is the infamous unexploded parachute mine and the home of the extremely lucky Joe Sadler in Ellerby Grove.

How lucky can you get?

One morning, after a raid, I was passing through Ellerby Grove, one of the streets which was on my usual shortest route and saw ahead a group of people with a smattering of police and soldiers. I asked someone what was happening and was told that a parachute mine had not exploded and had been defused during the night.

I pedalled up to the house in question and stopped to have a look. The mine had shaved the front window and buried itself into the concrete path in front of the window.

Unknown to me of course then, but in later years I was to work in the same firm as the gentleman of the house and he told me that he was sitting behind the window reading, in fact just about to join his wife in the shelter, when he was shaken by this mighty thump which shook the whole house. He lifted the blackout curtain and this massive light-grey object of destruction was outside the window about two feet from his nose.

'How lucky can you get?' he said, smiling, in later years. His name was Joe Sadler.

John Cottrell-Smith's diary

145: This is often all that was left after the bombers had gone.

83

146: *Hull dockside scene. London and North-Eastern Railway lighter Number 39 appears to have survived relatively unscathed.*

147: *The extensive timber yards surrounding all the docks in Hull made excellent targets for the Luftwaffe. Despite the damage, the city, somehow, kept going. Charles Pearson the ladder makers have covered the roof of their premises with temporary sheeting and what appears to be a brand-new ladder leans against the wall.*

148: *These are some of the warehouses alongside the Alexandra Dock, quite possibly destroyed in the air raids of 6-7 May 1941 and which were still burning when John Cottrell-Smith made his escape from the area..*

149: Chas. Ware and Sons have moved... A scene in the devastated High Street in Hull.

150: This appears to be the rear of a terrace of shops, somewhere in Hull after the Luftwaffe had visited.

151: There is no doubt about this location. Derwent Street was one of many streets in East Hull where the mostly working-class families living there were hard hit. Before and just after the war, in the days before supermarkets, every street had at least one small grocery shop. Unfortunately, a great deal more than Sanpic and Brasso will be needed to get this shop back into habitable condition. Note the white paint around the lamp post to help visibility in the blackout.

85

7th May 1941:

Moonlit night. First hits were the oil mills with BM 1,000's. Then heavy bombing followed.

The day after my birthday, I arrived home from school that evening, and I started to read my adventure book and studied my other presents which included a metal model of HMS Eagle, the aircraft carrier, and a set of metal soldiers labelled 'Finnish Ski Troops in Winter Fighting Dress'. I added them to my collection of other lead soldiers and numerous aeroplanes, tanks and ships, with which I played many imaginary war games, swooping the planes, pushing the tanks and trucks and steaming the ships into ports on the floor.

We had tea of home-made sausage-rolls and Spam, and cakes which she had baked.

After enjoying the evening with my family, I sensed the usual tenseness which seemed to effect everyone about nine o'clock, obviously wondering what fate would have in store during this night.

One could not relax whilst in bed, even on a peaceful night, expecting from hour to hour to be rudely disturbed and urged to the shelter. Sure enough, we spent that night in our shelter. For most of the night, the centre of the city was blasted and burned, but although close enough, we managed to escape the main brunt of the bombing, at intervals watching with awesome disbelief, the fantastic glow from the holocaust of burning buildings.

In the morning, long after the last Aryan visitors had departed for home, the dock staff, arriving for their shift and looking downcast and holloweyed after the night's experience, told many tales of destruction and death.

Of most of the large stores destroyed, of hotels, the station, Stoneferry mills, Ranks mill and the centre of the city still burning fiercely. Of rows of terraced homes flattened. Police, firemen, ambulancemen and women and rescue workers continuing to search for survivors amongst the heaps of rubble that, the evening before, had been peoples' homes.

I stayed in all day with Mo, reading and listening to the wireless. We waited for the BBC news. After a summary of news from the battlefronts, the announcer informed us that 'a north-east coast town was bombed last night. There are reports of considerable damage and casualties'.[15]

'Not even mentioned the town's name', *we grumbled, after hearing, on other previous occasions, the names of other unfortunate places such as London, Coventry, Plymouth and Liverpool.*

That evening we automatically settled into our four inch thick, concrete blockhouse that we called our shelter. It was as if we knew that it was our turn next after the pounding of the city the night before. And it was!

Getting on towards midnight, the first waves of bombers droned overhead, dropping hundreds of incendiary bombs. They were everywhere, one or two rolling through our blast wall, to be put out by dad and his colleagues with sand and water which were kept in red buckets inside the entrance. After a lull, the next waves of aircraft spewed down high explosives and oil bombs, with which they were about to concentrate on our eastern docks. The shelter shook amid the din of explosions. 'I'm frightened!' *I whispered to Mo, laying next to me on the bunkbed.*

'We'll be alright', *she answered, but the tone of her voice was not convincing.*

I thought a silent prayer: 'Please God, make this war end soon.' *During a let-up we heard mens' shouts and running feet coming towards us.*

The R.A. gun crew had found things a trifle too hot crouching in their emplacement and had run across to our shelter. 'Where's my *** boot? Who's got my right *** boot?'

The man was insistant about its whereabouts, having aquired two left ones.

When his eyes were accustomed to the semi-darkness, he saw my mother and apologised profusely for his language.

I felt warmed and more confident in their company. The bombing continued.

'Where's Frank?' one of the artillerymen asked.

'The stupid bugger must have stayed on sentry-go', suggested another soldier.

The first chance they got, two of them dashed across over the lock-gates to trace his whereabouts and returned minutes later obviously very upset.

'We found him on the road near the billet', stammered one of the men.

Frank was dead, laying with both legs blown off. One of the worse sounds was the scream of the bombers diving. We thought that they could have been Ju 87s or Stukas, but were probably Ju 88s. To avoid going too fast in their dive, they had air-brakes on the wings, hence that awful scream.

Many of the ships in dock contributed to the ack-ack defence, especially a Free-French destroyer, berthed on the river side of our western jetty shed on the other side of the lock.

These French sailors were blasting away with their Bofors, Pom-poms and Lewis guns.

When an oilbomb hit the shed that they were berthed at, they set to with the vessel's equipment

[15] This was probably done to accord with Churchill's wishes that 'disproportionate publicity was not given to these raids. Our attacks on Germany were inflicting much greater damage'. Despite the use of decoy 'starfish' sites to mislead enemy bombers, Hull and the Humber mouth are unmistakeable from the air. It may be that in order to discourage the enemy from sustained attacks upon the east coast's most important port it was decided it was not to be mentioned by name.

to extinguish the flames. Sadly some of them were killed from another bomb falling nearby. We all owed a great debt to these brave men!

On Hedon Road, running along the north side of the dock, was the jail.

It had been taken over by the military and used as a 'glasshouse', the name known by all ex-squaddies.

The bombs were slicing down the multi-storeyed cells, killing the shouting inmates, apparently, no one answering their desperate calls to be let out and take shelter. Opposite the jail, on the dock side, was a large shed where all the ammunition was stored. This was supplied to the vessels in dock, for their anti-submarine guns (placed on the poop-deck of vessels) and their assortment of antiaircraft guns. Also inside were, apparently, torpedoes and depthcharges. During the early morning the building was hit and started blazing fiercely. For the rest of the night and into the day time, the contents of the shed exploded continuously, with the incessant popping of small arms, the background to the heavy blasts of large shells and charges. The tracers gave a bright visible display over the glow of hell below.

The pit-prop yard behind the house was blazing also and mum voiced her fears about some bags of sugar that she had saved since the outbreak of war and pleaded with dad to bring it across during a lull. It amazes me, when I look back, that in the middle of the situation that we were in, all she could worry about was her precious sugar! Luckily the wind changed and the fire did not spread to the house.

We finally emerged from our lucky haven about 5 am. Acrid, bitter smoke filled the air from the cargo sheds burning. I couldn't see any fire-fighting anywhere, it was hopeless anyway as all were infernoes, beyond saving. Some vessels had been hit and varied items of cargo floated around in the dock, some blocking up the lock-pit, such as bales of wool and timber. With heavy hearts, we slowly walked the short distance to the house, relieved that the terrible night was over, but thinking about the future and what further evils it had in store for us.

Most of the windows had gone again and tiles from the roof, but apart from shrapnel holes, partly dug into the walls, the house had escaped; an arrogant tower amidst the scene of surrounding chaos. We couldn't live in the house anymore so we cleared up our possessions best we could. I tried to wash not realising that the soap had glass splinters in it, so cutting my hands and face quite badly. After being patched up I searched and found more items for my collection of the litter of warfare. During that morning I hated the Germans with all my body and soul, swearing to myself that one day I would succeed in killing one to satisfy my young rage. If only an enemy airman would parachute down and I could help my dad to club him to death! That was how I felt on that second day after my eleventh birthday.

John Cottrell-Smith's diary

152: All too often people would leave their places of work and return the following day to find a sight something like this waiting for them. The still-smouldering wreckage of an unidentified business somewhere in Hull.

Facts: Hull suffered more from bombing than any other British city apart from London in World War II.
Between September 1939 and April 1945 there were 82 air raids on Hull in which bombs or incendiary devices were dropped.
Over 1,200 people were killed in these raids (more than in Coventry or Plymouth). 3,000 people were injured.
370 air raid shelters were destroyed.
152,000 people — about half the population — were made homeless at some point.
86,715 houses were destroyed or damaged — almost 94% of the total. (Coventry lost 50,479)
There were 815 air raid warnings, leading to 1,000 hours under alert.

87

153: This is the Salvation Army Hall in Franklin Street in East Hull, probably soon after the raid of 18 July 1941 when the air raid shelter there was hit with the loss of 18 lives.

154: The interior of the Franklin Street Salvation Army Hall in 1941 showing extensive damage to the roof.

155: Franklin Street Salvation Army Hall in July 2005, now besieged by cars, but otherwise remarkably little changed from 64 years ago.

156: *The gaunt ruins of St. Andrew's church in Prospect Street.*

157: *Not definitely identified, this may be the ruins of the railway station at the old Humber ferry terminal.*

158: *This appears to be the sandbagged remains of a quayside metal shelter or railway wagon with a warehouse in the background which has been struck a glancing blow by a bomb or debris.*

a relatively minor nature involving only a small number of bombers. Even so, during one such attack on the night of 15/16 April, more than 50 people were killed in Hull when a 1,000kg parachute mine exploded on a crowded communal air raid shelter in Ellis Terrace off Holderness Road.

Away from Hull, Bridlington was attacked again during the night of 9/10 April. Several HEs fell on the town, killing a man on Hamilton Road and a child on New Burlington Road. Elsewhere in April, bombs fell at Sewerby, York, Catfoss, Hornsea, Mappleton, and between Hedon and Paull; there was little damage and few casualties. Again, all the raiding bombers escaped, with one exception. Junkers Ju 88A-5 *Werk Nr* 0541, 4D+KK, of 2/KG 30, ditched somewhere off the Humber during the night of 7/8 April after experiencing engine failure. There were no survivors from *Uffz* Helmut Owich's crew. Could this have been the aircraft which dropped one 500kg HE and one 1,000kg HE on Spring Bank West and Kirklands Road in Hull at approximately 0040 hours on Tuesday 8 April?

The next heavy raids on Hull came during the night of 7/8 May and in the early hours of 9 May 1941. In the first of these attacks, 72 Heinkel 111s and Junkers 88s were involved while 120 of the same type of aircraft participated in the second one. In Hull, there were lengthy 'Red Alerts' – from 2315 hours on Wednesday 7 May to 0508 hours on Thursday 8 May and from 0005 hours until 0555 hours on Friday 9 May. The people of Hull were distinctly unfortunate with regard to the first of these May raids in that the primary target for the Luftwaffe in the North that night was Merseyside. Adverse weather conditions west of the Pennines, however, resulted in the German bomber crews heading for their secondary target, Hull.

These were terrible times for the people of the city, the Luftwaffe's latest onslaught resulting in more massive damage and devastation to docks, industries, the shopping centre, the transport system, and the inevitable destruction of hundreds of homes. Also, the Central Fire Station was hit, as were several banks, churches and schools. Around 450 people died and another 350 were seriously injured in the May 1941 Blitz, while approximately 30,000 Hull residents were rendered homeless.

From Beverley and surrounding villages it appeared as though the whole of Hull was alight as fires quickly grew into huge, terrifying conflagrations. In Hunmanby, some 30 miles to the north of Hull, we watched in horror at the growing glow in the southern sky. For the author's mother, a native of Hull with a sister and two brothers living in the city, it was a deeply depressing experience.

Outside Hull, there were fatalities during the May raids in Hedon, Woodmansey and at a military camp near Preston, while a small number of people were injured at Wawne. One enemy bomber, apparently lost over the region, jettisoned its bombs, which fell harmlessly in farmland between Kilham and Thwing.

This time, however, RAF night fighters hit back with some success. First, during the early hours of Thursday 8 May, P/O Richard Stevens flying a 151 Sqn Hurricane from RAF Wittering in Northamptonshire, engaged and shot down a Heinkel 111. The aircraft, Heinkel He 111, *Werk Nr* 3987, 5J+ZB of Stab I./KG 4 from Eindhoven in Holland, came down in shallow water a few hundred yards south of Withernsea.

This is how the incident was reported by ARP personnel in East Yorkshire:

"Unidentified plane has dropped in the sea at 0228 hours. I am informed by Coastguard and Observer Corps that part of the plane is visible in the sea, 600 yards south of Withernsea."

(Withernsea Sub-Control to Beverley Control 0315hrs)

"It has now been ascertained that the plane previously reported is an enemy plane. Two enemy airmen have been taken prisoner and another two injured airmen are being attended to by First Aid Services. The ambulance driver has been instructed to take the injured airmen to Patrington Military Hospital. Police Sergeant Calvert is accompanying the ambulance."

(Withernsea Sub-Control to Beverley Control 0345hrs)

"It is now reported that it has been found impossible to get the injured airmen out of the machine[16]. The two prisoners have been taken in charge by the Hampshire Regiment."

(Controller Beverley to Regional Control Leeds 0504hrs)

The two captured German airmen were the Heinkel's observer and captain, *Oblt zur See* Paul Tholen, and his pilot, *Ofw* Hans-Karl Schröder. *Fw* Willi Schreiber and *Ofw* Alfred Hoffman were the crew members that died before they could be extricated from their aircraft.

Next, early on Friday 9 May, night fighters of 255 Sqn from RAF Kirton-in Lindsey in Lincolnshire became spectacularly involved in aerial combat over East Yorkshire.

Within half an hour, between 0120 and 0150 hours, the squadron claimed six enemy bombers destroyed, five by Boulton Paul Defiants and one by a Hawker Hurricane. However, there are only details available with regard to the three enemy bombers and their crews, which crashed on land in East Yorkshire following combat over the region.

First, at about 0125 hours, a Defiant delivered a blistering attack on a Heinkel 111 over Keyingham. The enemy bomber, Heinkel He 111, *Werk Nr* 4006, A1+FM of 4./KG53, caught fire and dived into the ground at Sunk Island. Of the five Germans on board, only *Uffz* Franz Magie, the observer, was able to parachute to safety. A second crew member, most probably the wireless operator, *Uffz* Jakob Kalle, also baled

Incident:
5 May. Junkers Ju 88A-5 3Z+FP, Werk Nr 7117, of 6./KG 77 forcelanded in the sea off Bridlington at 0015 following engine failure (cause unknown). Oblt Baumann, Fw Hopfer and Ofw Auernhammer were all killed. Ofw Schieting was resued by a passing ship and captured; the aircraft was lost.

[16] First Aid Personnel abandoned their rescue attempt as the incoming morning tide gradually submerged the Heinkel. If the two trapped German airmen were still alive at this point, then they subsequently drowned, inside their aircraft.

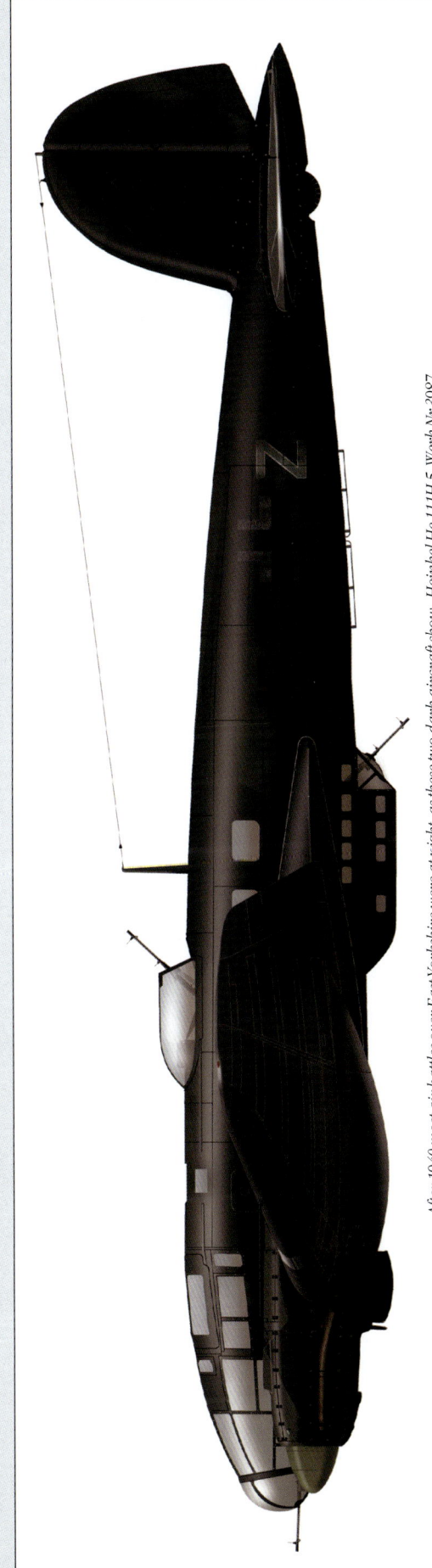

After 1940 most air battles over East Yorkshire were at night, as these two dark aircraft show. Heinkel He 111H-5, Werk Nr 3987, 5J+ZB, of Stab I./KG 4, was shot down off Withernsea on 8 May 1941 by a 151 Squadron Hurricane. No photos are known to exist of the aircraft so this illustration is a likely reconstruction.

Hurricane IIB V6931, DZ-D, served with 151 Squadron at Wittering in 1941. The finish of overall sooty black RDM2 Special Night is typical for RAF aircraft used at night at this time, as are the Medium Sea Grey code letters. The nose emblem is a fernleaf and the letters 'NZ' suggesting that the regular pilot originated from New Zealand

ILLUSTRATIONS NOT TO SAME SCALE

out but his parachute had been badly burnt in the cabin fire and failed to open. The Heinkel's pilot, *Uffz* Günter Reinelt, the flight engineer *Ogefr* Rudolf Lorenz and the air gunner, *Gefr* Heinrich Wülf were still in the Heinkel when it crashed and exploded. The bodies of Reinelt and Lorenz were later recovered from the scattered wreckage, but there was no trace of Wülf whose body must have been totally destroyed as the Heinkel exploded. Günter Reinelt, Rudolf Lorenz and Jakob Kalle were all buried in Brandesburton churchyard.

Shortly afterwards, one of the raiding Heinkels made a successful wheels-up landing in a field between the villages of Long Riston and Catwick, about six miles east-north-east of Beverley. The aircraft, Heinkel He 111, *Werk Nr* 3000, G1+FP of 6./KG55, was attacked by a 255 Sqn Defiant to the north of Hull, the night fighter's bullets inflicting critical damage on both of the Heinkel's engines and killing its pilot, *Fw* Gerhard Ender. Two of the bomber's crew baled out at a dangerously low level; *Fw* Georg Schopf landed heavily and awkwardly and broke his leg, while wireless operator *Uffz* Bruno Schakat had no hope of survival when his parachute wrapped itself around the Heinkel's tail unit. Still on board the crippled bomber, observer *Fw* Heinrich Müller struggled desperately with the aircraft's controls but managed to pull off a brilliant belly-landing. Soon, both the slightly injured Müller and the badly injured Schopf were in the hands of Catwick Home Guard before being transported to hospital in Beverley. The two dead German airmen, Ender and Schakat, were buried locally but later transferred to the German War Cemetery at Cannock Chase in Staffordshire.

Next, at 0140 hours, several witnesses on the ground witnessed an air battle over Winestead between a Defiant and a Heinkel 111. The enemy bomber, Heinkel He 111 (*Werk Nr* 4042) A1+CW of 6./KG53, then plunged to the ground and exploded a half mile northeast of Patrington railway station. Usually, in an incident of this nature, the pilot had little chance of escaping from a crashing aircraft, but on this occasion it was the Heinkel's pilot who was the sole survivor from the crew of five.

Uffz Helmut Teschke parachuted to safety and captivity while the bodies of his crew – *Gefreiters* Willi London, Johannes Kaminski, Hans Stieglitz and Hermann Decker – were recovered from their shattered Heinkel and buried in Brandesburton churchyard.

The Heinkel 111 which made a wheels-up landing between Long Riston and Catwick was definitely shot down by F/Lt Richard Trousdale DFC (pilot) and Sgt Chunn (air gunner) in a 255 Sqn Defiant. Ten minutes later, the same combination was responsible for the destruction of a second He 111, which crashed into the sea off Withernsea.

The other four Heinkel 111s destroyed over the region during the early hours of 9 May 1941 were the victims of 255 Sqn Defiant crews P/O Wyvill and Sgt Maul, P/O Wynne Willson and Sgt Plant, and P/O Wright and Sgt McCheaney, and the squadron's CO S/Ldr Roddick Smith in a Hurricane, but who shot down which Heinkel is not clear.

The early hours of 9 May 1941 had certainly been a very successful period for the RAF's night fighters, but once again the people of Hull had been desperately unlucky. Luftwaffe bomber crews had been briefed to attack steelworks at Sheffield at that time, but poor weather conditions over South Yorkshire had forced them to head instead for East Yorkshire and their secondary target, Hull.

Enemy bombers continued to be active over Hull on moonlit nights in June, although their attacks lacked the ferocity of the March and May air raids. The minor raid during the night of 2/3 June 1941[17] was a particularly sad affair as events turned out. Only one German aircraft took part in the raid, yet 27 people died and another 11 were seriously injured. The reason why there were so many fatalities in the course of this 'light' attack is that the aircraft's bombs fell on Hull after the 'All Clear' had sounded. The sequence of events was as follows:

2230hrs, air raid warning – people take to their shelters; 2355hrs, 'All Clear' sounds – people leave shelters and return home; 0001hrs, four bombs (2 x 50kg) and (2 x 250kg) fall on Marlborough Avenue, Park Avenue, Blenheim Street and Margaret Street. This regrettable episode saw one family completely wiped out; Mr and Mrs Ellston and their five children had left an air raid shelter after the 'All Clear' and were returning home when they were hit by the blast from one of the exploding bombs and killed instantly.

Elsewhere in East Yorkshire, Bridlington fared the worst when, at 0206hrs on 18 June, two 1,000kg parachute mines exploded on Lamplugh Road and St Anne's Road. Several houses in the area were completely destroyed and many others badly damaged, while St Anne's Convalescent Home was also hit and part of it wrecked. Seven civilians were killed in this raid and several others seriously injured.

Worse was to follow for Hull when the Luftwaffe launched major raids on the city during the early hours of 11, 15 and 18 July. By far the worst of these attacks was the one on 18 July, when 108 bombers from Luftflotte 3 dropped more than 170 tonnes of HEs and parachute mines, plus more than 6,000 IBs. Hundreds of houses in East Hull were completely wrecked or severely damaged, Victoria Dock was hit and large fires were started at Spillers, Reckitts and East Hull Gas. Furthermore, 140 people were killed and more than 100 seriously injured.

Away from Hull, Bridlington suffered again when, at 0028hrs on Thursday 17 July, four HEs exploded along the Promenade. Residential properties at 103 and 105 received a direct hit and were totally destroyed while adjoining dwellings were badly damaged. Three people were killed and several others

Facts:
Defiant aircraft with 255 Sqn on 8 May 1941:
N1687, N1740, N1810, N3310, N3312/YD-T, N3316, N3318, N3319, N3329, N3335, N3364, N3378, N3398, N3422, N3458, N3481

[17] This was raid no 50 on Hull.

Incident:
14-15 June, 1232hrs. Junkers Ju 88A-5 V4+GP, Werk Nr 6263, of 6./KG 1 shot down by ship's guns off Spurn Head. Oblt *Karl Schröder* (pilot), Ofw *Dietsch* both killed. Stabsfw *Wingenfeld* and Uffz *Fridel* made prisoner. Aircraft lost.

159: A Defiant nightfighter, JT-S, of 256 Sqn sometime in 1941. The very rough matt black RDM2 'Special Night' finish is wearing badly, as usual, and obscures the serial number.

160: This is the business end of a Defiant; the rotating Boulton and Paul gun turret mounted four .303 Browning machine-guns. Considering that the aircraft used basically the same engine as the Hurricane and Spitfire, yet had to carry the weight of the turret and its gunner, with only half the firepower of the single-seaters, (with no fixed forward-firing guns) it should have been no surprise that the Defiant squadrons were decimated when they eventually met up with Messerschmitt Bf 109s in daylight.

161: A serious problem after any major air raid on Hull was the large number of unexploded bombs (UXBs). Here soldiers from a Royal Engineers bomb disposal team pose for the camera with a 250kg high explosive bomb they have just defused. Considering the hazardous nature of their duties the men look surprisingly cheerful.

By early afternoon, it was possible to walk past the sheds and make our way to the main gates. The heat was so intense and the smoke so bad that we had to walk down the middle of the road with sheds either side, until we reached the open area of the more widely spaced timber sheds. With our essential belongings we walked past many craters and shelters that had been damaged. When nearing the flattened kennels where the police dogs were kept, we came upon a squad of troops who had been sent in to attempt the clearing up operation.

They appeared to have just arrived and were obviously in a low state of morale, looking dejected and two men were even fighting over some disagreement or other.

When we came into sight they became quiet and stared blankly at us. 'Where the 'ell 'ave they come from?' I remember one of them exclaiming. Hell was the operative word!

After passing through the gates onto Hedon Road, the contrast was remarkable. From the deserted dockland to the bustle of the main road, we joined people in the exodus to escape the ravages of their former homes. Some to stay with relatives, friends or to community centres. People with desperate expressions on their faces, struggling with their belongings, many guiding bemused or crying children.

Carts, prams and wheelbarrows were utilised in the procession. We heard many a shouted joke, either about themselves or what they were going to do with the 'Jerries'.

We were thankful to find that the bus service was running from the cleared rubble of the city centre to west Hull destinations, but were stunned by the sights we saw in this place that we used to call Hull. The Cecil cinema was an empty shell and looking up to the top of the wall-less girders, I saw an unburnt poster hoarding advertising that week's film Gas Bags, *and showed the Crazy Gang in cartoon form on a barrage balloon. This poster was to remain on display for many months after. On the bus garage roof, a double-decker bus was laid on its side hanging precariously over the edge. The shell of Hammonds and someone talking of a German airman on that night before last, parachuting onto the edge of the roof screaming down to the firemen to help, then being devoured by the flames. 'Frying in his own bloody fire!' one man behind me pointed out.*

John-Cottrell Smith's diary

162 Above left: Shortly after 2230 hours on 31 March 1941 a 1,000kg parachute mine exploded outside the ARP Control HQ at the corner of Ferensway and Spring Bank. There were several fatalities, including Hull's Deputy Medical Officer of Health, Dr David Diamond.

163 Above: As dawn broke and under now silent skies, rescue workers continued to search the rubble for any sign or sound of survivors. This was such a scene on Buckingham Street in Hull following one of the May raids.

164-167 Left: Gravestones in Brandesburton churchyard, of four of the twelve German airmen killed during air raids on Hull, 8/9 May 1941. From left: Obfw *Alfred Hoffman*, died trapped in his Heinkel 111 which came down in shallow water near Withernsea; Obgefr *Rudolf Lorenz*, killed when his Heinkel 111 crashed at Sunk Island; Gefr *Willi London*, killed in the Heinkel 111 which crashed at Patrington and Gefr *Hans Stieglitz*, also killed in the Patrington crash.

Facts:

The Küstenfliegergruppen had been steadily poached from the Kriegsmarine by Hermann Göring since April 1940. By May 1941 almost all had become Kampfgruppen, wholly under Luftwaffe control with only a nominal maritime strike role. That this was so can be gauged from the fact that the Luftwaffe sank only 19 merchant vessels in British coastal waters in 1942.

were trapped in the collapsed buildings before being brought out by ARP rescue teams, which included personnel from Driffield and Beverley. Also, water, gas and electricity supplies in the vicinity were disrupted for a time and one gas main caught fire.

No enemy bomber was shot down in the June raids, but during the night of 9/10 July two Junkers 88s crashed in rather mysterious circumstances at Speeton. A third Ju 88 from the same unit also came to grief that night when it flew into high cliffs at Staithes in North Yorkshire.

These three Junkers 88s were not from a bomber group, but from an anti-shipping unit, Kampfgruppe 106, based at Schipol in Holland. The purpose of their operation on 9/10 July was to patrol the North Sea from Whitby up to the Farne Islands. Each aircraft carried four high explosive bombs and their crews had orders to attack any British ships located in the patrol area.

Their flight plan was to fly the first leg of the operation in a north-westerly direction to a position 120 miles east of Middlesbrough. The second leg would take them to a point ten miles east of Whitby. They would then fly a third leg, west-north-west towards West Hartlepool, before heading north-north-west to the Farne Islands and then returning to Schipol.

Take-off was shortly before 2200hrs with Junkers Ju 88A-5 (*Werk Nr* 4386) M2+AL, piloted by *Hptm* Heinrich Moog, acting as the lead aircraft. Moog was *Staffelkapitän* of 3./KGr 106 and had recently joined the unit from 5./KG 30. The other two aircraft in the formation were Junkers Ju 88A-5, *Werk Nr* 3245, M2+CL, piloted by *Lt* Helmut Sinz, and Junkers Ju 88A-5, *Werk Nr* 2227, M2+EK, with *Oblt* Edgar Peissert at the controls.

Everything went according to plan until the three Ju 88s started on their second leg towards Whitby. They then encountered thickening mist but, even more important, they lost contact with the Noordwijk radio beacon in Holland. The three crews were now lost; they were in big trouble not knowing whether they were over land or sea. Actually, Peissert was not far from his patrol line, but he was flying on the wrong bearing and was heading straight for the towering cliffs at Staithes. Moog and Sinz meanwhile were 40 miles or so away, in the vicinity of Flamborough Head.

First to crash at Speeton, at 2348hrs, was Sinz's M2+CL. Chris Coleman, son of local farmer Arthur Coleman, was in bed asleep at Church Farm when:

"I was woken up by a terrible roaring in the sky. I heard explosions and a huge ball of fire passed by my window and then there was a huge explosion not far away."

The German bomber had hit the roof of a barn at Philip Jackson's Millholme Farm, and then clipped the farmhouse itself before crashing into a field and disintegrating. *Lt* Sinz, *Fw* Harald Beuting, *Uffz* Wilhelm Quodt and *Fw* Otto Donder all died in the crash. When NFS firemen from Filey arrived on the scene they were shocked to find four unexploded high explosive bombs in the wreckage. These bombs were later successfully defused by an Army bomb disposal squad. The remains of the four German airmen were buried in Bridlington Cemetery on Monday 14 July 1941, but later transferred to the German War Cemetery at Cannock Chase in Staffordshire.

Hptm Moog and his crew were more fortunate when their bomber flew into the ground to the east of Speeton and finished up on the cliff top about half a mile away from Sinz's aircraft. What had happened was that M2+AL had hit gently sloping ground before sliding on its belly across one and a half fields and coming to rest in a turnip field on the cliff top. Moog and his crew had been very lucky indeed; their Ju 88 had come to halt just feet away from the cliff edge with four HEs still on board. Amazingly, *Hptm* Moog, *Lt* Werner Blome, *Ofw* Alfons Wiefer and *Fw* Heinz Rieme had all escaped serious injury in their spectacular crash. Then, after setting fire to their aircraft, they had moved off down the clay cliff with their rubber dinghy and a supply of emergency rations, apparently with the intention of escaping out to sea. The four Luftwaffe men then had their second lucky break of the night — they were captured by soldiers of the Yorks and Lancs Regiment before they reached a minefield towards the bottom of the cliffs...

Meanwhile, 36 miles to the north-west of Speeton, the third Junkers 88 in the formation, M2+EK, had also crashed, into high cliffs at Staithes. *Oblt* Peissert, *Lt* Rudolf Bellof, *Gefr* Gerhard Vogel and *Fw* Karl Kinder were all killed on impact. Their remains were buried in Acklam Road Cemetery at Thornaby, North Yorkshire.

Back at Speeton, Moog and his crew were held in a military guardroom overnight. As young Chris Coleman was making his way to the local school at about 0830hrs on 10 July, he passed the guardroom and caught a glimpse of the four Luftwaffe men in there. He noticed that one of them had a bandage round his head.

Later that day, Moog, Blome, Wiefer and Rieme were interrogated by a RAF Intelligence Officer. Initially, they were not very cooperative; in fact a follow-up intelligence report noted that the four German airmen were *"Insolent as well as uncommunicative."* Also, they flatly refused to identify the bodies of Sinz and his crew. Over the next few days, however, a meticulous search of the crashed Ju 88s, coupled with further interrogation of the four survivors, provided a considerable amount of interesting information for Air Intelligence. Of particular interest were a number of maps upon which Luftwaffe routes to various British targets had been drawn in. For example, it was discovered that for an attack on RAF Dishforth in North Yorkshire, the landfall feature for German bombers was not Flamborough Head but Carr Naze, the narrow promontory of boulder clay, which leads to the rocky Filey Brigg at the northern end of Filey Bay.

Hptm Heinrich Moog was the most senior Luftwaffe officer to have been captured in East Yorkshire up to this point in the war. He was the *Staffelkapitän* (Commanding Officer) of 3./Kü.Fl.Gr. 106 and at 33 was one of the oldest and most experienced pilots in the Luftwaffe, having flown on more than 100 operations. In Luftwaffe circles, Moog was acknowledged as an expert on the Junkers 88 and had trained many young and raw Ju 88 pilots while with 5./KG 30.

Moog's *Bordfunker* (wireless operator) was another very experienced airman who had flown most of his operations with KG 3 and KG 30. On Monday 16 October 1939, Alfons Wiefer had been on board one of the nine KG 30 Ju 88s, which carried out the first air raid on Britain in World War Two, the attack on shipping in the Firth of Forth. Subsequently, Wiefer had flown on operation over Norway, Holland and France prior to the Luftwaffe's 1940-1 bombing campaign against Britain.

Initially, some people thought that the two Ju 88s, which crashed at Speeton, might have been involved in a mid-air collision, but RAF Air Intelligence personnel quickly dismissed this theory. The two aircraft were certainly not brought down by a RAF night fighter as none were in action over the region that night, and there were no reports of any East Yorkshire heavy AA battery firing at an enemy plane during the night of 9/10 July. However, the author has seen on ARP message, which states that an enemy aircraft had been *"… fired at by a destroyer in the bay."* It is possible that the Ju 88, which was on fire when it crashed at Millholme Farm, had been shot at and damaged by a warship in Bridlington Bay. As for Moog's bomber, former Speetonian Alan Staveley told the author that this aircraft was cruising along straight and level when it hit the ground and gouged its way across one and a half fields.

It had been said that Moog's M2+AL had only just cleared the high cliffs to the east of Speeton before it crashed. This seems highly unlikely as the aircraft was flying straight and level on a west-north-west heading when it came to earth. A more likely explanation is that Moog had flown in low across Bridlington Bay, cleared the 120 ft high cliffs along the southern side of Flamborough Head, but had then found himself flying toward rising sloping ground between Buckton and Speeton where the land is of the order of 350 ft. It could well be that the highly experienced Heinrich Moog saw the ground just in time for him to execute a brilliant crash landing.

Circumstances surrounding the crashes of the three Küstenfliegergruppe Junkers 88s during the night of 9/10 July 1941 may have varied, but there does appear to have been one common root cause — disorientation. It has been suggested that the three Ju 88 crews lost their way because of the misty conditions, which prevailed that night along the Yorkshire Coast. Yet Moog, Sinz and Peissert were three of Kü.Fl.Gr. 106's most experienced pilots. Furthermore, Heinrich Moog and Edgar Peissert had alongside them two of the anti-shipping unit's senior navigators in Werner Blome and Rudolf Bellof respectively. A more likely explanation is that the three crews had been the victims of British countermeasures in the 'Radio War.'

From the examination of downed Luftwaffe aircraft and the interrogation of captured German airmen, along with the work of code-breakers at Station X at Bletchley Park in Buckinghamshire, it became apparent that German bomber crews were being guided to their targets in Britain by a series of radio beams transmitted from medium frequency radio beacons in Belgium, Holland, France and Germany. Consequently, radio countermeasures would become a vital element in the work of the signals branch of the RAF. No 80 (Signals) Wing was formed with its HQ at Radlett in Hertfordshire, from where the 'Battle of the Beams' would be conducted.

At first, attempts were made to jam the enemy's beacon signals, using systems code-named 'Aspirin' and 'Bromide'. Once such systems had been perfected at Radlett, small outstations were established, usually in fairly remote areas, to put the jamming process into operation. Each outstation was manned by a small team of signals personnel who were usually billeted with local families. In East Yorkshire, there were outstations on the Yorkshire Wolds near Market Weighton and at Millington, a small village three miles north-east of Pocklington.

Also of importance were listening stations where operators monitored the source and frequency of German radio transmissions. At RAF Staxton Wold, receivers to pick up enemy radio signals were installed at the top of the radar station's three transmitting masts. In nearby Scarborough, there was a listening station in the grounds of Scarborough Castle where a team of four, operating in a cramped ten feet by ten feet hut, kept a close watch on *Knickebein* and other German navigational beams.

Enter the Meacon

Next came 'Meacon', a clever but simple radio countermeasure system whereby German beacon signals were re-transmitted on the same frequency from a small number of 80 Group outstations, thus giving Luftwaffe crews a faulty bearing and at times causing near panic as pilots and navigators realised that they were hopelessly lost.

There were no Meacon stations in East Yorkshire, but the approach to the full length of the Yorkshire coast was covered by Meacon stations at Marske and Brotton in North Yorkshire and Legbourne and Louth in Lincolnshire. German bomber crews usually knew when their beacon signals were being jammed, but could not tell when they were being Meaconed as

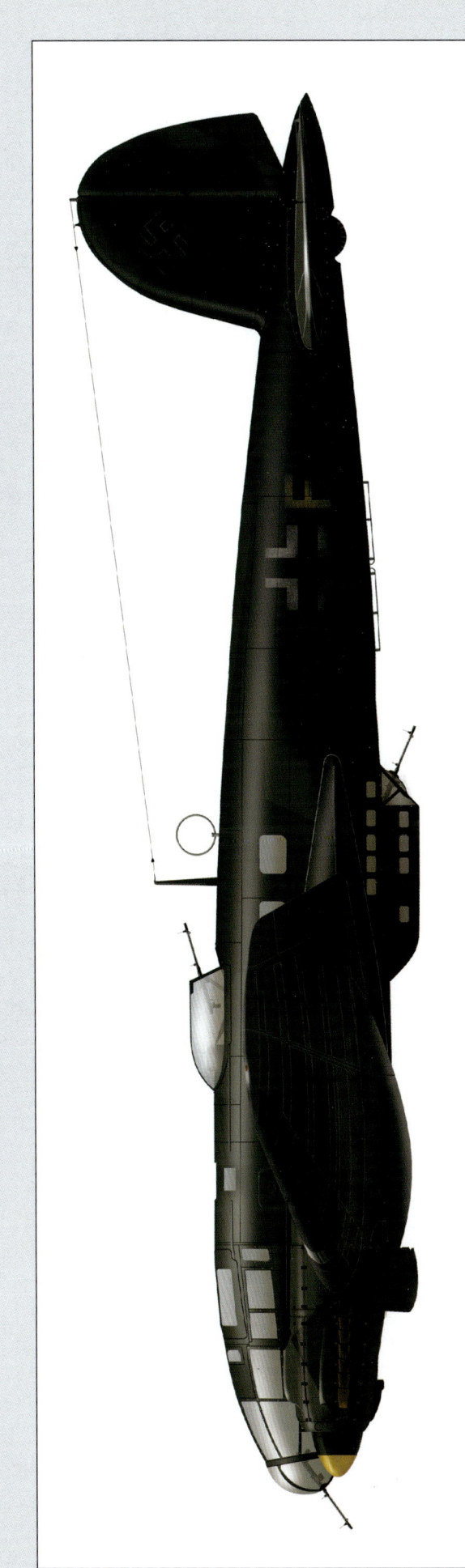

This Heinkel He 111P-4, Werk Nr 3000, G1+FP, of 6./KG 55, crashlanded at Long Riston on 9 October 1941 after it was shot down by a Defiant of 255 Squadron. It wears the typically scruffy night camouflage of the time.

Defiant Mk I N3340, YD-D, of 255 Squadron in typical all-black finish, but with an interesting fuselage roundel variation.
ILLUSTRATIONS NOT TO SAME SCALE

their original signals were being re-transmitted using the same frequency. Many a German bomber crashed in Britain or came down in the North Sea as a result of the Meacon radio countermeasure and not because of 'bad weather', 'engine failure' or 'technical trouble', reasons frequently given by the Luftwaffe for aircraft losses.

One can reasonably assume that the crashes of the two Junkers 88s at Speeton, and the third at Staithes, were the result of a successful RAF radio countermeasure operation.

Early on 11 July 1941, the Luftwaffe lost another of its bombers over the region when a Heinkel 111 of KG 4 came down in the sea off Flamborough Head. After dropping its bomb load on Hull, Heinkel He 111, *Werk Nr* 3956, 5J+ES of 8./KG 4 piloted by *Fw* L. Weitz was engaged in combat by a RAF night fighter, a few miles north of Hull according to statements made by the three German airmen who survived the ditching. It is thought that the night fighter, which attacked the Heinkel was a 255 Sqn Defiant from RAF Hibaldstow in Lincolnshire. One of the Squadron's Defiants, crewed by Sgt Cox (pilot) and Sgt Fitzsimmons (air gunner), was definitely involved in an air battle with a Heinkel 111 to the north of Hull during which Fitzsimmons was injured by return fire from the enemy aircraft. Cox and Fitzsimmons, however, only claimed, *"... one He 111 damaged."* The three survivors from the Heinkel, Fw Weitz along with his observer and wireless operator, were rescued from their rubber dinghy by a Royal Navy minesweeper and landed at Hartlepool. The Heinkel's air gunner could not be found and was presumed drowned.

Throughout the remainder of 1941, there were only two air raids of any significance on East Yorkshire. First, during the early hours of 18 August, a small number of Luftwaffe bombers attacked Hull. Their intention was to raid the docks, but poor bomb aiming resulted in most of their bombs falling on houses in East Hull. Casualties that night totalled 20 killed and 15 seriously injured. Next, during the night of 30/31 August, a sharp attack on the city led to more misery for the people of East Hull where many houses and several communal shelters were destroyed or badly damaged. In this latest raid on Hull, more that 40 people were killed and another 36 seriously injured. All the enemy aircraft participating in the August raids on Hull returned safely to their Dutch bases.

Elsewhere in East Yorkshire, the only fatality in the course of night-time bombing incidents during the latter part of 1941 occurred at Flamborough when, on the night of 12/13 September, a civilian was killed when a high explosive bomb exploded on council houses.

Before leaving the Luftwaffe's 1941 bombing campaign against East Yorkshire, reference must be made to one dramatic daylight attack by an enemy aircraft on a target in the region. This was on Monday 10 November and lessons were well underway at the village school in Hunmanby when, at 1330hrs, the air raid siren on Mallinson's shop in Bridlington Street sent out its wailing warning. Children living near the school were sent home while the others, including the author, were seated in corridors, which now had blast walls in place outside the windows. Shortly afterwards, loud bangs were heard from the direction of Speeton.

What had happened was that an LNER passenger train travelling from Hull to Scarborough, its locomotive belching out smoke and steam on the steep

Incident:
8 August. A Messerschmitt Bf 110C-5, 4U+XH, Werk Nr 2306, from the reconnaissance unit 1.(F)/123 was shot down about 65 miles off Flamborough Head by two Spitfires of the newly-formed 129 Sqn from Leconfield. The crew of Mende and Pietras were posted 'missing'.

168 Below: *Retribution. A Whitley Mk V bomber (actually of 51 Sqn at Dishforth) being loaded up with 250 lb HE bombs in July 1940. Note the freshly-applied matt Night finish on the fuselage and how de-icing fluid has removed the paint from the propeller blades. Aircraft such as this flew from Driffield and bore much of the load when it came to taking the fight back to Germany in 1940-41.*

Facts:

1942 saw the release of the all-time classic film, Casablanca, *starring Humphrey Bogart and Ingrid Bergman and its immortal song* As Time Goes By. *Bing Crosby sang* I'm Dreaming of a White Christmas, *probably the most popular song of World War II. Rowntree's plain York chocolate bars cost 2½d (1p) and 2 rationing points each.*

climb from Bridlington up to Speeton, had been spotted by a lone German bomber. As the train emerged from the cutting between Bempton and Speeton, the enemy aircraft dived down on its target, first machine-gunning the train and then releasing its four high explosive bombs. It was quite remarkable that no passenger on the train or any of the three-man train crew was hurt. The LNER men, Robert Langford (driver), Richard Porter (fireman) and Ernest Fewster (guard), who were all from Bridlington, and the train's passengers had quite a tale to tell when they eventually arrived home later that afternoon.

Away from the Home Front, 1941 was a busy year for the 4 Group Bomber Command Squadrons based in East Yorkshire. Apart from continued night attacks on key German ports, industrial towns and cities, oil installations and marshalling yards, East Yorkshire's bombers were also involved in a new bombing campaign, against German U-boats. These submarines were causing chaos among our North Atlantic convoys, which were bringing vital supplies of food and raw materials into British Ports. Too many Allied ships were being sunk by them and too few U-boats were being destroyed by escorting Royal Navy corvettes and destroyers or RAF Coastal Command aircraft. This situation was all too much for Prime Minister Winston Churchill who decided that the U-boat menace should be tackled in a different way. Bomber Command aircraft would now bomb U-boats in dock at Lorient and Bordeaux on the Bay of Biscay, attack U-boat building yards at Bremen, Hamburg and Kiel in North Germany, and raid the marine diesel engine works at Mannheim and Augsburg.

Serious threats to the convoys were also posed by the presence in the North Atlantic of two German battle cruisers, *Gneisenau* and *Scharnhorst*, (colloquially known as *'Gluckstein'* and *'Salmon'* to RAF crews) and the ability of a long-range reconnaissance bomber, the Focke Wulf Fw 200 *Condor*, to locate and attack convoys well out in the North Atlantic. Consequently, the RAF's bombing campaign was broadened still further to take in German aircraft factories at Bremen and Dessau, Condor airfields at Stavanger in Norway and Bordeaux in France, and the *Gneisenau* and *Scharnhorst* when they docked in the French port of Brest.

Bomber Command's response from East Yorkshire airfields was strengthened in the spring of 1941 by the re-opening of RAF Driffield as a bomber station. The bombers had left Driffield at the end of August 1940 following a series of Luftwaffe raids on the airfield but, in April, the bombers were back with the Vickers Wellington II having replaced the now outdated Armstrong Whitworth Whitley V. The 'Wimpey', as the Wellington was affectionately known, was first flown from RAF Driffield by 104 Sqn and 405 (RCAF) Sqn. Then, towards the end of June, 405 Sqn transferred to another East Yorkshire bomber station, RAF Pocklington. Bomber Command's presence in East Yorkshire was further strengthened in August by the arrival at RAF Holme-on-Spalding Moor of 458 (RAAF) Sqn, equipped with Wellington IVs.

1941 had been a memorable but miserable year, especially for the people of Hull, but what would 1942 have in store? In 1941, Bomber command had opened new airfields at Pocklington and Holme-on-Spalding Moor, while others were under construction at Breighton, Elvington, Lissett and Melbourne and would be operational in 1942. Also, new squadrons were being formed in the region and soon most of East Yorkshire's bomber airfields would be welcoming a new aircraft, the four-engined Handley Page Halifax II. It now seemed highly likely that Hull and other heavily bombed British towns and cities would be avenged in 1942 as Bomber Command prepared to launch massive raids on Germany. But, how would the bombers of the Third Reich respond — could the citizens of Hull expect more misery in the year ahead?

169: *Retribution II. British bombers began to get bigger in 1942 and so did their bomb-loads. This is a 2,000 lb armour-piercing bomb about to be loaded into a Wellington. The bomb is painted a dark green with a lighter green nose. Behind that are three rings, white/red/white respectively.*

BAEDEKER 1942

The raids on Hull and York

170 Above: The sinister silhouettes of Dornier Do 217E bombers of KG 2 setting out from their Dutch bases on a bombing or minelaying mission over Britain.

During the Luftwaffe's Blitz on Hull in 1941, East Yorkshire's night defences had suffered badly from a shortage of equipment and limited technology. There were insufficient searchlights and heavy anti-aircraft guns, while our night fighters also depended heavily on the searchlights, plus good visibility. Considering the thousands of rounds of ammunition fired by the AA batteries defending Hull and the number of night patrols flown by RAF fighters, the number of German bombers actually shot down over the region in 1941 had been disappointingly small.

Scientists, however, had been working for some time on new technology which would revolutionise Britain's night fighting capability. Of particular importance was the development of Ground Controlled Interception (GCI) and Airborne Interception (AI), the latter being on-board radar. A GCI controller at, for example, RAF Patrington, would direct a night fighter pilot towards an unidentified aircraft until the AI operator in the night fighter obtained a contact on his screen. The AI operator would then guide his pilot towards the 'bogey' until visual contact was established. This new radar system meant that RAF night fighter crews could now locate enemy aircraft in the dark without having to depend on searchlight illumination and clear skies.

AI sets had first been tried out in Bristol Blenheims in 1940, but the early sets had proved largely ineffective. The latest AI sets were installed in an aircraft which would become a highly successful night fighter; the powerfully armed twin-engined Bristol Beaufighter. First success for an AI-equipped Beaufighter came during the early hours of Wednesday 20 November 1940 when a 604 Sqn Beaufighter, crewed by F/Lt J. Cunningham and Sgt J. Phillipson (AI operator) shot down a Junkers 88 over Sussex. This was the first of many nocturnal victories for John Cunningham who became known as 'Cat's Eyes' Cunningham. The press knew nothing of AI, a very closely guarded secret, and the story which circulated in the newspapers of the day was that Cunningham was on a special diet of carrots to improve his night vision. *"Carrots DFC is Night Blitz Hero"* read one headline!

Even so, it was the spring of 1942 before the first AI equipped Beaufighters arrived in Yorkshire, with 406 (RCAF) Sqn at RAF Scorton in North Yorkshire. None of these highly effective night fighters were ever to be operational from an East Yorkshire airfield. RAF Leconfield, which had played such an important part in the defence of the region during the Battle of Britain, had reverted to Bomber Command control. A new fighter airfield, RAF Hutton Cranswick, opened in January 1942 when 610 Sqn moved in with their Spitfires, but in the year ahead the new Fighter Command station had a training rather than operational function.

It was also hoped that 1942 would be a more successful year for East Yorkshire's ground-based night defences, with the introduction of more radar-controlled searchlight and heavy anti-aircraft guns in the region.

During the first quarter of 1942, there were no major air raids on Hull, much to the relief of the inhabitants of that battered city, although the presence

Incident:
26-27 February. Dornier Do 217E-4 U5+ST, Werk Nr *1176*, of *9./KG 2* went missing over the Humber, cause unknown. Lt *Josef Scharnbacher*, Uffz *Sylvester Mischalla*, Uffz *Bruno Przibilla* and Uffz *Hans Kappenberg* all lost.

Incident:
27-28 February. Dornier Do 217E U5+AS, Werk Nr *5346*, of *8./KG 2* was shot down by naval gunfire over the Humber. Uffz *Helmut Günther*, Ofw *Karl Erber*, Uffz *Christian Pollok* and Uffz *Wolfgang Volz* all missing.

Incident:
8-9 March. Dornier Do 217E-4, U5+LT, Werk Nr *5335*, of *9./KG 2* was lost in a raid on Hull, cause unknown. Oblt *Helmut Hedler*, Uffz *Heinz Stelter*, Fw *Günter Kowalski* and Uffz *Hermann Materne* all missing.
8-9 March. Heinkel He 111H-2, G1+KU, Werk Nr *5393*, of *10./KG 55* was lost in a raid on Hull, cause unknown. Ofw *Engelbert Beisser*, Oblt *Anton Schneider*, Fw *Willi Walz* and Fw *Gustav Kuberka* all posted as missing.
8-9 March. Junkers Ju 88A of *10./KG 30* missing in a raid on Hull.

[18]*Eagle squadrons were composed of American citizens who had volunteered to fly with the RAF. Later in the year, from 29 September, these US flyers would transfer to the USAAF (United States Army AirForce) to join the 4th Fighter Group.*

of enemy aircraft over flying the region meant that air raid sirens were being regularly activated. The first deaths to result from an air raid on East Yorkshire in 1942 occurred during the night of 13/14 April when bombs fell on Hull (four killed) and Patrington (one killed).

There was a dramatic change in the air war over Britain later in April 1942 when the Luftwaffe resorted to bombing historic towns and cities in retaliation for the heavy and destructive RAF raids on the relatively unimportant German towns of Lübeck and Rostock. Lübeck was primarily noted for its beautiful Gothic architecture and it would appear that this old medieval town was targeted on 28 March 1942 because Air Marshal Sir Arthur 'Bert' Harris, the new Commander-in-Chief of Bomber Command, was desperate for a major morale-boosting success in his bombing campaign against Germany. A series of raids on Essen in the Ruhr industrial region had yielded only disappointing results, but had cost the RAF dearly in men and aircraft.

Harris, who had coldly observed that Lübeck was built *"... more like a firelighter than a human habitation"* was proved right as the old, tightly-packed timbered buildings were easily blown apart by HEs and razed to the ground as thousands of IBs detonated and spread huge fires across the town.

The destruction of Lübeck was followed by a series of RAF raids, starting in 23 April 1942, on a similar tinderbox town, Rostock. Results were equally satisfying for Harris, and the attacks on Lübeck and Rostok were collectively regarded as being a personal triumph for the Commander-in-Chief of Bomber Command.

There was immense anger and resentment in Germany following the savage raids on Lübeck and Rostock and a furious Adolf Hitler promised the German people *Terrorangriffe* (terror attacks) against the civilian population of Britain. German newspapers turned to the long-established Karl Baedeker tourist guide to Great Britain, promising their readers that the Luftwaffe would now proceed to wipe out every British town and city described in Baedeker's handbook. Consequently, when such attacks materialised they became known as the 'Baedeker Raids'.

On the night of 23/24 April 1942, Exeter was attacked, then on 25/26 April it was Bath, followed by a heavy raid on Norwich on 27 April; then, during the early hours of Wednesday 29 April, it was the turn of York.

Between approximately 0230 and 0400 hours, small waves of enemy bombers swept in to attack the city, preceded by pathfinder aircraft which dropped flares to illuminate the target area.

One wave came in over Flamborough Head before heading west-south-west and overflying the Yorkshire Wolds to York. Other groups, in an attempt to outwit the region's night defences, flew north off the Yorkshire coast before making staggered turns inland between Filey and the Cleveland Hills. Although the Luftwaffe claimed that 74 of their bombers had attacked York that night, the RAF estimated that no more than half those numbers were involved in the raid. Whatever the number, the German bombers, Dornier 217s, Heinkel 111s and Junkers 88s, gave York quite a hammering. The bombing wrecked or seriously damaged houses, schools, churches, shops, Bar Convent, the Guildhall, the waterworks, the gasworks, factories and warehouses, the railway complex and RAF York. There was also serious disruption to the city's electricity, gas and water supplies, and the road network. Furthermore, 79 people were killed and another 90 badly injured in the raid. The devastation and high number of casualties brought home to the people of York the horrors associated with a major air raid and probably made them more aware of what Hull folk had been going through in 1941.

The response of our night defences to the 29 April raid on York depended almost entirely upon aircraft. Unlike Hull, York did not have a searchlight/heavy anti-aircraft shield and so an armed response to German bombers would perforce have to come from any available night fighter squadrons. However, with RAF Leconfield now a bomber base, with the airfields at Catfoss and Church Fenton being used for training purposes, and with RAF Hutton Cranswick and RAF Catterick being no more than transit stations, any night fighter response had to come from RAF Scorton in North Yorkshire and fighter airfields in Lincolnshire.

Some people in York have been quoted as saying that there were hardly any RAF night fighters up during the 29 April attack on their city, and that those which were flying were not scrambled until after the first bombs had fallen on York. The facts suggest something different. The first point to make is that 26 RAF night fighters were sent up after radar operators in East and North Yorkshire had obtained several plots of 'hostiles' both off the Yorkshire coast and moving inland. RAF aircraft in action during the York raid were as follows:

3 Beaufighter IIs of 406 Sqn – RAF Scorton
2 Havoc IIs of 1459 Flight – RAF Hibaldstow
9 Hurricane IIs of 253 Sqn – RAF Hibaldstow
12 Spitfire Vs of 133 (Eagle) Sqn[18] – RAF Kirton-in-Lindsey

First up were a 253 Sqn Hurricane, piloted by F/Sgt Russo, and a 1459 Flight Havoc crewed by F/Lt Winn and P/O Ferry. These two Hibaldstow-based aircraft took off at 0145 hours, 45 minutes before the first bombs fell on York. Their orders were to patrol together over East Yorkshire and intercept any enemy aircraft. The US-built twin-engined Douglas Havoc was equipped with both on-board radar, AI Mk IV, and a Turbinlite, which was a powerful searchlight in the nose of the aircraft. The concept was for

101

171: *The far more capable Beaufighter soon began to replace the Defiant in the RAF nightfighter squadrons. Not only was it much more heavily armed, it had more endurance and could carry radar. This is an all-black NF Mk II, R2270, which went to Scorton-based 406 Squadron after it had completed trials and photography with the Aeroplane and Armament Experimental Establishment at Boscombe Down. Note the AI radar antenna projecting from the nose.*

172: *Hurricane IIB pilots of 'B' Flight of 253 Sqn pose for the photographer as they prepare for a night mission from their base at Hibaldstow on 23 December 1941. The nearest all-black machine is Z3971/SW-S, 'Samasthans II'. Behind it is Z3171/SW-P, 'Hyderabad City', an appropriate name as all the aircraft were supplied with funds from the Indian State of Hyderabad.*

173: *A Turbinlite Havoc (AH470) of 1459 Flight showing the mammoth searchlight in the nose. It crashed on take-off on 27 July 1943 and was not repaired.*

174: F/O D.C. Furse, seen here at the board, flew the Beaufighter which shot down a Dornier 217 near Malton after the 29 April raid on York. P/O J.H. Downes, Furse's radar operator/gunner is seated first left. (Goss/Rauchbach Archive)

175 Below: Do 217E-4s of 9./KG 2 during a test flight in Holland. The middle aircraft, U5+KT, Werk Nr 4314 was attacked and damaged by a Beaufighter over the North Sea on 15-16 September 1942. The flight-engineer parachuted, but the aircraft returned safely to base.

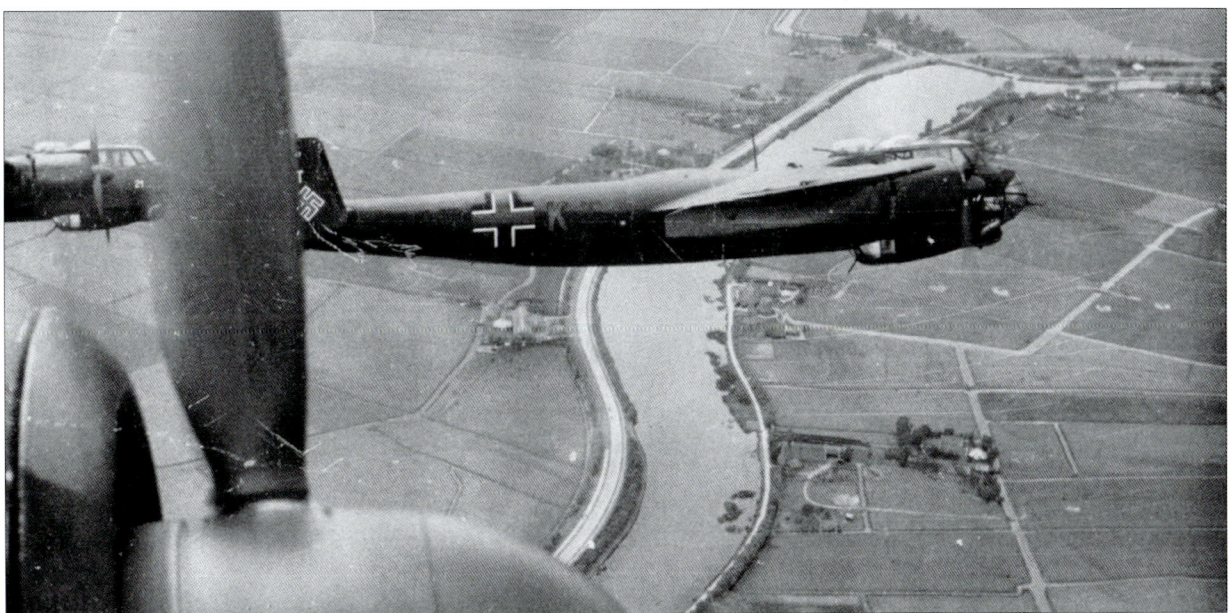

176: The crew of the Dornier shot down by F/O Furse. Lt Karl-Heinz Mühlen (second left) was the pilot. The aircraft in the background is a Dornier Do 17Z. (Goss/Rauchbach Archive)

103

the Hurricane to operate in close proximity to the Havoc so that when the Havoc had locked on to a 'bandit' its pilot would switch on his searchlight, illuminate the enemy plane and then watch as the Hurricane roared in to shoot down the raider. This was all very simple in theory, but far from straightforward in practice. For example, the Havoc's searchlight was powered by huge batteries stored in the aircraft's bomb bay; this made the Havoc cumbersome and sluggish and an inappropriate partner for the fast and highly manoeuvrable Hurricane. Two further drawbacks were that the batteries only provided a two and a half minute duration illumination and the Havoc did not carry any weaponry.

In Yorkshire, the first night fighter to be scrambled was a 406 Sqn Beaufighter which took off from RAF Scorton at 0200 hours. Crewed by F/O D.C. Furse (pilot) and P/O J.H. Downes (AI operator), this aircraft was to carry out a patrol between York and Flamborough Head. Between 0215 and 0230 hours, a second Havoc/Hurricane duo took off from RAF Hibaldstow. The Hurricane, piloted by a Frenchman, Lt Beguin, would fly as satellite to the Havoc crewed by P/O Beveridge and P/O Scott. Once airborne, the two pilots were instructed to make for York and orbit the city. At 0230 hours, a second 406 Sqn Beaufighter, crewed by Sgt Stephen and Sgt Bradshaw, was scrambled at RAF Scorton to patrol East Yorkshire between York and the coast. From 0230 hours, twelve Spitfires of 133 (Eagle) Sqn were sent up on patrol from RAF Kirton-in-Lindsey. Six of these aircraft were to orbit York while the others were to carry out orbits over the coast of East Yorkshire. Next, from 0245 hours, another seven 253 Sqn Hurricanes were scrambled at RAF Hibaldstow with orders to patrol the York area. Finally, at 0308 hours, a third 406 Sqn Beaufighter, crewed by P/O Lawrence and Sgt Wilmer, took off from Scorton to patrol the area between York and the coast.

The first waves of Luftwaffe aircraft enjoyed a surprisingly trouble-free operation, approaching and exiting the target area well away from the heavy AA guns in Holderness and not encountering any RAF night fighters — but for three German bomber crews these would be no safe return to their bases in Holland.

Bombs had been falling on York for about three-quarters of an hour when a Junkers 88 fell to the guns of a young Frenchman, W/O Yves Mahé of 253 Squadron. Hurricane pilot Mahé was over flying the city at a height of 6,300ft when he saw a trail of flares dropping from approximately his own altitude. Using full throttle, the very determined Frenchman was heading in the direction of the flares when, at 0315hrs, he spotted an enemy bomber about 1,000yds on his port side, flying a south-south-east course away from York. A tight turn took Mahé's Hurricane into a firing position slightly astern of the 'bandit':

"...delivered a 2 second burst and saw a big flash and start of fire in his starboard engine. E/A then went into steep spiral dive. I followed him down to 3,000ft where I lost contact. The flames had then gone out, but the E/A was still diving down, at least 300mph."

Mahé's victim was Leeuwarden-based Junkers Ju 88D-1 *Werk Nr* 1334, M2+CH, of 1./KGr 106, which carried a crew of four: *Lt* Werner Boy (pilot), *Uffz* Karl-Heinz Kugler (observer), *Gefr* Willi Schindler (wireless operator) and *Gefr* Heinz Müller (air gunner). These men had been distinctly unlucky in that on their initial run over the target area their four high explosive bombs had 'hung up' (failed to release). Their brave young pilot, Werner Boy, aged 19, opted to try again and it was on their second bombing run that cannon shells from Mahé's Hurricane had ripped into their aircraft.

As M2+CH spiralled out of control, Boy ordered his crew to bale out. Kugler, Schindler and Müller all leapt from the uncontrollable Ju 88 over Naburn and parachuted to safety and internment. Werner Boy was still in the diving bomber, however, and was killed when it ploughed into the ground at Crockey Hill, three and a half miles south of York.

Later, during interrogation, the three German airmen were quietly cooperative and one of their number, Willi Schindler, made it very clear that he was glad to be out of the war and still alive. It also emerged that Kugler had succeeded in releasing their four HEs shortly before their Ju 88 was attacked by Mahé's Hurricane.

Dornier Do 217E-2 *Werk Nr* 1164, U5+KP, of 6./KG2, operating out of an airfield at Soesterberg in Holland, was the next Luftwaffe bomber to fall to the guns of a RAF night fighter during the early hours of 29 April. Crewed by *Lt* Karl-Heinz Mühlen (pilot), *Uffz* Otto Hacker (observer), *Uffz* Fritz Kälber (wireless operator) and *Fw* Otto Fussnecker (flight engineer/air gunner), had experienced a comfortable inbound flight before dropping four 500kg HEs on York gasworks, at approximately 0300hrs, from a height of 9,000ft. It was on their return leg, when approaching the East Yorkshire coast, that the crew's good fortune finally deserted them.

Confident that in a little over two hours they would be landing back at Soesterberg, Mühlen and his crew were in for a most unexpected and unpleasant shock as they neared Flamborough Head. Suddenly, cannon shells and machine gun bullets tore through the thin skin of the fuselage and the Perspex canopy of the crew cabin, filling the plane with choking acrid fumes. Inside the cabin, Mühlen had been wounded in the left calf, but Hacker and Fussnecker had been more seriously injured. Hacker had cannon shell splinter wounds to thigh and buttocks while Fussnecker was in a most distressed state — an exploding cannon shell had left his left hand dangling uselessly and connected to his arm by only sinews and shattered bones.

With wind whistling and roaring through the

Facts:
Despite the danger of a German invasion being apparently long past, highly secret resistance cells made up of carefully selected civilian volunteers, known as 'Auxiliary Units', who were meant to stay behind after a German invasion, gathering intelligence and making sabotage raids, were still being formed. Men (and women) were recruited in the East Riding and were intended to make use of many concealed 'Operational Bases' where they stored weapons and explosives. One known to the writer was at Little England Hill near Withernsea. These units and their purpose were of the utmost secrecy and their existence was only revealed in the late 1990s.

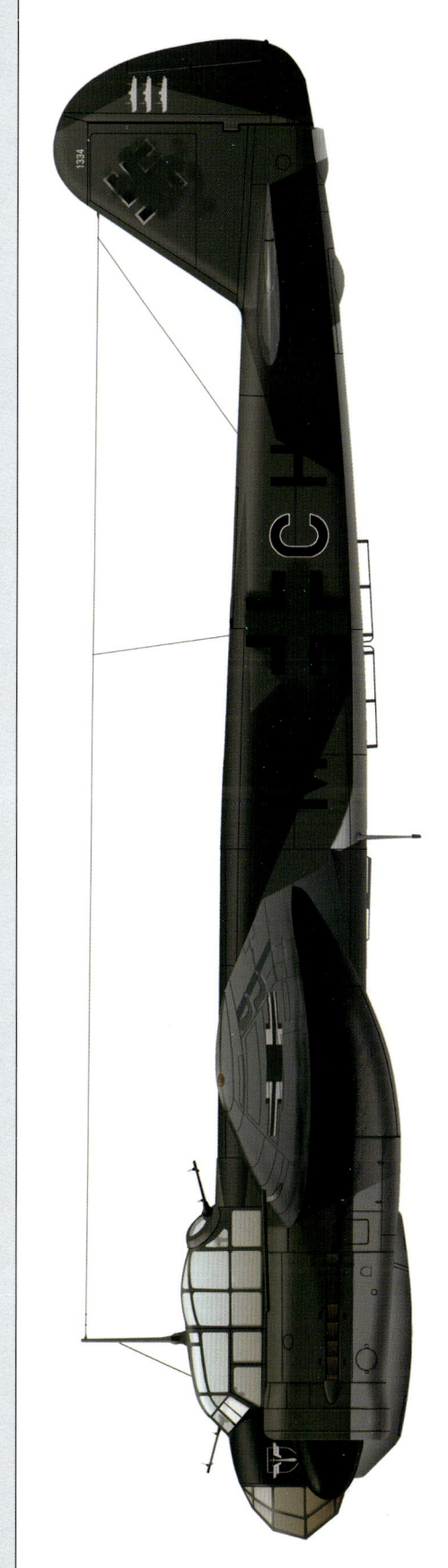

Junkers Ju 88D-1, Werk Nr 1334, M2+CH, of 1./KGr 106 and piloted by Lt Werner Boy was shot down during the Baedeker raid on York on 29 April 1942 by W/O Yves Mahe in a Hurricane of 253 Squadron. The primary role of KGr 106 was anti-shipping strikes (as shown by the tail markings), but the Luftwaffe was so stretched to support these raids that this aircraft was used as a conventional bomber. Note how the fuselage cross and swastika have been obscured. This suggests that the undersides were probably temporary black, but photos only show the top surfaces.

Hurricane Mk IIB Z3971, SW-S, 'Samasthans II', of 253 'Hyderabad' Squadron in all-black 'intruder' finish in April 1942. At the time the squadron was operating in collaboration with the Turbinlite Havoc unit, 1459 Flight. *ILLUSTRATIONS NOT TO SAME SCALE*

105

badly holed aircraft and with the port engine out of action, the four German airmen were in desperate straits. In a bold manoeuvre, Mühlen banked his bomber sharply to port and then dived steeply. Now, the Dornier was heading back towards York and was too low for the crew to bale out. A crash landing seemed inevitable and, with the aircraft in such an unstable state, the impact with the ground was likely to be heavy and life-threatening. Despite Mühlen's valiant efforts to safely land U5+KP in an open field, the bomber's nose hit the ground first, causing the aircraft to bounce back into the air before crunching down and sliding across the field. Soil and stones poured into the crew cabin during the dramatic landing, but the Germans were still alive.

Then, as the crew struggled to extricate themselves from their mangled Dornier there was a massive explosion as the main fuel tank exploded. The four Luftwaffe men managed to get clear of the blazing wreckage but all four were badly injured. Mühlen, apart from the bullet wound in his left leg, had now sustained severe burns to his face, while Hacker and Fussnecker were both in great pain and suffering from shock as a result of their cannon shell injuries. But the crew member in the greatest distress was Kälber. Mühlen was shocked and sickened when he located his wireless operator. Kälber's face was scorched, his smouldering uniform and helmet burnt to his body and head, and any metallic part of his flying suit was still glowing from the heat generated in the explosion. Fritz Kälber, in great agony, knew that he was dying.

Mühlen was now so desperate to get help that he fired his pistol in an attempt to attract attention. Despite the pistol shots ringing out loudly across the moonlit countryside, nobody appeared at the crash site. There was now no alternative but for the tenacious pilot to set out into this foreign landscape in search of assistance. Eventually, he stumbled across a house where he was promptly taken into custody by a group of soldiers; the time was approximately 0530 hours. Mühlen immediately told the soldiers about his three badly injured comrades and was assured that help would soon be on its way. He was then provided with soap and water to clean up his burnt and blood encrusted face.

From statements subsequently made by *Leutnant* Mühlen, one gets the impression that he appreciated the attitude of the British soldiers towards him. He clearly enjoyed speaking to the soldiers in English and getting involved in conversation about Churchill, Hitler, the RAF, the Luftwaffe, and the war in general. But what made Mühlen glow with pride was when the soldiers admired his flying suit, uniform, fur-lined flying boots and his Iron Cross.

Next, Mühlen was taken by armed guards to Malton Police Station where he was searched and questioned. The injured pilot was then transported to the local hospital, accompanied by a local police-man in a car driven by a young ATS woman. After treatment for his injuries, Mühlen discovered that Kälber had died, Fussnecker had had his left hand amputated and Hacker was having to lie face down on account of the shell splinter injuries to his posterior. To Karl-Heinz Mühlen, Oskar Fussnecker and Otto Hacker war was no longer such a glorious adventure.

In a RAF Air Intelligence Report, it is recorded that Mühlen's Dornier crashed "...*at Coneysthorpe, Nr Malton, 16 miles NE of York. 29.4.42. 033hrs*".

RAF documents suggest that Mühlen's Dornier was shot down by the Beaufighter crewed by F/O Furse and P/O Downes. This 406 (RCAF) Sqn. Scorton-based night fighter was patrolling between York and the East Yorkshire coast when contact was made with a Dornier 217 E-2 which was heading east in vicinity of Flamborough Head at a height of 6,000ft. Shortly after 0320hrs the Beaufighter engaged the Dornier in an attack from astern, with cannon and machine gun fire seen to be striking both sides of the bomber's fuselage. The Dornier then made a sharp climbing turn to port and disappeared when heading back inland. When Furse and Downes returned to base they could only claim 'One Dornier Do 217 E-2 damaged'. However, following interviews with Furse and Downes, the interrogation of the three Luftwaffe survivors and an inspection of the wreckage of U5+KP, their claim, was upgraded to 'One Dornier DO 217 E-2 destroyed'.

The third Luftwaffe bomber which failed to return from the 29 April raid on York was a Junkers Ju 88A-5, *Werk Nr* 0289, 3Z+AV, of 11./KG 77. This aircraft had bombed York and was overflying the coast of North Yorkshire in an easterly direction when it was intercepted by a 406 Sqn Beaufighter, crewed by P/O A. G. Lawrence (pilot) and Sgt H. J. Wilmer (navigator-radar). Accurate cannon and machine gun fire resulted in the Ju 88 bursting into flames and falling into the sea approximately 50 miles east of Whitby. There were no survivors from *Lt* Armin Körfer's crew.

A number of other Luftwaffe aircraft had narrow escapes in the course of the York operation. W/O Yves Mahé, who had already shot down one raider, was soon in action again, attacking a Heinkel 111 to the east of York. On this occasion, however, the bomber's pilot put his aircraft into a steep dive and escaped eastwards. Mahé then realised that he himself was now in serious trouble; his instruments showed that oil pressure was zero and oil temperature was 110 degrees. After advice from Sector Control, Mahé made a safe emergency landing at RAF Church Fenton at 0340 hours. It had been an exciting, and at times dramatic, patrol for the young Hurricane pilot.

Another Heinkel 111 was spotted firing its machine guns into the streets of York. F/O H. D. Seal, in a 253 Sqn Hurricane, gave chase and was able to fire two bursts before the Heinkel's pilot took effective evasive action and disappeared into the smoke and haze over the target area. Then, a Dornier 217

177: *A Rowntree's warehouse in York burns. 29-30 April 1942.*

178: *York's historic Guildhall burns.*

179: *Despite severe damage to the station on 29 April and many gaps in the roof, York station was fully operational again in less than 48 hours. At one point as the ticket office burned, staff carried the money to safety in Wellington boots!*

107

180: Wrecked homes in Westminster Road, York. (Evening Press, York)

181: The tail of Junkers Ju 88D-1 M2+CH, Werk Nr 1334, of 1./KGr 106 which crashed at Crockey Hill near York following combat with the Hurricane flown by Frenchman W/O Yves Mahe. Based at Leeuwarden in Holland, this bomber had previously been employed in attacking shipping rather than land targets, as can be seen from the three ship silhouettes on the tail, each one denotes a ship sunk.

182: A York family owed their lives to this Morrison shelter, which stayed intact when their house was destroyed by a high explosive bomb on 29 April 1942. (Evening Press, York)

108

Incident:

When York Station was hit by bombs, at least thirty trucks, several coaches and four locomotives were destroyed, among them the streamlined Gresley A4 Pacific No 4469, Sir Ralph Wedgewood, a contemporary of the famous Mallard, *now in the National Railway Museum at York.*

183 Right: *Five nuns were killed when a high explosive bomb hit Bar Convent on Nunnery Lane. (Evening Press, York)*

184 Far right: *The church of St Martin le Grand was completely gutted in the same raid.*

was very fortunate to escape when being pursued by a 1459 Flight Havoc Turbinlite, piloted by P/O Beveridge, and a 253 Sqn Hurricane piloted by Frenchman Lt Beguin. The Dornier was illuminated by the Havoc's nose searchlight but, as the Hurricane dived in to attack, the Havoc came between the bomber and the night fighter, thus preventing Lt Beguin from using his guns. Contact was then lost as the Dornier swung east and headed for the coast.

Finally, how did the American airmen of 133 Sqn fare during their patrols in the early hours of 29 April? Actually, it was a most disappointing operation for the squadron, with only one of its pilots making contact with an enemy aircraft. This was Irish-American P/O E. Doorly who, while orbiting York, was in combat with a Dornier 217 shortly before 0400 hours. However, as Doorly was attacking the Dornier his own Spitfire was hit by return fire from the enemy bomber. The temperature of his aircraft's engine rose alarmingly and the engine finally cut, leaving P/O Doorly with no option but to bale out. He parachuted down and landed safely about six miles from Church Fenton.

As dawn broke on 29 April 1942, NFS crews were still damping down at the scene of major fires in York. The Mansion House had been saved, but the Guildhall and the church of St Martin le Grand had been gutted. Elsewhere, ARP Rescue Parties continued with their search for trapped civilians, burrowing deep into the rubble of shattered homes. Sadly, at some addresses there were no survivors, just bodies. One York family had a miraculous escape when their house received a direct hit from a high explosive bomb. As their home collapsed around them they were saved by a sturdy Morrison shelter inside which they had taken refuge when the air raid sirens sounded.

At York railway station, a massive clean-up was already underway. The station buildings had to be made safe, the railway lines had to be cleared of wrecked engines, carriages and rubble from the roof, some railway lines had to be replaced, while the signalling system was in urgent need of repair.

The major air raid on York on Wednesday 29 April 1942 had not been much of a success for the Luftwaffe. They had lost three of their bombers, with six airmen killed and another six taken prisoner, while the railway system at York, at the centre of the Luftwaffe's target area, was functioning again within a few hours of the raid. Nor had any lasting damage been inflicted on RAF York, the home of 48 MU (Maintenance Unit). Hangars, buildings and runways had been hit by high explosive bombs but the work of the resident unit – taking delivery of, repairing and rebuilding aircraft damaged in combat or air accidents – was soon back to normal.

Also, one of the navigators on the York raid had been guilty of an incredible navigational blunder. Briefed to instruct his pilot to turn onto a west-south-west heading at Flamborough Head and then fly a 40-mile leg to York, the hapless fellow had ordered his pilot to change to a WSW heading at Spurn Head. The result of this careless miscalculation was that the pilot flew on this heading for 40 miles and then bombed Gainsborough in Lincolnshire!

Nor had the night been much of a triumph for the RAF. Shooting down only three of the raiding bombers was a poor return considering the number of RAF night fighters in action over East Yorkshire – 26. Furthermore, the RAF had lost one of its Spitfires. We have already seen how two of the German aircraft shot down during the raid on York were the victims of two of the three 406 Sqn Beaufighters which were operational that night. But why had only three of the squadron's Beaufighters been scrambled out of twelve serviceable aircraft?

Finally, had the raid really been a *Terrorangriffe*

109

(terror attack)? An analysis of where the bombs had fallen and the interrogation of captured German airmen suggest that it was no such thing. Also, a Luftwaffe briefing photograph for the raid clearly shows that the principal target area was the railway station/engine sheds/marshalling yards complex. Other targets were the gasworks and RAF York. All three were legitimate military targets. Damage to residential property and civilian casualties would appear to have been the result of poor work by the German bomb aimers rather than a deliberate attempt to terrorise and destroy the civilian population of the city. Furthermore, if the Luftwaffe crews had wanted to destroy the historic heart of York, dealt with at length in the *Baedeker Guide*, then surely the aiming point for at least some of the bomber force would have been York Minster, so clearly visible in the moonlight and under the falling flares.

Scarborough Street dies

Heavily bombed and battered Hull had enjoyed a period of relative calm during the first four months of 1942, with only two relatively minor raids on the city. Then, on the night of 19/20 May, the dreaded sound of a formidable force of enemy bombers was heard overhead. In the course of the 'Red Alert', which lasted from 2339hrs to 0116hrs, fewer bombs fell on Hull than had been dropped in any of the major attacks in 1941, but this time most of them were of the 500kg variety plus one 1,000kg HE and one 1,800kg HE. Luftwaffe bomber crews had been briefed to target the docks, but the inaccuracy of their bombing led to domestic property adjacent to the docks, especially along and off Hedon Road and Hessle Road, bearing the brunt of the attack. One such street, Scarborough Street, located between Hessle Road and St Andrew's Dock, fared the worst when it was hit by the largest and most destructive bomb dropped on Hull so far, a 1,800kg monster (known as a 'Satan' to Luftwaffe armourers). In this street of tightly-packed terraced housing, several properties were completely flattened while many others were rendered uninhabitable. There were 50 fatalities in the street and more than 100 people received serious injuries. Some bomb loads did land in the dock area and huge fires were started which took many hours to bring under control.

On the same night, the Blackburn Aircraft Company's premises at Brough were bombed and there were reports of HEs exploding around Hedon, Hornsea and Withernsea. There were no fatalities in any of these bombing incidents and the only serious damage was to the Blackburn buildings at Brough.

The Luftwaffe lost three aircraft during the 19/20 May raid on Hull. They were:

Dornier Do 217E-4 (*Werk Nr* 5362) U5+JK of 2./KG2, piloted by *Lt* Heinz Scholz;

Junkers Ju 88A-4 (*Werk Nr* 1610) S4+BH, of Kü.Fl.Gr. 1./506, piloted by *Fw* Hans Bleek;

Junkers Ju 88 A-4 (*Werk Nr* 1514) S4+AH, of Kü.Fl.Gr. 1./506, piloted by *Hptm* Alfred Rumpf.

Exact circumstances surrounding the loss of these three bombers are not known, but it is thought that they must have come down in the North Sea.

Inspired by Bomber Command's successful attacks on Lübeck and Rostok, Sir Arthur Harris next produced an ambitious plan which entailed despatching 1,000 RAF bombers in a single raid on a major German city. Three such raids were carried out in May and June 1940; they were collectively referred to as 'Operation Millennium'. First on the night of 30/31 May, more than 1,000 RAF aircraft were sent to attack Germany's third city, Cologne, on the eastern bank of the River Rhine. Next, on 1/2 June, just under 1,000 bombers flew to the Ruhr industrial region and raided Essen, the home of the mighty Krupps iron and steel, engineering and armaments factories. Then, on 25/26 June, around 1,000 of our aircraft bombed Bremen, a city with vital aircraft factories and shipyards in northern Germany.

East Yorkshire's airfields contributed Wellingtons, Whitleys and Halifaxes to each of these massive raids. The 1,000 bomber operations saw the introduction of the 'bomber stream', a vast air armada within which each aircraft had a set route, height, speed and timeslot to and from the target area. This bomber stream concept was later used for other major raids on Germany. Whenever the chosen target was in northern Germany, say Bremen or Hamburg, the spectacular bomber stream could be seen leaving East Yorkshire over Flamborough Head.

On the Home Front, there was little Luftwaffe activity over East Yorkshire in June and July 1942 with the exception of the evening of 25 July, when a single bomber brought death and destruction to the seaside town of Withernsea, and the night of 31 July when enemy aircraft were back over Hull. It was at 1826hrs on 25 July when a stick of HEs fell on Withernsea, killing 12 people and seriously injuring eight others, and destroying several houses, some shops and a cafe. This turned out to be Withernsea's worst night of the war. Six nights later came the raid on Hull. It is difficult to tell what exactly the German bomb aimers were targeting that night as the bombs were so scattered. Most of the resulting damage was to residential areas where 27 civilians were killed and many others seriously injured.

During the remainder of 1942 there were only a few minor raids on East Yorkshire, some carried out by just a single aircraft. August started with daylight raids on York (Sunday 2 August) – one person killed, and Beverley (Monday 3 August) – two people killed. But the region's most tragic incident in August occurred on the night of 28 August at Hornsea. What happened was that a Luftwaffe bomber, while being pursued over East Yorkshire by a RAF night fighter,

185: By 1942 the standard day fighter in use by the American-manned 'Eagle' squadrons in the RAF was the Spitfire Mk V, armed, as here, with two 20mm cannon in the wings. Those used by 133 Sqn in their attempts to defend York on 29 April were finished as seen here. It is not known for certain if this aircraft was in use by one of the Eagle squadrons, but the fancy yellow aircraft letter under the nose is typical of the free-thinking Americans' approach to such matters.

186: Rescuers frantically scouring the wreckage of Scarborough Street on 20 May 1942 for survivors after it was hit by the most powerful bomb to be dropped on Hull, the 1,800kg 'Satan'. This view appears to be looking north towards Hessle Road. Today a modern industrial estate occupies much of the site.

187: The scene at Queen Street Withernsea on 26 July 1942, showing the wreckage of Turner's shop. Ms Turner, who still runs the shop, but was then a child, was in the rear of the building when the bomb hit. She relates how the bureaucracy of the time operated; as the shop had received a direct hit, it was assumed that everyone had been killed and therefore no compensation was forthcoming, unlike for those on either side who were less affected. Bullet damage from an attacking German aircraft can still be seen on the shop opposite.

jettisoned two 500kg bombs as it was passing over Hornsea at approximately 2330hrs. One of the bombs hit and demolished the SE Yorkshire Light and Power offices and showroom at the corner of Cliff Road and Eastgate. Three elderly women and a young girl were killed as they walked past the building. The other bomb exploded at the back of 'Beechwood', a house on Belgrave Drive, doing a considerable amount of damage but not resulting in any casualties. Regrettably, the German aircraft responsible for bombing Hornsea on 28 August succeeded in evading the pursuing RAF night fighter and escaping out over the North Sea.

A distinctly unproductive period for the RAF night fighters came to an end during the night of 23/24 September 1942 when a 25 Sqn Beaufighter shot down a KG 2 Dornier 217 off Flamborough Head. It was a beautiful night with cloudless skies and a full moon, perfect conditions for a night fighter pilot, as P/O R. Peake (pilot) and Sgt T. R. Parry (navigator – radar) took off from RAF Church Fenton in an AI-equipped Beaufighter at 2245hrs. This was to have been a routine practice flight over the East Yorkshire coast involving P/O Peake's aircraft and a similar 25 Sqn Beaufighter crewed by P/O A. M. Hill (pilot) and Sgt J. M. Dymock (navigator-radar). Both crews would be operating in close cooperation with Patrington GCI radar station. Then at 0035hrs, P/O Peake was informed by the Patrington controller that there was "*a possibility of trade*" and instructed to switch to Easington CHL radar station. The Easington controller immediately reported that there was a 'bogey' 20 miles ahead at 14,000ft.

After being given a series of vectors by Easington, Sgt Parry was able to guide his pilot to within 3,000ft of the unidentified aircraft. P/O Peake was still unable to positively identify the bogey and was closing in for another look when a burst of machine gun fire, from the dorsal turret of the other aircraft, swept past the Beaufighter. Undeterred by the return fire, Peake moved in ever closer on the diving, twisting twin-engined aircraft which he was now able to identify as a Dornier 217. At a range of 600ft, Peake opened fire with his cannon and machine guns, the shells and bullets shattering the Dornier's engines and ripping holes in the bomber's fuselage. Another return burst, this time from the ventral turret, passed uncomfortable close to the Beaufighter and Peake was forced to curtail his pursuit. Then, as Peake executed a climbing turn to port, he saw a bright glow in the sky which became brighter as it descended towards the sea.

From his position a few miles away, P/O Hill saw the stricken bomber break into two pieces, which then fell into the sea and continued to burn for several minutes, approximately 15 miles ENE of Flamborough Head. There were no survivors from the 1./KG 2's Dornier Do 217E-4, *Werk Nr* 4294, U5+FH, piloted by *Oblt* Alfred Cornelius and based at Eindhoven in Holland.

At 0130hrs, P/O Peake and Sgt Parry landed safely at RAF Church Fenton. What had started as a routine practice flight ended up with a double first for the two 25 Sqn airmen — their first combat experience and their first 'kill'.

The last quarter of 1942 was a hectic time for RAF bomber squadrons based in East Yorkshire, as their aircraft continued to raid industrial targets in Germany and Italy. By now, most of these squadrons had switched from the twin-engined Vickers Wellington to the four-engined Handley Page Halifax. In October, another four-engined 'heavy' arrived in East

188 Above: Halifax B Mk IIs of 10 Sqn on the way out to a mission in mid-1942. Earlier, commanded by the famous Australian Wg Cdr D.C.T. 'Pathfinder' Bennett, on 27 April 10 Sqn had attacked the German battleship Tirpitz, then lurking in a Norwegian fjord. On this raid 10 Sqn's aircraft carried a special spherical mine which it was hoped would rupture the vessel's hull from below. German countermeasures, however, prevented the squadron from carrying out accurate drops.

190 Right: A closeup view of the business end of a brand new Beaufighter IIf. R2375 served with 219 and 409 Sqns, lasting until February 1944, when like too many others, it crashed while serving with an OTU (No 54). The antenna of the early AI radar sets are clearly visible.

Incident:
10 December. Uffz Max Reüthe and crew in Dornier Do 217 F8+AP of KG 40 dropped mines off Spurn.

Incident:
17 December. Lancaster I SR-N/W4319 of 101 Sqn was returning to base at Holme-on-Spalding Moor after a mine-laying operation when it was shot down near Redcar by 'friendly' fire. The IFF was apparently not working. Sgt M. A. Fussell and his crew were all killed.

Incident:
20 December. Uffz Max Reüthe and crew in Dornier Do 217 F8+AM of KG 40 dropped bombs on Hull.

189: Two 102 Sqn Halifaxes collided while landing in thick fog at Holme-on-Spalding Moor on 24 October 1942. Nearest is DT512, DY-Q. On its belly is W1181/DY-D. Sadly W/C Bruce Bintley and his wireless operator were killed in 'Q'.

Yorkshire, namely the Avro Lancaster which would be flown by 101 Sqn from RAF Holme-on-Spalding Moor. By the end of the year, only 466 Sqn and 196 Sqn of the East Yorkshire-based bomber squadrons were still flying the Wellington, from RAF Leconfield.

RAF Driffield, with its grass runways, was unsuitable for the new heavy bombers and, in December 1942, it closed down as an operational Bomber Command airfield so that concrete runways could be constructed. However, the airfield remained open for training purposes until the summer of 1943 with 1484 (Bombing) Gunnery Flight and 1502 Beam Approach Training Flight in residence. The 1484 Flight flew Battles, Lysanders and Whitleys in a target towing capacity to provide air-to-air gunnery practice for 4 group air gunners. This unit also used Defiants, with the gun turret removed, to provide extra training for the Bomber Command gunners. The 1502 Flight was engaged in training 4 Group pilots in using the Beam Approach Landing System, which enabled pilots to land their aircraft in most adverse weather conditions, with the notable exception of thick fog. For the greater part of 1942 the flight had used Whitleys for this training but in November they were replaced by Airspeed Oxfords.

During the same period, there was very little Luftwaffe activity over East Yorkshire. On Saturday 24 October, at 2140hrs, four 500kg HEs were dropped on Hull, causing considerable damage to the railway system and to domestic property on Anlaby Road, Campbell Street and Walker Street. Seven people were killed in this latest raid on Hull.

There were no attacks in November, while in December there were only two air raids of any note. In the first, on the night of Thursday 17 December, 15 KG 2 Dornier 217s took off from their Dutch bases to attack York. Most of the aircraft crossed the East Yorkshire coastline in the vicinity of Flamborough Head, headed over the Yorkshire Wolds and bombed the city from 2200hrs. A mixture of HEs and IBs caused a number of large fires to develop, the most spectacular one being at the gasworks. Several houses were destroyed or badly damaged and a number of civilians were seriously injured.

Two of the raiding Dorniers 217s never reached York, encountering strong winds and driving hail and rain and flying into high land in North Yorkshire. *Fw* Wilhelm Stoll's aircraft crashed on Wheeldale Moor, four miles south-west of Goathland, at 2200hrs. *Oblt* Rolf Haussner's hit a hillside near Hawnby, a small village six miles north-west of Helmsley, at 2215hrs. Both Dorniers disintegrated on impact and all eight airmen on board were killed.

Finally, at 1925hrs on Sunday 20 December, seven 500kg HEs were dropped on Hull. Although this was only classified as a minor raid, many homes were wrecked or severely damaged on Holderness Road, Staveley Road, Carden Avenue, Tunis Street and at Bilton Grove. Three people died in the raid and several others were seriously injured. The two Luftwaffe bombers involved in the attack returned safely to their Dutch bases where preparations were well underway to celebrate Christmas 1942.

113

COMING IN ON A WING AND A PRAYER
Drama in Filey Bay

Before leaving 1942, let us take an in-depth look at an air drama, which unfolded over the northern part of East Yorkshire in December of that year. It is the story of an air battle with a difference, an RAF bomber crew's fight for survival without a Luftwaffe night fighter or enemy flak battery within hundreds of miles. It exemplifies one type of danger faced by Bomber Command aircrew every time they climbed into their aircraft.

This is a story, which starts eight miles north-west of York at the 4 Group Bomber Command airfield of Linton-on-Ouse, the home of 78 Sqn equipped with four-engined Halifax II heavy bombers. The date was Friday 11 December and it was late morning when orders were received for 78 Sqn to contribute ten Halifax aircraft for the coming night's raid on the industrial city of Turin in Italy. Consequently, the afternoon was a busy one at Linton as the selected machines were checked over, re-fuelled and bombed up while their crews were briefed in preparation for the Turin operation.

Third in line to take off for Turin was Halifax II W7764, piloted by P/O K.T.Watson. There were seven other men on board the Halifax: Sgt G.E.Coleman (navigator), Sgt J.L.Goldby (bomb aimer), Sgt L.H.McKinnon (wireless operator), Sgt G.E.Bailey (flight engineer), Sgt T.R.Galbraith (mid-upper gunner), Sgt W. Bamford (rear gunner) and Sgt R.C. Head (second pilot). Sgt Head had joined P/O Watson in the cockpit to gain operational experience before becoming captain of his own aircraft.

Watson, Coleman, Goldby, McKinnon and Bamford had first got together as a Whitley crew while training with 10 OTU (Operational Training Unit) at RAF Stanton Harcourt in Oxfordshire. The Watson crew's first operation had been a particularly tough assignment, namely the third of 'Bomber' Harris's 1,000 bomber raids, to Bremen on 25 June 1942, while the five men were still at OTU. Then, in August, they were sent on loan to Coastal Command, carrying out lengthy, tedious and uncomfortable anti-submarine sweeps over the Bay of Biscay while they were based at RAF St. Eval in Cornwall. Next, in the autumn of 1942, Watson and his crew moved to 1652 HCU (Heavy Conversion Unit) at RAF Marston Moor in North Yorkshire.

There they were joined by Bailey and Galbraith, forming a seven-man crew to fly the Handley Page Halifax. After their training at HCU had been completed, Watson and his men were posted to an operational Halifax Squadron, 78 Sqn at RAF Linton-on-Ouse. Their 11 December 1942 flight to Turin would be their fourth operation in ten days.

At 1636 hours, P/O Kenneth Watson eased his Halifax into the air. The flight plan was to head south, over-flying Reading, and then crossing the English coast at Beachy Head before flying across France to northern Italy. But, just minutes into the flight and

191 Above: Similar to the Halifax flown by P/O Watson and his crew, this is Mk II W1245 'B' of 78 Sqn. This aircraft was one of four from the squadron lost on a raid to Mainz on 11/12 August. The others were W1061, W1115 and W1233. Twelve of the 28 crewmen survived; eleven becoming prisoners of war, F/Sgt Fay of the RCAF evaded capture.

at a height of only 500 feet disaster struck; the port inner engine suddenly burst into flames. With the fire spreading towards the fuselage, P/O Watson was faced with a distinctly critical situation.

Bomb aimer in Watson's aircraft, Sgt John Goldby, later described what happened on board the crippled Halifax:

> *"The original plan was to fly to the coast and jettison our bombs in the sea. This plan was changed a number of times as unforeseen circumstances arose. The plan unfolded as follows:*
> *Plan A. To jettison our bombs in the sea and return to Linton.*
> *Plan B. As the fire could not be extinguished and the pilot was having difficulty in maintaining height, it was decided that we should bail out. I therefore jettisoned the bombs and front hatch in preparation for this and was ready to jump. However, I could see that we were too low and told the pilot so.*
> *Plan C. The pilot informed us he would crash land and ordered us back into our crash positions further back in the fuselage.*
> *Plan D. The pilot said he intended to make for the sea and ditch the aircraft. As we crossed the coast just to the south of Filey, we were told to stand by for ditching and the pilot talked us through it, down to the tail of the aircraft striking the sea first in the approved manner.*
> *Of course, with the front hatch gone the sea poured in. A number of the crew had failed to plug in their intercom and were expecting to experience a crash landing. They were therefore extremely surprised to find themselves in the sea!*
> *The pilot was already in the dinghy when we got to it, having got through his window onto the port wing without even getting wet; the rest of us were soaked to the skin. We realised that we would soon be rescued because our ditching must have been seen by quite a number of people."*

The final moments of the Halifax's gentle descent to the inky waters of Filey Bay, at about 1710hrs, had indeed been seen by several people in Filey. David Baker (near Coble Landing), Geoff Cappleman (on Belle Vue Street), brothers Dick and Jim Haxby (at home on Mitford Street), Colin Ross (outside the school on West Road), Bob Watkinson (bottom of Cargate Hill), and Rodney Court in Crescent Gardens had all heard and seen the low-flying bomber trailing smoke from one engine as it dropped down to the sea and ditched about one mile out from Bempton Cliffs.

Retired local fisherman Dick Haxby was 13 years old at the time and his father, Jim Haxby Senior, was one of a group of Filey fishermen who set out to rescue the ditched airmen. According to Dick:

"The thinking was that cobles launched straight away from Coble Landing could get to the 'plane quicker than Filey Lifeboat. Two cobles were launched; one was the 'Jean and Barbara' crewed by Tom Jenkinson (skipper) with Bill and Frank Cammish, while the other was the 'Matthew and Edward', crewed by George Mainprize (skipper) with my father Jim Haxby and his brother Jack".

The Halifax's bomb aimer, John Goldby, picks up the story:

"It was not long before two fishing boats arrived on the scene; one took us on board while; the other took the dinghy in tow. Subsequently, Filey lifeboat joined the party. The aircraft had sunk before we left the scene.

We were landed at Filey (Coble Landing) and then taken to the local RAF Regiment camp at Hunmanby Moor. P/O Watson telephoned Linton to report our whereabouts and our Squadron Commander, Gerry Warner, decided to leave us where we were and send transport for us the next morning. We returned to Linton on the morning of 12 December, expecting to be granted the usual seven days survivors' leave. Our expectations were rudely shattered. We got nothing"

In fact, just three days after their dramatic ditching in Filey Bay, P/O Watson and his crew were back in the air and flying a 'Gardening' (mine laying) operation off Heligoland and the Friesian Islands.

It later emerged that, upon receiving a report of a Halifax bomber down off the coast of East Yorkshire on 11 December, the Air Sea Rescue station at Bridlington had launched two of its vessels – pinnace *1292* and seaplane tender *1501* – to search for the missing bomber and its crew. Unfortunately, however, no person thought of contacting the ASR unit at Bridlington to confirm that the Halifax crew had been rescued and landed at Filey. Consequently, it would be after 2100 hours on 11 December before the two rescue craft returned to Bridlington following a painstaking four hours search of the sea off Flamborough Head.

Regardless of the confusion over communications, the most important thing was that a dramatic incident, which could so easily have ended in tragedy, had such a happy ending. The fact that not one of the eight airmen on board Halifax W7764 was injured in the Filey Bay ditching is a testimony to the skilful, focused flying of the aircraft's pilot, P/O Kenneth Watson, a Lancastrian from Clitheroe. P/O Watson did have the advantage of a reasonably calm sea with little wind, and was helped in the emergency by the fact that it was still daylight – Double British Summer Time continued through the 1942/3 winter – but his exemplary text book ditching (tail well down, wings kept level, into the wind) saved his crew from serious injury, or worse.

Back in May 1942, when Coleman, Goldby, McKinnon and Bamford first met Kenneth Watson, they had been astonished and a little concerned to discover that the pilot they had been crewed with was wearing an Army uniform! What had happened was that Kenneth Watson had recently transferred from the Royal Engineers to RAF Bomber Command. However, after numerous training flights followed by actual operations they realised that P/O Watson was a very cool, calm and collected character. Following the dramatic events of 11 December they knew that in Kenneth Watson they had an exceptionally good pilot.

The one sad development arising from the Filey Bay episode on 11 December was that the rescue operation led to one almighty row in Filey. Apparently, one of the fishermen in the rescue cobles should have been on the town's Lifeboat. The fact that he had acted independently of the RNLI triggered off a period of argument and recrimination.

The story of the final flight of Halifax W7764 is, however, not quite complete. What, for example, happened to the aircraft's bomb load — a 1,000lb high explosive bomb and nine canisters of incendiaries — which bomb aimer John Goldby had jettisoned minutes before the ditching?

The first piece of evidence, which the author came across in an attempt to answer this question, was in RAF Staxton Wold's records for 11 December 1942:

"A HALIFAX bomber on an operational flight passed over STAXTON with its fuselage on fire. A load of incendiary bombs and a 1,000lb high explosive bomb was jettisoned in an adjacent field. The burning incendiaries were extinguished by Station Personnel"

At first, the author assumed that P/O Watson's Halifax must have over flown RAF Staxton Wold's 'A' site, the technical site high up on the Wolds above Staxton village, and that the aircraft's bomb load had fallen dangerously close to the RAF Station's important radar equipment. Later, when this was put to John Goldby, the man responsible for jettisoning the bombs, he was clearly not happy; and rightly so as the author was soon to discover while studying the Civil Defence for Filey and District at the County Archives Office in Beverley. Copies of the relevant documents: a letter from an irate farmer and an unexploded bomb report, are included in this chapter and prove conclusively that the Halifax's bomb load had fallen on open farmland – Flixton Carr – just as bomb aimer John Goldby had intended.

P/O Watson had flown the safest route to the coast, over the low and flat Vale of Pickering. The reference in RAF Staxton Wold's records to the jettisoned bombs having fallen *"in an adjacent field"* clearly refers to their position in relation to the radar station's 'B' site, the accommodation site, which was located on the eastern side of the A64 and just a few hundred yards north of that road's junction with the A1034 road to Flixton and Muston.

The bombs had fallen on land farmed by a Mr G.W. Patrick of Carr House Farm. Mr Patrick was not happy about the existence of unexploded munitions on his land, as can be seen from his letter of complaint. Farmer Patrick's frustration over the time being taken in removing unexploded bombs from his land is understandable, but the task of retrieving the 1,000lb bomb by RAF bomb disposal men proved to be a most difficult and dangerous operation owing to the marshy nature of the ground in the vicinity.

By the time Mr Patrick's land had been cleared of all munitions, 26 February 1943, P/O Watson and his crew had flown eleven more operations over enemy territory, fortunately without any further mishaps. Watson was later promoted to flight lieutenant and on completion of his tour of duty on 22 March 1943 was recommended for, and duly received, the Distinguished Flying Cross, partly on the strength of his highly successful ditching in Filey Bay.

Watson's bomb aimer on 11 December, Sgt J.L.Goldby, was also subsequently rewarded for his own particular skills. After promotions to first Pilot Officer and then Flight Lieutenant, John Goldby was awarded the Distinguished Flying Cross in July 1944, while serving with 640 Sqn as the Squadron's Bombing Leader at RAF Leconfield. Five months later he was a prisoner-of-war after parachuting from a crashing 640 Sqn Halifax over the German town of Osnabrück on 6 December 1944. It was 13 May 1945 before John Goldby was back in England.

As the fourth Christmas of the war approached, there was a feeling in Britain that the tide was slowly turning against Adolf Hitler and his ruthless regime. Luftwaffe air raids on East Yorkshire had decreased and most had been on a relatively minor scale compared with those experienced in Hull during the 1941 Blitz. Overseas, General Bernard Montgomery had led the British Eighth Army to a victory over the *Afrika Korps* at El Alamein. In the USSR, thousands of German troops had been tied up in the siege of Stalingrad. Before Christmas 1942, the Soviet forces broke in and inflicted horrendous losses on the Wehrmacht. Hopes were high that 1943 would bring more good news in the fight to overthrow Fascism.

192 Far left: *Now F/Lt K.T. Watson DFC, the pilot responsible for the successful ditching of burning Halifax bomber W7764 in Filey Bay on 11 December 1942. Kenneth Watson survived the war and died in the 1980s.*

193 Left: *Bomb aimer on board the doomed Halifax was Sgt John Goldby, seen after promotion to pilot officer. he later transferred to 640 Sqn at Leconfield where he became the squadron's Bombing Leader.*

THE FILEY NEWS

Filey had rather more "incidents" last week than is usual; for, in addition to three fires, there was a most exciting episode on Friday night when eight men were rescued from the bay. The cobles, as is often the case, were launched in quicker time than could be hoped for doing the same with the lifeboat, and so a happy ending was brought about to an incident which might have concluded in the deepest tragedy.

194: *This is all the local press were allowed to say about the ditching. Quite what purpose the excessive secrecy served is a mystery — the story ought to have made a good morale booster.*

195: This is the crew of the Filey fishing coble Jean and Barbara, *which picked up P/O Watson and his crew from their dinghy off Bempton Cliffs. L to r: Bill 'Codge' Cammish, Frank 'Tosh' Cammish and Tom 'Tint' Jenkinson. Sadly, the two Cammish brothers were drowned in 1948 when their salmon coble capsized off Primrose Valley. (Dick Haxby)*

196: The *Jean and Barbara was still going strong in the early 1960s, seen here in the hands of the Haxby brothers; Dick (in the boat) and Jim. (Dick Haxby)*

197: This is the letter mentioned in the text written by farmer G.W. Patrick complaining about the presence of unexploded RAF ordnance on his land.

```
COPY                    Carr House Farm,
                          Seamer,
                            Scarborough.

                        14th January, 1943.

Dear Sir,

        There is a 1000 lb unexploded R.A.F.
bomb in one of my ditches.  The R.A.F. have
made 2 attempts to get it out, but have failed
and have packed and gone away and they have
blocked the ditch up and caused one of my
fields to flood.  I am digging the ditch deeper
and opening out the other end to make the water
run the wrong way and this has releaved the
flooding a bit already.

        There is also a large quantity of un-
exploded incendary bombs in one of my fields
some are of the explosive type, buried out of
sight and these will make ploughing and tilling
difficult

                        Yours truly,

                          G.W. PATRICK.
```

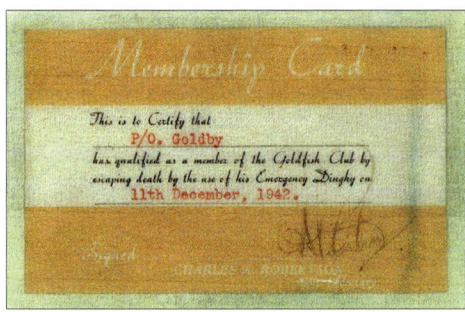

198 Far left: *Airmen who survived a ditching were entitled to wear a distinctive uniform badge.*

199 Left: *And were given membership of the 'Goldfish Club'. This is P/O Goldby's membership card.*

200: *This is the East Riding Constabulary report on the unexploded bombs on farmer Patrick's land at Flixton Carr Farm, compiled by Sgt Harold Walker of Filey Police.*

201: *A view through the gate at some of 406 Sqn's Beaufighters. Just visible to the left of HL-O is what appears to be a Merlin-engined Beaufighter in the later Dark Green/Medium Sea Grey nightfighter finish. This is most unusual for that model as most were finished in the sooty black finish known as 'RDM2 Special Night'.*

202 Above: *Beaufighter IF T4638/NG-F of 604 Sqn, showing how badly the ultra-matt black finish RDM2 weathered. In the event, it was found that a slightly glossy, much lighter camouflage was more effective at night. With four 20mm cannons and six machine-guns, plus airborne radar and a speed of 300mph, the Beaufighter was a potent antidote to German night bombers.*

203 Right: *The main gun used in Britain during World War II for anti-aircraft purposes was the superb 3.7 inch AA gun. Mobile and capable of firing a 28lb shell to 30,000ft at 3,000ft per second when it was introduced into service in 1938 it was probably the most advanced gun of its type and for for many years afterwards. By 1943 1,675 were in service in Britain, many equipping batteries in the East Riding.*

1943

Dorniers and Beaufighters down

We have already seen how in the spring of 1942 a new RAF night fighter had appeared in the skies above Yorkshire, namely the twin-engined Bristol Beaufighter. This aircraft, equipped with an on-board radar system (AI), packed a powerful punch with its four 20mm Hispano cannon in the nose and six 0.303in Browning machine guns mounted in the wings. Early in 1943, another highly effective RAF night fighter arrived in Yorkshire. This was the de Havilland Mosquito, also equipped with an AI system and with similar weaponry to the Beaufighter. These were the two main British night fighter types, which would now patrol the Yorkshire coast from the Tees to the Humber, guided by GCI radar stations at Goldsborough in North Yorkshire and Patrington in East Yorkshire.

The first Luftwaffe aircraft to be shot down over East Yorkshire in 1943, however, fell not to the cannon and machine guns of a RAF night fighter but to the heavy anti-aircraft guns of a Royal Artillery Unit in Holderness. It was on the night of 3 January when 23 KG 2 Dornier Do 217 bombers flew across the North Sea from their base at Soesterberg in Holland to attack port installations in Hull. The weather that night was atrocious, with thick cloud, rain, hail and strong winds over Hull and Holderness. As a result of the adverse weather conditions, some of the 'Holzhammer' (wooden hammer/mallet) Geschwader raiders dropped their bombs over rural East Yorkshire – at Seaton, Withernwick and between Mappleton and Goxhill – and in the sea off Hornsea, while others aborted the operation and returned to Soesterberg. One German pilot did reach Hull and dropped two 500kg HEs at approximately 2030hrs. These bombs fell alongside the River Hull where they demolished a section of timber wharf but did not cause any casualties. This was a mere pinprick of a raid compared with the heavy attacks in 1941 and gave the people of Hull the hope that the worst was now over.

One of the KG 2 pilots on the Hull raid that night made the fatal mistake of overflying a searchlight unit and heavy anti-aircraft battery near Skeffling, six miles south-south-east of Withernsea. The enemy bomber

119

was swiftly 'coned' by searchlight beams and then hit and critically damaged by the adjacent AA battery. At 2125hrs, Easington ARP wardens reported a plane flying very low followed by the sound of a crash and a fire being seen. Next, a message from Skeffling ARP stated that a Dornier 217 was down on the eastern side of the Skeffling to Out Newton Road. A follow-up police report said that two German prisoners had been taken to Withernsea Police Station and that two others were on their way.

The downed bomber, Dornier Do 217E-4 U5+KT (*Werk Nr* 4314) of 9./KG 2 and piloted by *Uffz* Anton Reis, made a safe wheels-up landing. Reis and the other three crewmembers, *Ogefr* Horst Küster, *Uffz* Arno Salz and *Uffz* Alfred Muschiol, were all unhurt and wasted no time in setting their aircraft on fire before they could be captured.

Twelve days later, shortly after 2000hrs on 15 January, air raid sirens sounded across Hull and along the coast of East Yorkshire as radar stations in the region detected a number of 'hostiles' approaching from the east. At 2015hrs and 2035hrs, two 25 Sqn Mosquito night fighters were scrambled at RAF Church Fenton and placed under Easington CHL control. After a number of Vectors from Easington, F/Lt J. Singleton (pilot) and F/Lt C.J. Bradshaw (navigator-radar) soon had visual contact on a Dornier 217 at an altitude of 7,500 ft. Joe Singleton got in three bursts of cannon and machine gun fire and strikes were seen on the Dornier's tail unit and at the port wing root. Visual contact was then lost as the Dornier's pilot put his aircraft through a series of weaving manoeuvres. When Singleton and Bradshaw returned to base at 2125hrs they could only make a claim for '*one Dornier 217 damaged*'.

The Luftwaffe later reported that Dornier Do 217E-4 (*Werk Nr* 4272) U5+AT of 9./KG 2, piloted by *Uffz* Hans Unglaube, had been lost that night in the Humber area. Could this aircraft have been F/Lt Singleton's 'damaged' Dornier? No trace was ever found of the Dornier's crew.

Next, on 3 February 1943, there was an air battle off the coast near Filey, which resulted in the destruction of another Dornier Do 217E-4 bomber, the latter crashing on the Hunmanby side of Muston. The RAF night fighter involved in the combat was a 219 Sqn Beaufighter VI equipped with Mk VIII AI radar and crewed by F/Lt J.E. Willson (pilot) and F/O D.C. Bunch (navigator – radar); the aircraft was based at RAF Scorton in North Yorkshire. F/Lt Willson's combat report graphically describes how the action unfolded. Later that night, a message was sent from 13 Group Fighter Command Intelligence to Fighter Command HQ at Stanmore in Middlesex to confirm the Willson/Bunch success.

Many people in the Filey-Muston-Hunmanby area witnessed the Dornier's dive to destruction. The author can remember standing at the back door of the family home in Station Road at Hunmanby and watching an orange flame in the sky, coming in from the sea in the direction of Filey, and getting lower and lower until it disappeared from view to the north of the village. As the blazing aircraft was descending we saw Hunmanby's NFS Unit, led by the author's father Syd Bright, turn out and head up Bridlington Street towards the crash site; Filey NFS also attended the crash.

The enemy bomber had narrowly missed roof tops in Muston before crashing into a field on the southern edge of the village and then bouncing, slithering, disintegrating and finally coming to rest almost half a mile south of Muston, not far from the Muston to Hunmanby road. The NFS units from Hunmanby and Filey were greatly relieved to find neither bombs nor bodies in the wreckage.

The 'Muston Dornier' was Dornier Do 217E-4, *Werk Nr* 5460, U5+GL, of 3./KG 2, based at Soesterberg in Holland and on an operation to bomb port installations at Sunderland. It would appear that *Ofw* Karl Müller, *Fw* Heinz Lewald, *Uffz* Friedrich

204: *Two Dornier Do 217E-4s of 3./KG 2 in flight over Holland. The aircraft in the background, U5+GL, was shot down and crashed at Muston on 3 February 1943. The dark night camouflage is compromised somewhat by the white fuselage band. This marking was required in the Mediterranean theatre of operations, where KG 2 was also required to carry out operations. It is also possible that the underside of the engine cowlings was given a coat of temporary yellow paint for the same reason.*

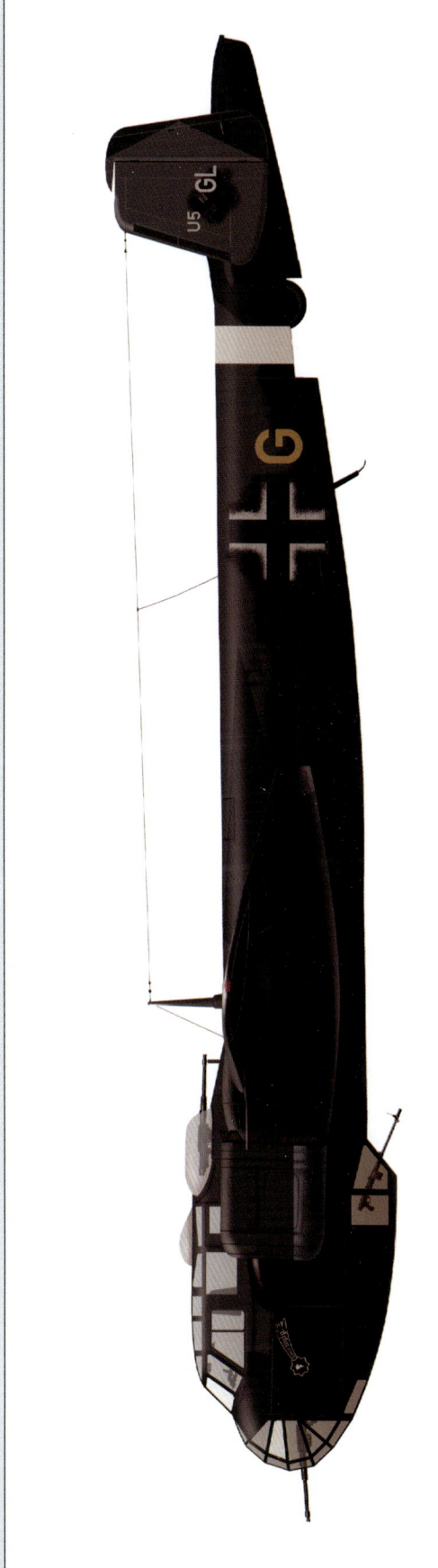

Dornier Do 217E-4 Werk Nr 5462, U5+GL, of 3./KG 2, 3/2/43 which crashed at Muston on 3 February 1943 after being shot down by a 219 Squadron Beaufighter. The undersides of the engine cowlings may have been yellow on account of KG 2's commitment to Mediterranean operations as well as over England.

Beaufighter Mk VIf MM856, NG-C, of 604 Squadron in 1943. The finish is the newer RAF nightfighter camouflage of overall Medium Sea Grey and Dark Green on the upper surfaces which replaced the all-black finish used previously. ***ILLUSTRATIONS NOT TO SAME SCALE***

121

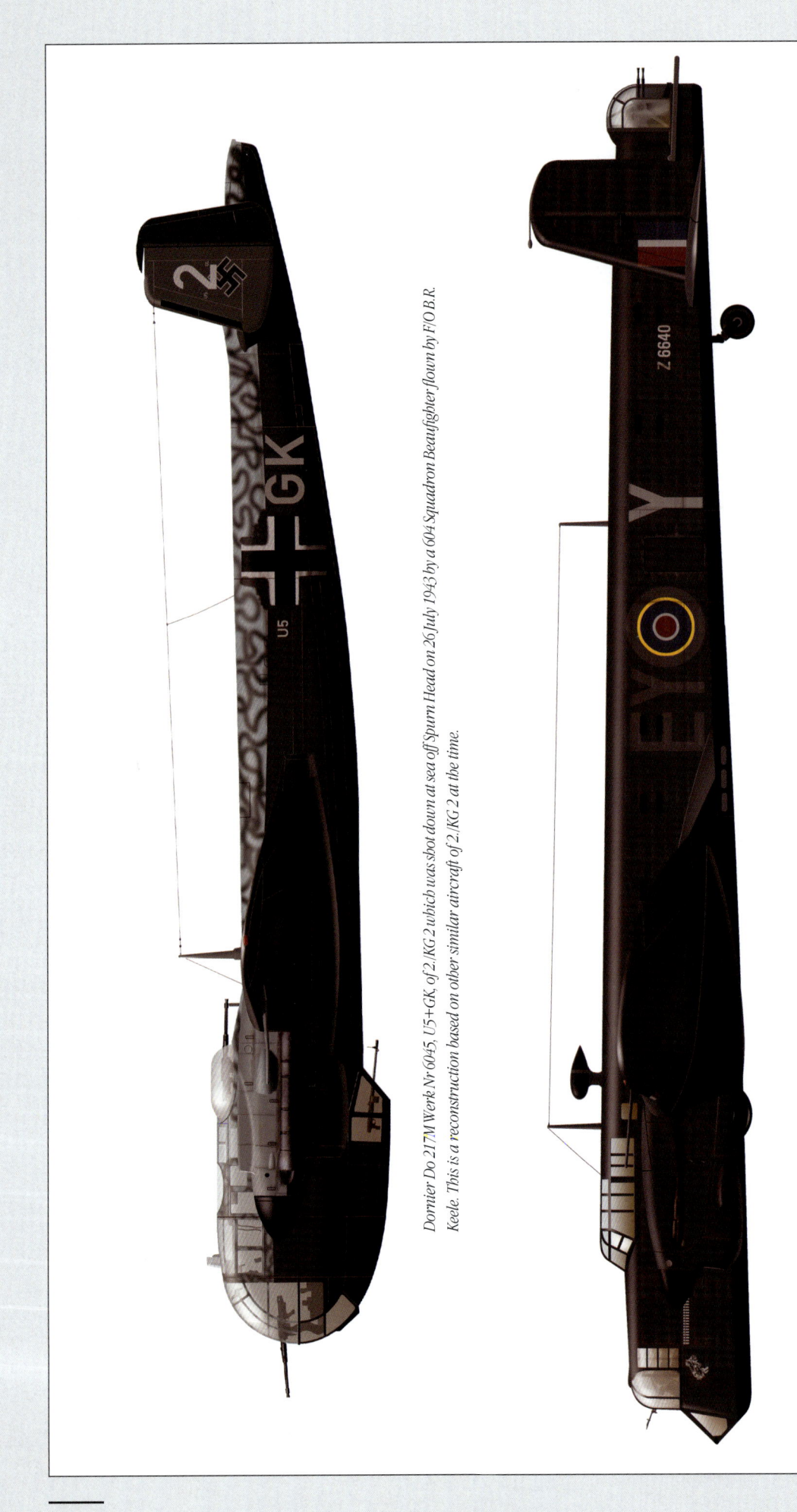

Dornier Do 217M Werk Nr 6045, U5+GK of 2./KG 2 which was shot down at sea off Spurn Head on 26 July 1943 by a 604 Squadron Beaufighter flown by F/O B.R. Keele. This is a reconstruction based on other similar aircraft of 2./KG 2 at the time.

Whitley Mk V Z6640, 'Y', ex-EY-R of 78 Squadron, shown here when with 1484 Target Towing Flight, Driffield, in 1943. Last used on operations on 10 January 1942, 'Yoke' retained its bomb log and nose art (apparently of a rampaging bull) on a non-standard all-black finish. Interestingly, modern RAF trainer aircraft now sport an all-black finish. The target towing yoke shown is speculative as available pictures show insufficient detail to be absolutely certain of the towing equipment used.

ILLUSTRATIONS NOT TO SAME SCALE

122

```
TO HQ FC INTELL
FROM 13 GROUP INTELL
AI/214      3/2/43.
        CATTERICK COMPOSITE NIGHT COMBAT REPORT 3-4/2/43.
========================================================
219SQD. ONE BEAU VI AI VIII 1950 - 2143 HOURS INTERCEPT E/A CONTACT
2029. E/A CRASHED 2037 AT WA 573985 NEAR FILEY.
    ONE DO. 217E. DESTROYED. OUR CASUALTIES NIL AS FAR AS IS KNOWN.
GENERAL.    F/Lt J.E. WILLSON (PILOT) F/O BUNCH (R/O)

        A/C UNDER SEATON G.C.I. (CONTROLLER S/L WILSON)
CONTACT AT 4/5,000 FEET HEIGHT. E/A TOOK EVASIVE ACTION UP AND DOWN
WITH COMPLETE ORBITS?. SPEED VARIED FROM 240 TO 170 M.P.H.
IDENTIFICATION AS DO. 217. PILOT GAVE ONE BURST OF X 2/3 SECS. AT
450 FEET RANGE AND E/A APPEARED TO OPEN FIRE SIMULTANEOUSLY.
FIRE THOUGHT TO COME FROM BELOW AND AMIDSHIPS. PILOT DOESN'T
THINK HE WAS HIT. COMBAT AT 4,300 FEET HEIGHT. E/A SEEN IN PIECES
ON GROUND BY FILEY RXXXXX  POLICE. NO BODIES FOUND.
WEATHER.
        HAZY WITH CLEAR STARLIGHT ABOVE.

T O O 2350 3/2/43.
CCCCCCC    IN PARA GENERAL   LAST LINE READ   FILEY POLICE
```

205 Above: The Air Intelligence Report sent from RAF Catterick to Fighter Command HQ concerning FLt Willson's victory over a Do 217, 3 February 1943.

206 Right: Two Catfoss-based Beaufighters of 2(C) OTU exercising over East Yorkshire on 17 March. Note that aircraft 'Q' has the 12 degree dihedral tailplane, fitted in an attempt to correct the Beaufighter's instability at low speeds, the cause of a number of fatal crashes.

207: On the very next day, the pilot and observer of this 2(C) OTU Beaufighter had a remarkable escape when their aircraft flew into the ground at Reighton. Seriously injured, they were extricated from the wreckage by Ted Bradshaw and other local farmworkers. (Ted Bradshaw)

INTELLIGENCE FORM "F".

PILOTS' PERSONAL COMBAT REPORT

F/Lt. J. E. Willson.

STATISTICAL.

Date	(A)	3. 2. 43.
Unit	(B)	219. Squadron.
Type and mark of our aircraft	(C)	Beaufighter VI. Mk. 8 A.I.
Time attack was delivered	(D)	20.30.
Place of attack and/or target	(E)	Filey area.
Weather	(F)	Hazey with clear starlight sky above.
Our casualties - aircraft	(G)	Nil.
Our casualties - personnel	(H)	Nil.
Enemy casualties in air combat	(J)	1. Do. 217. destroyed.
Enemy casualties - ground or sea targets	(K)	N/A.
Cine camera gun - carried Used	(L)	Not used.

GENERAL REPORT.

Razor 24 of 219 Squadron Beaufighter Mark 6. Mark 8A.I. F/Lt. Willson (Pilot) F/O. Bunch Nav/Rad, took off Scorton 19.50, Landed Scorton 21.45. At first Pilot was doing an exercise but this was soon terminated as there were some hostile about and Razor 24 was taken over by Seaton Snook, Controller S/Ldr. Willson. Pilot was ordered to patrol at about 11000 ft after some vectors A.I. contact was secured, target being below and to port range then about 2 miles, under directions from F/O. Bunch, the pilot was able to close in and reduce the range and secured a visual at about 1000 yards at the same time pilot reduced height to about 5,000 ft, during the whole of this time the E/A. took violent evasive action which consisted of, dives and turns and complete orbits variations of speed between 170. and 240 m.ph. The chase lasted about five minutes. Pilot was able to close in and reduced range to 450-500 ft and to identify the target as a Dornier by the 2 fins and the high mainplane. The target let go a flare. This must have illuminated our fighter. Our pilot closed in from slightly below and astern and opened fire, at the same time the Dornier opened fire from amidships and below, firing orange coloured tracer, but no hits were obtained. Our Pilot did not see any of his shots hitting so he continued firing giving about a 3-4 second burst, and then suddenly there was an explosion, and the target blew up and dived in flames, and was seen to crash on the land in the Filey area. Scene of crash Muston. Time 20.30.
Weather Haze with clear starlight above.
Our Casualties Nil.
E.A. 1. D.O. 217 destroyed on land Muston Nr. Filey.
Total rounds fired. 20. M.M. 174 S.A.A. 464 No stoppages.
Cinegun not used.

208: F/Lt John Willson's Combat Report relating to the shooting down of a Dornier Do 217 at muston, 3 February 1943. This is typical of the way in which such events were officially recorded by the RAF at the time.

209 Right: Daily reports were sent out from Headquarters at Bomber Command detailing important events and information relevant to the Command's operations. Classified as 'Secret', these yellow foolscap sheets of paper give a surprisingly accurate amount of information. This one for the night of 15-16 March 1943 records Luftwaffe ('GAF') operations over East Yorkshire. One of the aircraft noted shot down (over Lincolnshire) was another Do 217 of 6./KG 2 credited to F/Lt Willson. The Humber guns may have shot down a Ju 88 of KG 6.

SECRET.   IMMEDIATE.   BY TELEPRINTER.

To:- Headquarters, Nos. 1-6, 8 (P.F.F.) 91, 92 & 93 Groups and all
Bomber Command Stations in these Groups; H.Q. No. 26 Group;
Nos. 1, 2, 3 & 4 Bombardment Wings and Stations.

From:- Headquarters, Bomber Command.

BOMBER COMMAND INTELLIGENCE REPORT NO. 3255 - 17 MARCH, 1943

G.A.F. ACTIVITY (3255 - 17/3/43).

Night 15/16 March. Ten E/A, out of 25 which approached the Humber area,
crossed the Lincolnshire and Yorkshire coasts to make a short
attack for which there was no main target. There were few bombing incidents and little damage was caused.
Three E/A were destroyed by night fighters and one by the Humber
guns.

Day 16 March. Enemy activity was confined to 3 A/C on reconnaissance
over the Straits/Channel and a few defensive patrols.

FIGHTER COMMAND ACTIVITY (3255 - 17/3/43).

Night 15/16 March. 5 A/C of the Command took off on offensive patrols
over enemy territory.

Day 16 March. Nothing to report.

NAVAL AND COASTAL COMMAND SUMMARY OF NEWS (3255 - 17/3/43).

North Sea. A force of H.M. M.T.Bs attacked and sunk two M/Vs of 10,000
and 3,000 tons off the Norwegian Coast during the night of 14th March,
without loss except for one M.T.B. which struck a rock and sank, the crew
of which was taken off.

South Atlantic. A U.S.A. Warship is reported to have intercepted and sunk
a German blockade runner from the Far East, described as the KOTANOPAN
7092 tons, 400 miles W.N.W. of Ascension Island on the 10th March. Prisoners
were taken.

BALLOONS (3255 - 17/3/43).

LA PALLICE. 10 balloons are seen flying in and around the port on both sorties.
(Photos 9/3/43).

DANZIG. Balloons are seen close-hauled at their usual positions.
(Photos 8 - 11/3/43).

Distribution
As for previous reports.

Flight Lieutenant,
Duty Intelligence Officer.
T.o.O. 11.30/A.hrs.

210: Members of Hunmanby NFS, pictured here outsde their fire station in Depot Lane (Sands Lane) during a visit from inspecting officer Les Tranmer (centre, front row) in 1943. A team of firemen from this unit, led by the author's father Syd Bright (third from left, front row), attended the crash of the 'Muston Dornier'.

211: This Dornier Do 217M-1, Werk Nr 56158 of KG 2 was captured in Denmark at the end of the war and brought back to Farnborough for examination. The bulbous nose glazing and in-line engines clearly distinguish it from the 'E' variant which was the other mainstay of KG 2. Apart from those areas where British markings have been applied it wears its orginal Luftwaffe camouflage. Sadly for preservationists the aircraft was scrapped in 1955.

212: The wreckage of a Dornier Do 217 bomber brought down during a raid on Hull on 3 January 1943. This is most probably Do 217E-4 Werk Nr 4314, U5+KT, of 9./KG 2, which was shot down by heavy AA guns and which belly landed near Skeffling. It was subsequently put on display in Queen's Gardens in the centre of Hull and is being examined by the Lord Mayor of Hull, Alderman Leo Schultz. The photo appeared in the Hull Daily Mail on 20 January. (Hull Daily Mail)

Incident:
6 March. Uffz Max Reüthe and crew in Dornier Do 217 F8+LP of KG 40 dropped mines off Spurn Head.

Incident:
20 March. Lancaster I ED446/ SR-N of 101 Sqn crashed on the beach at Atwick, three miles north of Hornsea, during a low-flying air test. Sgt I. H. Hazard CGM and his crew were all killed.

213 Right: *Sgt I.J. Land, an RNZAF pilot from 2(C) OTU who was killed when his Beaufighter spun into the ground at Vicarage Farm, Hunmanby at about 0910 on 7 December 1942, today lies in Brandesburton churchyard.*

214 Far right: *Sgt Harry T. Clarke of the Pioneer Corps whose firefighting team, based at Hunmanby Hall, attended the crash of the Beaufighter which came down at Hunmanby on 4 January 1943. Originally from Clare in Suffolk, he married a local girl and settled in Hunmanby after the war.*

Fruth and *Uffz* Heinrich Wilensen had all baled out of their blazing bomber while it was over the sea, probably a few miles off Filey Brigg. However, no trace of their bodies or parachutes was ever found. Karl Müller was one of KG 2's most experienced and highly decorated pilots. He had flown on more than 200 operations and had been awarded the Ritterkreuz (Knight's Cross) in October 1942.

This had been quite a scalp for the Willson/Bunch team and the 219 Sqn Beaufighter crew went on to shoot down four more German bombers during the following month while patrolling the east coast between Northumberland and the Humber. It came as no surprise to their squadron when, during the summer of 1943, F/Lt John Willson and F/O Douglas Bunch received decorations, both being awarded the Distinguished Flying Cross.

A Beaufighter equipped with AI on-board radar was a brilliant night fighter and Luftwaffe bomber crews soon began to realise that once they had been tracked down by a Beaufighter then there was every likelihood that they would be blasted out of the sky. As production of the successful Beaufighter was stepped up, there was an obvious and urgent need for more pilots and observers – the latter would become AI operators when posted to operational squadrons – to crew these aircraft. This is where an airfield in East Yorkshire would play an important part in the training; namely RAF Catfoss, the home of 2 (Coastal) Operational Training Unit.

The powerful roar of Bristol Hercules engines became a familiar sound to people living in the Brandesburton area as training flights, by day and night, took off from the nearby airfield. Unfortunately, however, there was a problem side to RAF Catfoss's training programmes, notably the high number of air accidents involving 2 (C) OTU aircraft. For example, in the six months November 1942 to April 1943 inclusive, 2 (C) OTU at Catfoss lost 13 Beaufighters and 20 airmen in crashes. Twelve of these aircraft crashed on land – at RAF Catfoss (4), Hunmanby (2), Skipsea, Dunnington, East Bewholme, Westerdale (North Yorks Moors), Lissett and Reighton – and one in the sea.

Most of these accidents were the result of aircraft going into an uncontrollable spin, but the Beaufighter which crashed at Lissett on 22 November 1942 dived into the ground after a mid-air collision with a 316 Sqn Spitfire from RAF Hutton Cranswick. Both pilots were killed.

Several more of 2 (C) OTU's Beaufighters were badly damaged, some beyond repair, in accidents at RAF Catfoss itself. The Beaufighter proved to be a very demanding aircraft for trainee pilots, with a tendency to swing when taking off or landing and to stall at low speeds.

A group of Hunmanby schoolchildren, including the author, witnessed the final moments of the 2 (C) OTU Beaufighter which crashed at Hunmanby during the afternoon of 4 January 1943. Lessons had just ended at the village school on the first day of a new term and pupils were leaving the premises in Stonegate when a low-flying Beaufighter came into view, heading south. As the aircraft was about to overfly Hunmanby Hall, it suddenly rolled over and dived down below the tree line. A loud thud followed, whereupon the more inquisitive pupils rushed into the grounds of Hunmanby Hall to see what had happened to the aircraft. The Beaufighter was lying on gently sloping grassland, with its nose pointing downslope, and quite close to the trees which surrounded Hunmanby Hall Park. Army personnel based at Hunmanby Hall were already on the scene and attempting to extricate the two-man crew. It looked as though the Beaufighter had fallen fairly flat on the ground and seemed remarkably intact, but we later found out that the impact had killed the young Australian pilot, Sgt J.S. Dickson, and his observer Sgt J. Miles. Our curiosity came to an abrupt end when we were chased from the crash site by local policeman P.C. Harold Tilley.

A Beaufighter crash usually resulted in the death of both crew members, but on 18 March 1943, a 2 (C) OTU Beaufighter flew into the ground at Reighton and both pilot and observer, although seriously injured, survived the crash. Catfoss-based Beaufighter T5102 had been participating in an exercise with a Royal Navy vessel off the coast of East Yorkshire. As the pilot, Sgt R.E. Askew, prepared to return to base, he encountered a belt of low cloud as he approached land. Askew then appears to have lost height in an attempt to get below the cloud and establish his position. Unfortunately for Sgt Askew and his observer, Sgt McClymont, there was a layer of fog below the cloud and before the pilot could get his bearings his aircraft hit the ground, luckily a large and fairly flat field opposite the council houses which are next to the Dotterel Inn at Reighton. The Beaufighter was completely wrecked, as can be seen from the accompanying photograph, but when local man Ted Bradshaw reached the wreckage he found that both crew members were still alive. Ted and other farmworkers then succeeded in rescuing Askew and McClymont from the remains of their aircraft. Both airmen were then rushed to Scarborough Hospital and eventually made a complete recovery. For many years after this spectacular crash, Ted and Joyce Bradshaw would receive a Christmas card from the ever-grateful Sgt Askew.

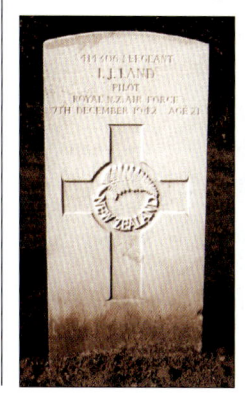

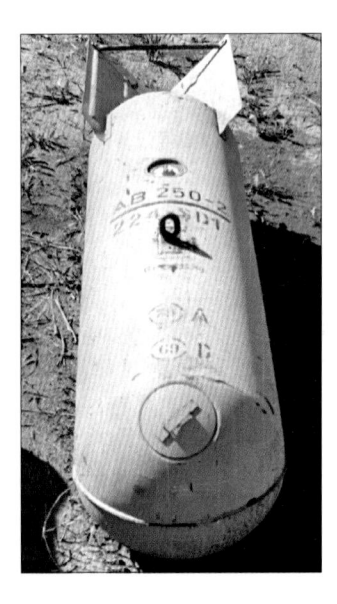

215 Far left: *A German AB 250-2 bomb container which held 144 of the lethal SD-2 'Butterfly' anti-personnel bombs.*

216 Centre left: *This is an SD-2 in the open position, the outer casing looking rather like a butterfly's wings when open.*

217 Left: *An SD-2 in the closed position in which it was loaded into the bomb container.*

The first major air raid on Hull in 1943 did not materialise until 0235hrs on Thursday 24 June, when a lethal cocktail of IBs and HEs fell on the city. Hull's central shopping area suffered badly and elsewhere in the city more than 1,000 houses were wrecked or damaged; 25 people died in the attack. A new type of German bomb fell on the streets of Hull that night, the 2kg SD2 anti-personnel bomb, which became known as the 'Butterfly Bomb'. This small explosive device was to become a constant worry for the people of Britain; to trip over one in the dark could prove fatal. It was a disappointing night for the region's defences as no enemy aircraft was brought down during the raid on Hull.

Then, on the night of 12/13 July 1943, radar operators in the region detected a large force of 'hostiles' approaching the Humber on a west-northwest heading. Was this to be yet another savage attack on Hull? But, as air raid sirens began to sound across Holderness and Hull, the raiding aircraft suddenly swung to port and attacked the Lincolnshire coastal towns of Cleethorpes and Grimsby. There was considerable bomb damage in both towns and 42 people were killed. Again, no Luftwaffe bomber was destroyed that night.

Twenty-four hours later, the same radar stations again warned of approaching 'hostiles' on a similar heading. This time, however their primary target was Hull. A force of Dornier Do 217s, from their Dutch bases at Eindhoven and Soesterberg, attacked the city between approximately 0123hrs and 0200hrs on Wednesday 14 July. Although the Dornier crews had been briefed to bomb docks and port installations in Hull, the bombing was very scattered and there was widespread damage to residential areas where most of the night's 26 fatalities occurred. Fortunately, however, only about half of the 50 Dorniers scheduled to attack Hull actually released their bomb loads over the city. Poor navigation resulted in several of the raiders dropping their bombs while overflying Lincolnshire. Grimsby was hit for the second night running and 25 people were killed in the town.

During the 14 July raid on Hull, six 604 Sqn Beaufighter VI night fighters were patrolling the Yorkshire coast yet only two of them were in combat with enemy aircraft. It was the Beaufighter of W/O D.W. Ray (pilot) and W/O G.A. Waller (navigator-radar) which had the only success of the night, shooting down a Dornier Do 217 which crashed into the sea some ten miles east of Scarborough. This was Dornier Do 217M-1 U5+EL (*Werk Nr* 56153) of 3./KG 2, piloted by *Uffz* Willi Spielmanns; there were no survivors. A second 604 Sqn Beaufighter, crewed by S/Ldr W. Hoy (pilot) and W/O E. Le Conte (navigator-radar) was in combat with a Dornier 217[19] off the Humber, but the air gunners in the enemy bomber put up a spirited resistance and their aircraft, although damaged, escaped out to sea.

Early on Monday 26 July, East Yorkshire's air defences enjoyed their most successful period of the year so far, shooting down three Luftwaffe bombers. In the thick of the action once again were the Scorton-based Beaufighters of 604 Sqn. During the night of 25/26 July, six of the squadron's aircraft were sent up between 2315 and 0030hrs and ordered to patrol the Yorkshire coast between Whitby and the Humber. Once airborne, two of the Beaufighters would operate under the control of Goldsborough GCI radar station, two would be guided by Patrington GCI, while the other two would be allowed to 'freelance' over the region.

"Strikes were seen on starboard engine..."

First to be engaged in combat was the Beaufighter crewed by F/O B.R. Keele (pilot) and F/O G.H. Cowles (navigator-radar) in air battles off Spurn Head between 0032 and 0046hrs. Under the control of F/Lt Fowler at Patrington GCI, Keele and Cowles were given a number of vectors until Cowles obtained a plot on his AI set at a height of 9,000ft and a range of four and a half

Incident:
24 June. Uffz *Max Reüthe and crew, now of KG 2, in Dornier Do 217K U5+CA of Stab/KG 2, dropped bombs on Hull, their aiming point being Paragon Station.*

[19] *This was the Do 217M-1 U5+EL, Wnr 56122, piloted by* Stabsfw *Wolk of 3./KG 2, whose radio-operator,* Uffz *Hugo Pankuweit was killed when they were attacked by a fighter.*

Incident:
14 July. Uffz *Max Reüthe and crew, in Dornier Do 217K U5+BA of Stab/KG 2, dropped bombs on Hull.*

Incident:
14 July. Uffz *Josef Rabl and crew, in Dornier Do 217E U5+AM of 4./KG 2, on their first operational mission, dropped 700 IBs (from four ABB500 containers) from 3,000 metres.*

miles. Despite desperate evasive action by the German bomber pilot, Keele soon had visual contact:

> "Fighter continued to close in with E/A taking fairly violent evasive action and when at 800ft (range) E/A was identified as a Do 217. E/A then started taking very violent evasive action and fighter closed to approximately 350ft and opened fire with 3 short bursts of cannon and MG. Strikes were seen on starboard engine, wing roots and on main plane and pieces were seen to break off. E/A caught fire and fighter had to break away to avoid collision. Fighter closed in again to give another short burst as E/A was descending rapidly with starboard engine and main plane in flames. Owing to the reduced speed of the E/A, fighter overshot and E/A was last seen disappearing into the haze in flames".

Almost immediately, Keele and Cowles were vectored towards another unidentified aircraft. Keele soon had visual contact with what turned out to be another Do 217. Accurate cannon and machine gun fire from the 604 Sqn Beaufighter soon had the Dornier in flames as it dived down out of control; it exploded as it hit the sea.

Keele and Cowles returned to RAF Scorton at 0150hrs, a job well done. The first of their victims, Dornier Do217M-1 U5+GK (*Werk Nr* 6045) of 2./KG 2 and piloted by *Uffz* Robert Fuchs, crashed into the sea a few miles out from Spurn Head. Only one body was recovered, that of air gunner *Uffz* Hubert Toeltsch. Their second victim was a Dornier Do 217K-1 (*Werk Nr* 4412) U5+BA of Stab/KG 2, occupied in minelaying, which also dived into the sea off Spurn Head. Observer *Uffz* Siegfried Ludwig and air gunner *Ogefr* Willi Schürleien baled out and were captured, but *Uffz* Max Reüthe (pilot) and *Uffz* Heinrich Böning (wireless operator) were still in their Dornier as it plunged into the sea and quickly sank. This was their 28th operational mission.

The third KG 2 Dornier to be definitely destroyed during the 26 July raid on Hull was shot down by a heavy anti-aircraft battery in Holderness. Dornier Do 217E-4 U5 + AN (*Werk Nr* 4395) of 5./KG 2 was hit in both engines by accurate AA fire and subsequently dived into farmland near Long Riston and exploded at about 0115hrs. *Uffz* Hans-Ulrich Colwe and his crew were killed instantly and their bodies were later buried in Brandesburton churchyard, where they still lie.

Primary targets for the KG 2 Dorniers during the early hours of 26 July had been docks, warehouses and port industries at Hull, but no bombs fell in the target area in the course of the attack. Although KG 2 bomber crews claimed to have dropped more than 100 HEs and 30,000 IBs in the raid, it would appear that most of these bombs had fallen in the sea or on farmland in East Yorkshire; farmers at Bewholme, Hatfield, Seaton and around Hornsea all reported bombs on their land between 0030 and 0120hrs. There was some minor damage to roofs and windows at some of these farms but no serious injuries had been reported. The Luftwaffe's latest attempt to inflict serious damage on Hull had been a dismal failure.

After the debacle of 26 July, there was no further attempt by the Luftwaffe to launch a major raid on Hull during the last five months of 1943, although some bombs did fall on East Yorkshire in this period. This was on the night of 17/18 August when Grimsby and Lincoln were targeted by KG 2 bombers. Two of the raiding aircraft strayed north across the Humber and dropped their HEs at Hedon and Roos. One civilian was killed at Hedon and two at Roos.

Aspects of the air war over East Yorkshire in 1943 led the people of the region to view the year ahead with growing optimism. There had been fewer major raids on Hull, smaller numbers of aircraft had participated in these raids, and there appeared to have been a marked deterioration in the quality of the enemy's bomb aiming. Furthermore, several

218 Below: *This is how the newspapers of the time presented war news to the public. The* Daily Mail *of 10 July 1943 showed a Halifax of 76 Sqn (DK193/MP-Y), based at Linton-on-Ouse, with a 2,000 lb HC high explosive bomb in the foreground.*

Luftwaffe bombers had been shot down. Morale had also been lifted by the almost nightly roar of RAF 'heavies' taking off from their East Yorkshire bases and heading for Germany. Between March and July, the main RAF offensive had been against the towns and cities of the Ruhr industrial region; Dortmund, Duisburg, Essen and Gelsenkirchen in particular had received a heavy pounding. Then, from July into August, attention had turned to Germany's largest port, Hamburg, where huge firestorms caused by RAF and USAAF bombs had left the city in ruins and 40,000 of its citizens dead. Finally, during the remainder of 1943, the principal target had been the capital city of the Third Reich, Berlin. Elsewhere, 4 Group Halifax bombers from East Yorkshire had joined other groups in raids on Cologne, Nuremburg, Frankfurt, Dusseldorf and Peenemünde, Germany's weapons research establishment on the Baltic coast.

Bomber Command activity in 1943 may well have boosted public morale in East Yorkshire but this was a worrying period for bomber squadrons based in the region. Major air raids, especially on targets in Germany, were proving to be very costly in terms of aircraft and airmen, but air accidents over East Yorkshire were adding to the death toll.

Earlier in this chapter, attention was drawn to the high incidence of air accidents in East Yorkshire involving 2 (C) OTU Beaufighters on training flights from RAF Catfoss. In 1943, East Yorkshire also became the graveyard for numerous Halifax bombers; some involved in air accidents when taking off for, or returning from, bombing operations, others while on air tests, training flights or exercises of one kind or another.

One of the most tense, worrying times for any bomber crew was the take-off when setting out on a bombing operation. With a full load of bombs and heavily laden with fuel, the bomber became a highly destructive weapon in its own right. This indisputable fact also led to many an anxious moment for civilians living within the circuit of a bomber airfield.

Let us look at just two of the air accidents in East Yorkshire which resulted from crisis situations at take-off. On 11 February 1943, Halifax W7879/DY-O of 102 Sqn took off from RAF Pocklington to bomb the German port of Wilhelmshaven. Engine failure as the aircraft got airborne resulted in 'O-Orange' crashing at North Dalton, just eight miles east of the airfield, at 1839hrs. Of the eight men on board there was only one survivor, Sgt Hill, the second pilot. The second example also involved a 102 Sqn aircraft from RAF Pocklington, but the circumstances were very different. Halifax JB848/DY-G had lifted off perfectly, but soon after take-off the bomber was caught in the slipstream of another aircraft. This caused the pilot, F/Sgt W.P. Comrie, to lose control of the Halifax which suddenly turned over and dived into a field opposite Pocklington School. A massive explosion followed; the aircraft had been bound for Berlin with a full load of HEs, IBs and fuel and there were no survivors from the seven-man crew.

On a happier note, some bomber crews when faced with a critical development at take-off had miraculous escapes. For example, when Pocklington-based Halifax JD127/DY-U of 102 Sqn was taking off for Berlin during the evening of 23 August 1943, the heavy bomber suddenly swung off the runway and headed for the airfield's control tower. Luckily for the crew, at the controls of their Halifax that night was one of the squadron's most experienced pilots, W/Cdr S.J. Marchbank, who immediately retracted the undercarriage so that his aircraft slid and scraped to a halt short of the control tower. W/Cdr Marchbank and his crew were able to scramble free from their fully-loaded bomber before it blew up at 2043hrs.

Some of the worst air accidents in the region in 1943 occurred when Halifax bombers, returning to base from operations over enemy territory, were involved in tragic incidents just minutes away from a routine landing. For example, on 24 August two 78 Sqn Halifaxes, BB373 and JB874, were returning from a raid on Berlin when they were diverted from RAF Breighton to RAF Leconfield. As the two aircraft were overflying Beverley they collided. Both bombers spiralled down to crash at Hull Bridge on the outskirts of Beverley at 0430hrs and of the fifteen airmen on board there was only one survivor. Similarly, on 22 November, Halifaxes LW333 of 102 Sqn and LW264 of 77 Sqn were homeward bound from Berlin when, at 2345hrs, they collided in their overlapping circuits – for RAF Pocklington and RAF Elvington respectively – and crashed near Newlands Farm on York Road at Barmby. Flames swiftly engulfed the wreckage and all fourteen crew members were killed.

On 14 September 1943, there was a tragic air accident over East Yorkshire which involved an aircraft from a local bomber squadron while on a fighter affiliation exercise. Halifax LW246/NP-Z of 158 Sqn,

Facts:
Popular songs and tunes in 1943 had a strong morale-boosting flavour. Among them was Glenn Miller's American Patrol, *which today epitomises the 1940s for many people. Strangely, one of the most popular songs of the time was a hit with both sides. This was* Lili Marlene, *sung in English by anti-Nazi German Marlene Dietrich. In films, Jane Russell strutted her stuff in* The Outlaw, *thereafter appearing on the noses of many US heavy bombers. Booth's Dry Gin cost £1 5s 3d (£1.26) per bottle.*

Incident:
22-23 September. Halifax II HR924/ZA-N of 10 Sqn from Melbourne was abandoned by its crew over Patrington after it had been badly damaged by a nightfighter over Hannover. F/Lt J.G. Jenkins and his crew all baled out safely.

219-220 left: The last resting places, in Brandesburton churchyard, of the four unlucky crewmembers of the Dornier 217 which crashed near Long Riston on 26 July. From left: Hans Ulrich Colwe, the pilot; Helmut Gabriel, wireless operator; Fritz Pilger, navigator and Rudolf Trodler, air gunner.

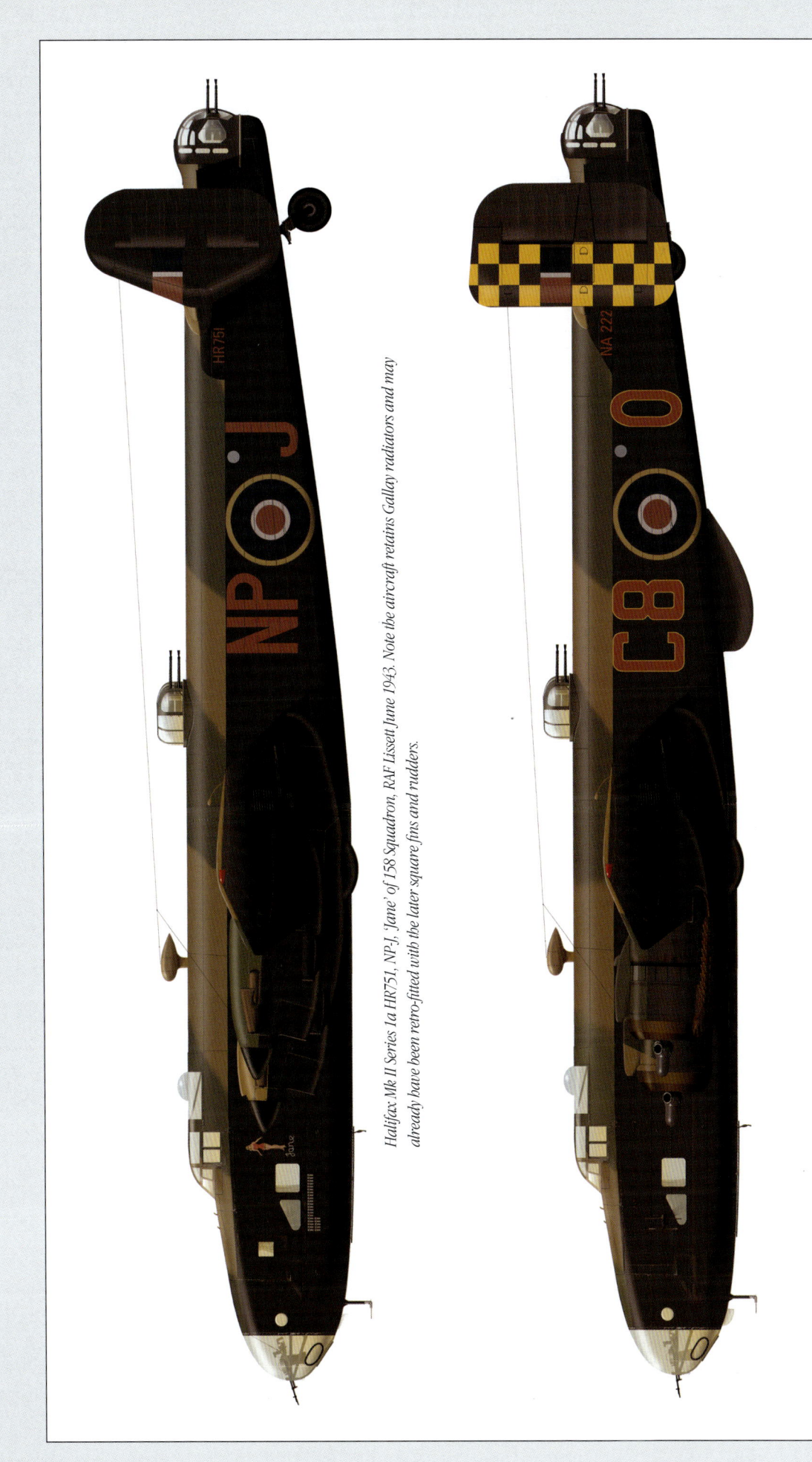

Halifax Mk II Series 1a HR751, NP-J, 'Jane' of 158 Squadron, RAF Lissett June 1943. Note the aircraft retains Gallay radiators and may already have been retro-fitted with the later square fins and rudders.

Halifax Mk VI NA222, C8-O of 640 Squadron in 1945. The yellow checks were for formation-keeping purposes during the daylight raids which Bomber Comand were increasingly asked to do during the last months of the war. The yellow outline to the red codes was also part of this purpose. It is not know if the aircraft carried any nose artwork.

131

based at RAF Lissett, was over the Yorkshire Wolds when disaster struck. A sudden major structural failure caused the bomber to fall out of the sky and crash on farmland at Fordon, five miles south-west of Filey at 1600hrs. This was a particularly costly accident as there were nine persons on board the Halifax and not the usual seven. The two extra RAF personnel were LAC Perrin, an armourer at Lissett, and Sgt Olive Moss, a WAAF who had been attached to RAF Lissett from 4 Group HQ at Heslington Hall, York. There were no survivors.

Eight days after the Fordon crash, the Dorniers of KG 2 were back over the region, only this time they were on a major minelaying operation to the Humber. For the majority of the Dornier crews this was a straightforward operation; they deposited their deadly weapons in the estuary and then flew back to Holland. For one KG bomber crew, however, this would be their final operation. It was shortly before 0100hrs on 22 September when a *Holzhammer* Geschwader Dornier 217 became trapped in the beams of several searchlights along the Holderness coast to the south of Withernsea. As the adjacent heavy AA guns opened fire, the Dornier's pilot, *Fw* Helmut Rumpff, put his aircraft into a steep dive in an attempt to escape from the searchlight beams. But Rumpff's bold manoeuvre went tragically wrong. It is possible that the pilot's vision was impaired by the intense glare from the searchlights as he failed to pull his bomber out of its dive in time and the aircraft hit the ground and disintegrated. Dornier Do 217K-1 U5+CM (*Werk Nr* 4620) of 4./KG 2 crashed about one-quarter mile west of the Easington to Out Newton road and a few hundred yards from Southfield Farm. *Fw* Helmut Rumpff, *Lt* Siegfried Von Weg, *Gefr* Arno Ehemann and *Ogefr* Kurt Stiegler were all killed instantly and their bodies were later buried in Hull North Cemetery.

Back at the crash site there was a major problem

221 Above: *A typical East Yorkshire airfield scene during the summer nights of 1943. Here 102 Sqn personnel at Pocklington wave good luck to the crew of DT743/DY-O as the pilot, Sgt T.H. Dargavel, prepares to take off late in the evening of 19 June. The night's target was the Schneider armaments factory at Le Creusot in France. 'O - Orange' returned safely to base early the following day.*

222: *RAF Lissett 29 June. The 158 Sqn crew of Halifax II HR837/NP-F had a narrow escape over Cologne when a 'friendly' bomb from a higher flying aircraft plunged through their own. The particularly fortunate mid-upper gunner, Sgt A.K. Young, sits in his battered turret. Pilot F/Sgt D.C. Cameron sits on top of the fuselage and Sgt Hulme, the flight engineer, peers through the hole. After repair 'F for Freddie' went on to complete several more missions before relegation to an HCU and eventual scrapping in January 1945.*

Incident:
2 October. Lt *Gehring and crew, in Dornier Do 217K U5+AS of 8./KG 2, dropped mines in the Humber mouth.*

— two unexploded 1,000kg sea mines were discovered among the wreckage of Rumpff's Dornier and a Royal Navy Mine Disposal Party was rushed to the scene. Sadly, as the three-man team attempted to defuse one of the mines it exploded. The three RN men were all badly hurt in the massive blast and were immediately transported to Withernsea Transfer Hospital. There, Lt Commander Peter Tanner was found to be dead on arrival while Able Seaman Percy Fouracre soon succumbed to his terrible injuries. Only Lt Frank Price survived the explosion.

At 2340hrs on 2 October 1943, a Junkers Ju 188E-1, Z6+GK (*Werk Nr* 260175) of 2./KG 66, which was also on a minelaying operation to the Humber, struck a sandbank in the estuary while taking evasive action from intense AA fire. The crash, about one-half mile out from Spurn Lighthouse, claimed the lives of *Lt* Gunther Beubler (pilot) and *Unteroffiziers* Heinz Urban, Albert Fischer and Erwin Pausch.

There was little Luftwaffe activity over East Yorkshire in the last quarter of 1943, with one exception. During the early hours of 20 October when a planned raid on Hull went embarrassingly wrong for the German raiders. A combination of poor navigation and adverse weather conditions over the target area resulted in thousands of IBs plus a scattering of HEs falling on rural East Yorkshire instead of on the city of Hull. The HEs caused little damage and no serious casualties, but the IBs set fire to many stackyards, especially in the Burton Fleming, Hunmanby and Rudston parishes, and also on the outskirts of Hornsea. There were so many fires in the East Yorkshire countryside that local NFS units had to request back-up from fire stations in North and West Yorkshire.

Away from the air war, good news had come in during 1943 from other battle fronts. On the Eastern

223: *The crew of Halifax III MZ 426/EY-G of 78 Sqn at Breighton in front of their mount. The only known crew member is the rear gunner, Sgt Barnet, holding the kitten. Named after a New Zealand Maori deity, 'Munga Taipo' survived the war.*

224 Below: *A Junkers Ju 188 A-3, G2+BD of III./KG 26 in typical late war Luftwaffe markings. This one carries anti-shipping radar and was captured in Norway at the end of the war. Similar aircraft were used by KG 66 for minelaying in the Humber.*

133

225: *As British bombers got bigger, so did the bombloads. Here a David Brown-built Ferguson tractor hauls a train of bomb trollies, each carrying five MC 500lb Mk XIII high explosive bombs.*

Front, the Russians had inflicted a crushing defeat on German forces in a series of savage battles fought during the winter and spring. In North Africa, in April, Montgomery's Eighth Army had finally won the two-year long desert war against Rommel's *Afrika Korps*. Soon, hundreds of defeated German and Italian troops would be seen in East Yorkshire as they were marched to prisoner-of-war-camps. This notable victory in North Africa had been followed in July by the invasion of Italy, the 'soft underbelly of Europe' by British, Commonwealth and United States forces.

So, as 1943 drew to a close, there was a strong feeling afoot in Britain that the tide had finally turned against Adolf Hitler and his Nazi regime. Talk of a German invasion of Britain had largely receded and been replaced by excited speculation as to when and where Allied forces would return to the European mainland and bring this wretched war to an end.

226 Left: *A young Luftwaffe soldier stands guard over Dornier Do 217M-1 U5+AT, Werk Nr 6325 of 9./KG 2 which crashed on landing at Gilze Rijen, Holland, on 19 April 1944. It was shot up on a mission to bomb Hull by a nightfighter of 605 Sqn, two of the crew baling out.*

227: *The wreckage of Halifax II JN909/DY-B of 102 Sqn, based at Pocklington, which was shot down by flak on a raid against Berlin on 1 September 1943. Of the two survivors, Sgt R.V. Wallace made his escape to Switzerland.*

Facts:
In World War II, Halifax bombers alone dropped 224,207 Imperial tons of bombs and pyrotechnics.

228: *Although there was a sense that the war was slowly turning to the Allies advantage, there was still a great concern over security, particularly in ports like Hull where so many were employed in shipping fishing and information reaching the enemy could have disastrous consequences. This poster says it all.*

A careless word...

...A NEEDLESS SINKING

229 Right: *This card belonged to Herbert Mallinson who was Head ARP Warden for the parishes of Hunmanby, Muston, Folkton, Flixton Reighton and Speeton.*

230 Far right: *Although in the eyes of the general public, there now seemed little likelihood of a German invasion of Britain, officialdom decreed that local invasion committees should stay in place, as can be seen from this special ID card. This also belonged to Hunmanby baker Herbert Mallinson. (via Jack Mallinson)*

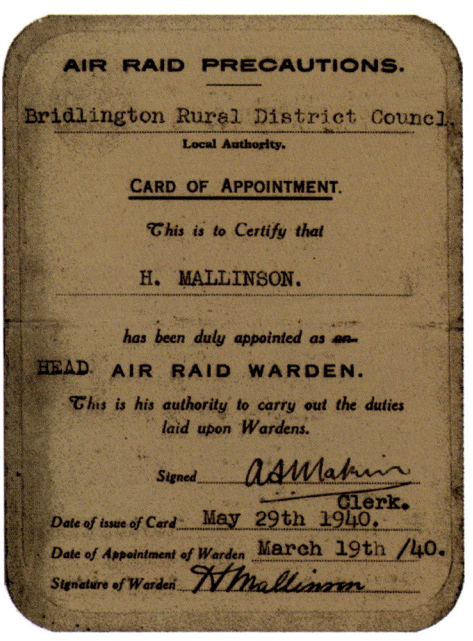

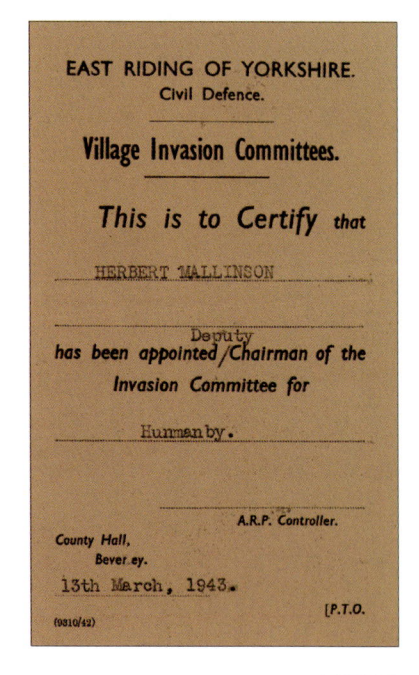

AIR RAID PRECAUTIONS.

Bridlington Rural District Council.
Local Authority.

CARD OF APPOINTMENT.

This is to Certify that

H. MALLINSON.

has been duly appointed as an
HEAD. AIR RAID WARDEN.
This is his authority to carry out the duties laid upon Wardens.

Signed *A.S.Makin*
 Clerk.
Date of Issue of Card May 29th 1940.
Date of Appointment of Warden March 19th /40.
Signature of Warden *H Mallinson*

EAST RIDING OF YORKSHIRE.
Civil Defence.

Village Invasion Committees.

This is to Certify that

HERBERT MALLINSON

Deputy
has been appointed/Chairman of the Invasion Committee for

Hunmanby.

A.R.P. Controller.
County Hall,
Beverley.
13th March, 1943.

(9310/42) [P.T.O.

135

1944 – A FORCED LANDING AT GRINDALE
Flamborough Head's link to D-Day

For people living in East Yorkshire in general, but for the residents of Hull in particular, the first two months of 1944 were remarkably peaceful as air raid sirens remained silent across the region.

Wartime winters in East Yorkshire had mostly been very severe so far, with blizzards, thick snow on the ground and temperatures hovering around zero, conditions which had frequently resulted in the grounding of RAF aircraft. In the middle of January 1944, however, a totally different type of weather problem interrupted RAF activity in the region — thick fog. For one RAF pilot this fog was to almost cost him his life.

It was Sunday 16 January 1944 and, at RAF Lindholme in West Yorkshire, it was F/Lt Peter French's 24th birthday. F/Lt French was a pilot with 1 Group Air Pool and was quite looking forward to his workload for the day, a straightforward flight to convey a senior RAF officer from RAF Lindholme to RAF St Eval in Cornwall. He was then scheduled to return to Lindholme by mid-afternoon. Little did Peter French realise what dramas lay ahead and that he would be celebrating the final hours of his birthday under arrest in the company of soldiers in East Yorkshire.

The day started well, with clearing skies giving rise to bright sunshine, although fog was forecast for later in the day. Then, just before takeoff, the first problem of the day; the Airspeed Oxford being used for the flight suddenly started to leak oil from one of its two engines. Next, the second hitch; RAF St Eval was now fog-bound, which meant that F/Lt French would have to divert to an airfield at Weston-super-Mare in Somerset.

Then, as he was standing around getting increasingly impatient with the groundcrew working on the oil leak, F/Lt French spotted a gleaming, very new-looking Airspeed Oxford in the vicinity. This was the personal aircraft of the Air Officer Commanding at RAF Lindholme. F/Lt French then made an audacious move; he asked the sergeant in charge of the groundcrew if he could borrow the AOC's Oxford for the day. Incredibly, the sergeant agreed:

"He's away on leave, he'll never know!"

So, after signing the necessary paperwork and running the engines, French was ready for a mid-morning takeoff for the West Country. About two hours later, the immaculate Oxford touched down

231 Above: Not the Oxford in which Peter French's escapade took place, but fairly typical of many others throughout the war. Seen here before June 1942, P8833 was one of two special ambulance versions used by 24 Sqn. This one was named Edith Cavell, *the other was called* Florence Nightingale. *Externally they were identical to most other Oxfords, which were used extensively for aircrew training and liaison work.*

232 Far left: F/Lt Peter French.

233 Left: An Oxford engine leaking oil, a trait which caused Peter French's problem.

safely at Weston-super-Mare. After offloading his passengers, French should then have flown back to Lindholme. However, his hunger overrode his better judgement and he went for lunch.

It was mid-afternoon before the refreshed pilot was airborne again and by the time he was overflying the Midlands all he could see below was a blanket of dense fog. Furthermore, on his port side the sun was dipping down towards the horizon. French was not unduly concerned at this stage as the Oxford was fitted with the Lorenz Radio Beam, a blind approach system to facilitate a landing in fog or poor visibility.

Minutes later, however, the young flight lieutenant realised that he was in big trouble for both his Lorenz system and his radio were not working. To make the situation even more critical, there was little fuel left in the tanks and it would be dark within the hour. It would be suicidal to attempt a landing in the thick fog; he would have to bale out.

F/Lt French:

"Simple in theory – fly towards the coast, point the aircraft out to sea, engage auto-pilot, then jump – and possibly end up in the fog beneath being impaled on a church spire, incinerated among electricity cables, or maybe drowned in a river. My mind searched desperately for some other way to escape the dangers now before me."

Fortunately, Peter French was no ordinary pilot. He was one of the most experienced pilots for his age in the RAF, having spent most of the war test flying virtually every type of aircraft to come into service with the RAF. His experience in remaining calm and logical in critical situations was to prove invaluable on that winter's afternoon over East Yorkshire. Also, he had a good basic knowledge of meteorology and this was to make all the difference between extinction and survival. His theory was that rising air above the relatively warm sea might have created gaps in the fog. So, he swung his aircraft towards the coast in the hope of finding such a clearance over the North Sea. F/Lt French:

"The sun was just scraping the western horizon when some miles ahead, staining the white quilt of fog that covered the ground, a darker patch with a ragged outline. With rising hope, I dived headlong towards the middle of the dark patch and peered downwards – and there, to my immense relief, I saw the black waters of the North Sea.

There was no turning back. I screwed up my courage, put the aircraft into a steep bank, spiralled downwards through the tiny gap in the fog, and flattened out just above the waves. Then I saw I was flying towards an unbroken wall of towering white cliffs.

Adrenalin kicked in – I heaved back on the control column – seconds later the Oxford swooped up the face of these monstrous cliffs and, by the grace of God, skimmed over the top with only feet to spare."

Once over what must have been Bempton Cliffs, and in rapidly fading light, he now had to search for a suitable landing place. He spotted two fields which were large enough to land the Oxford in but, there was yet another problem. One was a newly ploughed field, while the other was a grass field littered with vertical concrete anti-glider invasion posts. He opted for the grass field regardless of the obstructions.

"With undercarriage down, then flaps down, as slowly as I dared, I brought her hanging on the propellers, low over the hedge. I chopped the throttles and she dropped like a stone to the ground. Then, using brakes and engines alternatively in a life or death chicane, zigzagged violently the length of the field in the wildest ride of my life and by some miracle escaped crashing into the posts. My heart raced as the aircraft bucked and skidded its way to a standstill. Unable to believe my good fortune, I sat dazed for a while with the engines ticking over."

French then gently and carefully taxied the Oxford out of sight behind a haystack and switched off the engines, but tthere was still more drama ahead for the young pilot:

"I had just finished fitting safety locks to the flying controls when a convoy of Army vehicles swept into the field, headlights ablaze. Seconds later I was surrounded by a squad of soldiers. The young officer in charge treated me with courtesy, despite having thoughts, so I learned later, that I might be a spy. After a brief interrogation, I was put under arrest. While an armed guard was mounted over my aircraft, I was taken to the Headquarters of the Searchlight Battery at the village of Grindale, from which the soldiers had come".

Fortunately for F/Lt French, as the evening progressed at the Searchlight Battery HQ in Grindale and the drinks began to flow, suspicion quickly gave way to warm hospitality, especially when the soldiers discovered that it was their prisoner's birthday.

"The boundary hedge was fast approaching"

During the following morning, an RAF officer arrived at Grindale from RAF Lindholme and positively identified F/Lt Peter French, who was immediately released from custody and taken back to base. There was, however, still a major problem to be resolved — the Oxford had to be returned to Lindholme, preferably in an undamaged state. At that time, the RAF had a regulation which barred a pilot who had made a forced landing from flying the aircraft up again. So, another pilot was despatched to Grindale to fly the Oxford back to Lindholme. As soon as this pilot arrived on the scene at East Leys Farm and studied the situation the Oxford was in he quickly refused to attempt a take-off, arguing that it would be far too dangerous to do so. A second pilot was sent to East Leys Farm; he too refused to take the Oxford up.

At RAF Lindholme, F/Lt French was summoned

to his Flight Commander's office where he was told, quite bluntly: "*You put it in – you get it out!*"

On Saturday 22 January 1944, the flight lieutenant was flown over to RAF Lissett, six miles south of Bridlington, and then driven the ten miles to Grindale. Again, he was faced with yet another dangerous situation, which necessitated a calm rational approach and a considerable amount of courage. After two aborted attempts to take off across the field from which the concrete posts had now been removed:

> "I decided, as a last shot, to try a method I had used some years earlier during experiments towing giant tank-carrying gliders with equally huge four-engined heavy bombers. So I taxied back to the downwind boundary, swung the aircraft round to face into the strong wind, then locked on the brakes as hard as they would go. Next, I lowered the flaps a little, opened the throttles to their widest, and rammed the control column hard forward. Slowly the tail lifted. When everything was thundering and juddering fit to burst, I suddenly released the brakes.
> The Oxford leapt forward, and as she rocketed ever faster over the bumpy grass I hung on, and with all my might willed her desperately into the air. The boundary hedge was fast approaching when it dawned on me with sickening certainty that I was not going to make it this time either. In a now or never situation, I jerked back on the control column to lift the landing wheels momentarily from the ground, then quickly shoved it forward again to bounce the aircraft back into the air. Twice more I repeated the manoeuvre, and with each bounce the aircraft picked up a little more speed. Then, with a last giant leap into space, she sailed clear of the hedge, taking me with her."

Soon, F/Lt French was landing the Oxford back at RAF Lindholme, the AOC's aircraft, surprisingly, still in one piece. At base, he learned that on the day of his forced landing at Grindale, when he had failed to return by mid-afternoon, it was assumed that he had run out of fuel, crashed in the fog and been killed, probably in some remote part of the Yorkshire Wolds or North York Moors. For Peter French, Sunday 16 January 1944 was a birthday he would never forget.

Steinbock

The absence of Luftwaffe activity over East Yorkshire continued into March, but then the air of optimism prevalent earlier in the year was shattered when, just after 2130 hrs on Sunday 19 March 1944, air raid sirens began to sound again across the region. This was part of the Luftwaffe's Operation *Steinbock* (ibex) — the 'Baby Blitz' of January-May 1944. German sources later claimed that 131 of their bombers had raided Hull that night, yet when the 'All Clear' sounded at 2242 hrs not one bomb had fallen on the city. The bombs intended for Hull had dropped instead on rural parts of Lincolnshire and Norfolk, or into the North Sea. To make it an even worse night for the Luftwaffe, they had lost nine of their aircraft on the botched operation. Most of the air battles had taken place over Lincolnshire or over the North Sea off Lincolnshire and Norfolk. Only one enemy plane came down anywhere near Hull, a Junkers Ju 188 of 2./KG 66 which crashed into the sea near the Humber Lightship. There were no survivors.

The next attempted air raid on Hull came on the night of 20/21 April and the outcome was another humiliating failure for the Luftwaffe. Again, not a single bomb fell on Hull. Enemy bombing was even more scattered than during the March attack, with HEs and IBs falling harmlessly on rural parts of East and North Yorkshire, Lincolnshire, Norfolk and Northamptonshire.

During this latest fiasco, the Luftwaffe lost another eight aircraft: a Heinkel He 177 of KG 100[20] was shot down off Spurn Head by a 264 Sqn Mosquito crewed by F/O J.H. Corre (pilot) and P/O C.A. Bines (navigator-radar) from RAF Church Fenton; three Junkers Ju 88s from 5./KG 30, 2./KG 54 and 1./KG 66, plus a Dornier Do 217 of 9./KG 2 failed to return to base and were thought to have come down in the North Sea; and three Junkers Ju 188s of II./KG 2 crashed and were destroyed on the European mainland.

The mystery was why had these two attempted major raids on Hull in the spring of 1944 resulted in such humiliation for the Luftwaffe? The outcome of both attacks depended so much on the effectiveness of the *Pfadfindergruppe*, the German pathfinder force, which was responsible for dropping sky marker flares to indicate the final approach to the target area and flares and incendiaries to illuminate the TA itself. However, this procedure depended on accurate navigation which, in turn relied heavily on navigation beams transmitted by German radio beacons on the European mainland. Either the Luftwaffe was now using poorly trained or inexperienced navigators or the vital German navigation beams were being interfered with by the RAF's jamming and 'beam bending' techniques, outlined earlier. This could also explain why so many Luftwaffe aircraft failed to return from the two failed raids on Hull – they simply went missing, lost while overflying the North Sea.

Three nights after the second failed attack on Hull there was yet another awful air accident in East Yorkshire, high up on the Yorkshire Wolds at Folkton Wold, this time involving a 16 Group Coastal Command aircraft.

At 2215 hrs on 23 April 1944, Beaufighter JM279 of 143 Sqn took off from its base at RAF North Coates in Lincolnshire on a night training exercise, which entailed locating a pinnace from Bridlington Harbour. As the pilot, F/O R. Agnew (RAAF), and his navigator

---

Incident:
19 March. Lt Gehring and crew, in Dornier Do 217M U5+KS of 8./KG 2, attacked Hull; their 15th operational mission.

Incident:
19 March. Lt Richter and crew, in Dornier Do 217M U5+ET of 9./KG 2, attacked Hull on their fourth operational mission.

[20]*This was probably He 177A-3 Werk Nr 332357, 6N+IK of 2./KG 100 which was the only such aircraft lost by the unit on 20 April.*

Incident:
20-21 April. A Junkers Ju 88 was shot down near the Humber Lightship. It is not known for certain which unit it belonged to, but it was almost certainly a Ju 88S-1 of 1./KG 66 which failed to return on that day.

Facts:

The series of bombing raids against Britain between 21 January and 29 May 1944 were ordered directly by Adolf Hitler, who was adamant that war should once again be taken to the British. Known to the Luftwaffe as Operation 'Steinbock' (Ibex) these raids cost almost 10% of the attacking force, but by May, aware of the impending invasion, the Germans could no longer afford the losses.

Sgt H.B. Blackwell were flying at a low level in search of the pinnace, they unwittingly crossed the coast and flew into the ground at Folkton Wold. The time was approximately 2305 hrs. When firemen from Hunmanby NFS arrived at the scene they realised there was nothing that they could do for the two-man crew. The aircraft was a raging inferno, with cannon shells and machine gun bullets exploding in the intense heat. What had happened was that the Beaufighter had come down on its belly, slid across a field, but had then hit a raised track, which caused the aircraft to flip over and burst into flames. Remains of the two airmen were eventually recovered and taken to RAF Hunmanby Moor. Four days later F/O Agnew was buried with full military honours at Harrogate, while the body of Sgt Blackwell was transported to Wrexham for a private funeral.

While the Luftwaffe's spring 1944 air raids were going on over Britain, the RAF's bombing campaign against Germany intensified. In East Yorkshire, the construction of more Bomber Command airfields, the formation of new squadrons and the replacement of the twin-engined Whitley and Wellington bombers with the four-engined Halifax and Lancaster meant that there was a significant increase in aero engine noise over the region. Across much of East Yorkshire, the roar of our bombers taking off and climbing up and away into the evening sky became an almost daily occurrence. On the ground across the region, civilians and service personnel alike speculated as to what would the bomber boys' 'target for tonight'. Hamburg?, Essen?, Duisburg?, Cologne?, or perhaps the capital city of the Third Reich, Berlin?, RAF bombers continued to operate almost nightly over enemy territory. East Yorkshire's Halifaxes were heavily involved in raids on key German industrial towns and cities and attacks on important railway junctions and marshalling yards in France. The disruption of Germany's supply lines was essential in order to keep Wehrmacht reinforcements away from the planned Allied invasion zone in Normandy on the French coast.

Sadly, however, the RAF's massive air offensive was carried out at a heavy price. For example, on the night of 30/31 March 1944, out of a total of 795 RAF bombers despatched to bomb the German city of Nuremberg, 95 aircraft failed to return, which meant that more than 660 Bomber Command airmen would no longer be available for future operations. Lissett-based 158 Sqn lost four of its 16 Halifaxes sent to Nuremberg; this was a typical loss-rate for squadrons participating in the ill-fated Nuremberg venture. Luckiest of East Yorkshire's 4 Group Bomber Command squadrons were 77 Sqn, at RAF Elvington, and 102 Sqn at RAF Pocklington; they were spared the horrors of Nuremberg. Fortune also smiled that night on 466 (RAAF) Sqn at RAF Leconfield; all 16 of the squadron's Halifaxes returned safely to base.

On a much happier note, the spring of 1944 saw the opening of a new specialist airfield in East Yorkshire — RAF Carnaby. Back in the summer of 1942, the Air Ministry had decided that there was an urgent need for emergency landing grounds, close to the east and south-east coasts, which could handle Allied aircraft in distress. The sites chosen were at Manston in Kent, Woodbridge in Suffolk and Carnaby in East Yorkshire.

At Carnaby, work was started on a site approximately three miles south-west of Bridlington early in 1943 and was completed in the spring of 1944. During the summer of 1943, the author had the unforgettable experience of visiting the Carnaby site. The vastness of the project was awesome. Part of the massive runway had been more or less completed, while crawling over the landscape in the distance were huge earth moving machines, scraping and levelling the ground in readiness for the laying down of the rest of the runway. Adjacent to the runway were huge piles of building materials.

The single runway, running ENE – WSW would eventually measure 3,000 yards in length and be 250 yards wide, by far the largest runway anywhere in the north. Also, at each end of the runway 500 yards of land were cleared of all obstructions to provide grassy areas for overshoots and undershoots. The ultra-wide runway had three lanes, one for extreme emergencies when a pilot could land his aircraft immediately without needing permission and instructions from the control tower, the other two where normal landing procedures would have to be followed.

FIDO the fogbuster

RAF Carnaby was also provided with a new device called FIDO (Fog Investigation and Dispersal Operation). This system entailed pumping petrol through pipes lining the runway and then igniting

234: An Avro Lancaster comes in to land with the aid of FIDO. The heat generated by the burning petrol must have caused some interesting air currents for pilots while landing.

139

235: *Ground and aircrew gathered around an Heinkel He 177 of KG 100 in spring 1944. Although it appears to have only two engines, it fact it had four; two coupled in each nacelle. These were a constant source of trouble and caused many in-flight fires. The He 177 was the largest German aircraft to attack East Yorkshire.*

236: *The massive emergency landing ground at Carnaby. Note the distinctive 'frying pan' feature which was the dispersal loop where aircraft could be parked after landing. FIDO burners ran along each side of the runway and were supplied with fuel from storage tanks which are visible above the eastern end of the runway alongside the Hull to Scarborough railway line.*

237: *A Halifax B Mk II Series Ia of 78 Sqn, based at Breighton. The majority of the LW2xx serialled aircraft with 78 Sqn were lost on operations or otherwise written off by the end of 1943-early 1944.*

Incident:
20-21 April. A Junkers Ju 88 was shot down near the Humber Lightship. It is not known for certain which unit it belonged to, but it was almost certainly a Ju 88S-1 of 1./KG 66 which failed to return on that day.

the fuel. The resulting flames generated sufficient heat to clear fog from above the runway, thus enabling aircraft to land safely, something they could not have accomplished in foggy conditions at their home bases. Fuel for the FIDO system was brought by railway tankers to a specially constructed siding alongside the Hull to Scarborough railway line.

When Carnaby had its first 'burn', there was great consternation across much of East Yorkshire. A large red glow in the sky in the direction of Bridlington suggested that the town was on fire following an air raid. The author's father, on duty at Hunmanby's NFS station, telephoned Bridlington NFS to ask if assistance was required. Some NFS units actually left their home fire stations and headed for the resort. Throughout the remainder of the war, that glow in the sky near Bridlington would become a familiar sight for people living within a 50 mile radius of the airfield. From the air, it was visible over a far greater distance and many a long and tense air drama would end successfully on that massive runway at Carnaby.

The spring of 1944 was an exciting time for anyone with an interest in the air war as new types of aircraft began to appear over East Yorkshire. An appearance by one never-seen-before aeroplane caused a few moments of high drama for one East Yorkshire headteacher and a group of young school boys. This incident occurred one afternoon in Hunmanby while Mr W.S. 'Billy' Bray, head of the local school, was supervising a games lesson in a field at the top of Simpson's Avenue. Suddenly, there was a loud roar and a large black, twin-boom aircraft flew overhead at quite a low altitude

"Get down boys, flat on your face. Don't move until I give the order," shouted Mr Bray with great authority.

As increasing engine noise suggested that the plane was returning, the author could not resist a peep at the mystery aircraft. As it swooped over our heads, a large white star was clearly visible towards each wing tip; it was 'one of ours', an American aircraft. The aeroplane in question was a Northrop P-61A 'Black Widow'. It later emerged that the P-61As seen over East Yorkshire were operating out of RAF Scorton in North Yorkshire, where the 422nd NFS (Night Fighter Squadron) and the 425th NFS were based prior to flying to France later in the year.

Then there were the gliders, the Horsas and Hamilcars, towed by RAF bombers above the East Yorkshire countryside as their crews prepared for the Allied invasion of Europe. Both the gliders and their towing aircraft had broad black and white stripes painted across their wings and round their fuselages. At the time, we could not understand the significance of these markings but later learned that they were for identification purposes during the invasion and subsequent advance across German-occupied Europe.

On 14 May 1944, people living on Flamborough Head were aware of a lone RAF four-engine bomber, which was flying in towards the headland, turning back over the sea and then coming in again, a procedure which was repeated several times. To any onlooker, this must have seemed a rather pointless exercise on the part of the RAF. What they were witnessing, however, was an important experiment to test a theory which, if proved correct, could make an invaluable contribution to the coming Allied invasion of Europe.

At the hub of the experiment was a piece of captured German coastal radar equipment which was installed on Flamborough Head. The other vital component was a 617 'Dambusters' Sqn Avro Lancaster from RAF Woodhall Spa in Lincolnshire. This aircraft was to fly a series of elliptical circuits consisting of straight inbound and outbound legs, each one linked by a tight turn to port. On each straight leg, eight miles in length, the Lancaster was to drop a mass of 'Window' — thin metal foil strips on black backing paper. The theory was that as the bomber flew closer to the coast on each successive circuit, the falling

238: *A trio of Northrop P-61A Black Widow nightfighters of the Scorton-based US 422nd Night Fighter Sqn, shortly after D-Day. Nearest aircraft is 42-5536, 'Hustlin' Hussey', which still wears the early Olive Drab/Neutral Gray camouflage with a yellow nose cone (courtesy of the RAF). Centre is all-glossy black 42-5564 'Jukin' Judy', while at rear is 42-5573 'Lovely Lady'. The 422nd NF Sqn formed part of the US Ninth Air Force and went to Europe not long after D-Day.*

141

'Window' would give a coastal radar operator the impression that a fleet of ships was approaching the coast in that vicinity. If the Flamborough Head trials proved successful, a major deception operation, using several 617 Sqn Lancasters carrying 'Window', could be launched towards a certain stretch of the French coast to hoodwink German coastal radar operators and keep German reinforcements away from the actual Allied invasion zone on D-Day.

What happened on 14 May was that a contingent of 617 Sqn pilots and navigators flew from RAF Woodhall Spa to RAF Driffield, from where they were transported by aircrew buses to RAF Bempton, the radar station on Flamborough Head, to observe the crucial trials. Also present that day was Mr. Charles Bellringer from the Telecommunications Research Centre at Defford in Worcestershire. Mr. Bellringer, quickly given the nickname 'Ding Dong' by 617 Sqn aircrew, had over several weeks become familiar with earlier experiments into the use of 'Window' for deception purposes, conducted by electronic scientists led by Dr. Robert Cockburn at Tantallon Castle, on the south bank of the Firth of Forth in Scotland. Charles Bellringer's important role was to liaise between the 'boffins' at the TRE and the aircrew of 617 Sqn.

The airmen, Mr. Bellringer and a number of scientists gathered around the German coastal radar set on Flamborough Head while the 617 Sqn Lancaster flew in and out in a series of elliptical circuits, dropping 'Window' on each straight leg. After several other similar exercises in the same area, the boffins and RAF personnel concluded that they now had the basis for a major deception operation, code-named *Taxable*, which could be put into effect whenever the invasion came. To ensure that everything went according to plan on the big day, sixteen 617 Sqn Lancasters carried out a full-scale dress rehearsal off Flamborough Head in late May.

During the early hours of 6 June 1944, D-Day, the RAF's *Taxable* operation played its part in the successful Allied invasion of Europe. The first wave of eight 617 Sqn Lancasters was led by S/Ldr Les Munro, a New Zealander, piloting aircraft LM482/KC-W. Flying alongside Munro as co-pilot was none other than the redoubtable Leonard Cheshire, now Wing Commander Cheshire DSO, DFC, and the Commanding Officer of 617 Sqn. On the *Taxable* operation, each Lancaster carried a crew of 14 airmen, as opposed to the usual seven. So precise had to be the elliptical circuits, so accurate and well-timed the dropping of 'Window', that each aircraft had two pilots, two navigators, plus several extra personnel to handle the dropping of 'Window'. After two hours of 'Windowing', the eight Lancasters led by Munro and Cheshire were replaced by a second wave of eight aircraft led by Lancaster LM 492/KC-Q, piloted by two veterans of the Dams Raid in May 1943, S/Ldr Joe McCarthy DSO, DFC and S/Ldr Dave Shannon DSO, DFC. Another notable participant was the pilot of Lancaster ME557/KC-S, F/Lt Bill Reid VC, decorated for his heroic efforts during a raid on Dusseldorf in November 1943.

239 Far left: W/Cdr Leonard Cheshire.

240 Left: S/Ldr Les Munro. During the 'Taxable' operation Munro flew the lead Lancaster with Cheshire as his co-pilot, four years and a day since Cheshire had arrived in East Yorkshire to join his first squadron, 102 at Driffield.

241: Strips of window showing the metal foil front and black backing paper. This is a picture of a piece which was found on the clifftop at Filey Bay.

242 Below: This diagram shows how a Lancaster made six circuits off Flamborough Head on 14 May 1944. Each successive circuit took the aircraft 2,400 yards closer to the coast. The falling 'Window' suggested to operators using the captured German radar at RAF Bempton that a convoy was approaching. On D-Day itself, eight 617 Sqn Lancasters flew parallel circuits with a two mile horizontal separation between them.

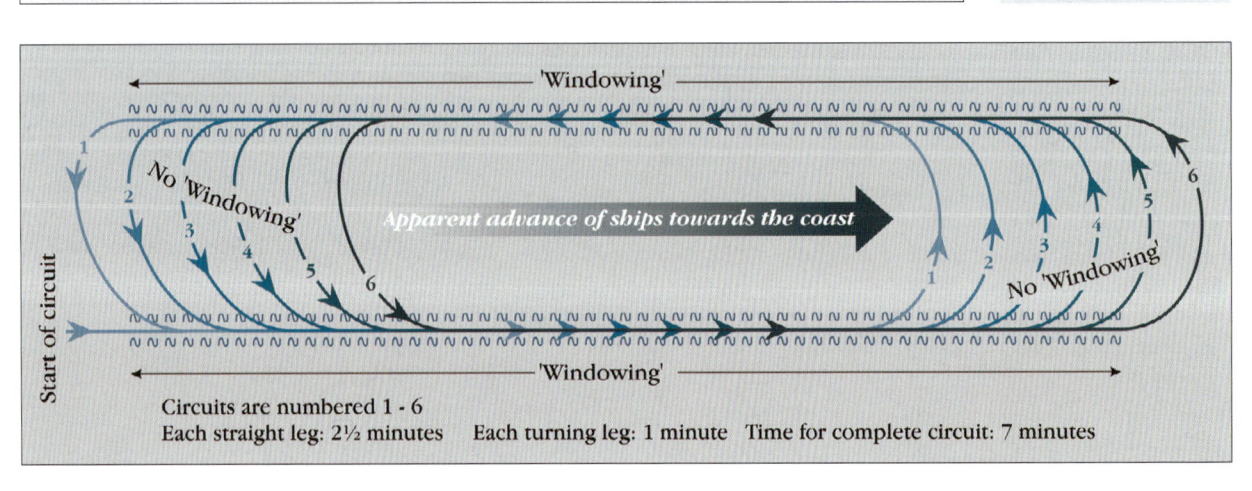

Circuits are numbered 1 - 6
Each straight leg: 2½ minutes   Each turning leg: 1 minute   Time for complete circuit: 7 minutes

243 Above: *A 4 Group Halifax attacking the V-3 gun site in northern France on 6 July 1944.*

244 Right: *Allied victory did not come cheap and people were encouraged to subscribe to all sorts of government schemes, as this American poster demonstrates.*

245 Below left: *By 1944 there was cause for hope—A Needler's chocolate advertisement from the period.*

246 Below right: *But it was still a time of make-do and mend. Everyone in the services was issued with one of these 'housewives'.*

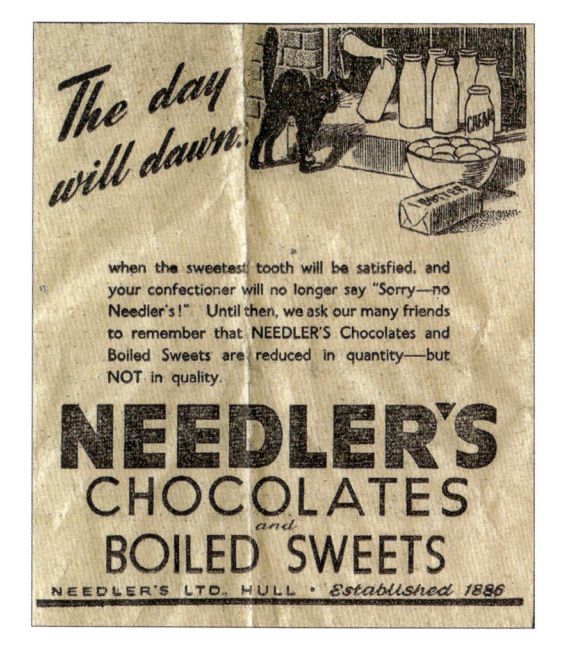

143

For four hours, 617 Sqn Lancasters flew a series of parallel elliptical circuits towards the French coast between Fécamp (35 miles west of Dieppe) and Le Treport (15 miles east of Dieppe), dropping 'Window' on each straight leg and edging ever closer to the French coast on each successive circuit. The falling thin foil strips suggested to German coastal radar operators studying their screens that an invasion fleet, sixteen miles wide and eight miles long, was approaching the French coast in the vicinity of Dieppe. *Taxable*, the brilliant deception operation, worked. As a result of disturbing reports from the German coastal radar operators, eleven German infantry divisions and two Panzer armoured divisions were kept on alert to the east of the River Seine, some sixty miles from the Allied landing zones.

As the second wave of Lancasters turned for home, around dawn, some of the aircrew caught a glimpse of the real invasion fleet, surging across the English Channel and heading for the beaches of Normandy. Those initial, monotonous trial flights off Flamborough Head in May had played their part in the least spectacular, but most important, of 617 Squadron's wartime operations.

A second RAF deception operation, code-named *Glimmer*, was carried out at the same time by Short Stirlings of 218 Sqn heading across the English Channel towards Boulogne, thus causing more confusion for German forces in north-western France.

Enter the V-1

Back in East Yorkshire, 4 Group bomber squadrons continued to make their contribution to the Allied invasion of Europe by bombing coastal gun emplacements, airfields, railway junctions and marshalling yards, and oil installations. Then, in the middle of June 1944, something happened in the South of England which was to have a bearing on Bomber Command operations throughout the latter part of June and into July. From 13 June a new German weapon, the V-1 or *Vergeltungswaffe* (Vengeance Weapon 1) began to descend on London. This pilotless aircraft, which became commonly known in Britain as the 'doodlebug' or 'flying bomb', was 25 feet long, had a 17 feet 6 inches wingspan, flew at 350 mph and carried a highly destructive warhead. The weapon's pulse-jet motor was programmed to cut out over London, whereupon it would dive down and cause death and destruction on a frightening scale. Although the primary target was London, many of the V-1s went off course and detonated across SE England and East Anglia. Launched mainly from the Pas de Calais in France, and with a limited range of 130 miles, these deadly weapons would never threaten East Yorkshire, or so it seemed at the time.

With 100 or more V-1s hitting London in one night, Bomber Commands attention now turned to attacking V-1 launch sites and storage depots. One such raid, a daylight operation on Wednesday 28 June against a V-weapon site at Wizernes, 15 miles south-south-east of Calais, was carried out by 103 Halifaxes from East Yorkshire, led by five Mosquitoes and two Lancasters from 8 Group's Pathfinder Force. One particularly enthusiastic participant on this raid was RAF Lissett's Station Commander, Group Captain Tom Sawyer DFC, who piloted one of 158 Sqn's 24 Halifaxes. This appears to have been a typical example of Tom Sawyer's hands-on approach.

From September 1944, London, SE England and East Anglia came under attack from Germany's second vengeance weapon, the V-2. The latter was an extremely destructive long-range rocket, 46 feet long with a 1,000kg warhead, which could reach an altitude of 60 miles, travel at over 3,000 mph, and had a range of approximately 225 miles. Unlike its predecessor, the V-1, the V-2 did not require a permanent launching ramp; it could be transported around the countryside on a trailer and then launched vertically from a mobile platform. However, the launching of a V-2 did require the presence of a number of back-up vehicles and did take between four and six hours preparation time. This lengthy operation enabled RAF reconnaissance aircraft to obtain photographs of where V-2s were being deployed in Holland. Again, East Yorkshire's Halifax bombers would play their part in attempting to nullify the threat from these terrifying weapons.

Despite the need to destroy V-weapon sites, East Yorkshire's bomber squadrons were in action almost nightly during the second half of 1944, attacking

---

Facts:
1944 saw the war irrevocably turn in favour of the Allies, who began to look to post-war issues. One of the most popular songs that year, I'll be Seeing You, *reflected the hopes of those separated by war. Films of the time represented patriotism — as portrayed by Laurence Olivier in Shakespeare's* Henry V *— and escapism with Walt Disney's cartoon* The Three Caballeros, *which gave rise to numerous examples of aircraft nose art. Eggs — if you could get them in 1944 — cost 2 shillings per dozen (10p).*

247: *The sinister shape of a V-1 in flight. Several thousand of these flying bombs were launched against Britain. Defeating them cost 7,810 lives and the Allies a financial sum of £47,635,190 (1945 figures). This against an estimated cost to the Germans of about £12,600,670.*

248: *An American Douglas A-20 Havoc, 41-3379, 'F', of the 2nd or 3rd Gunnery Tow Target Flight based at Goxhill, in flight over the northern suburbs of Bridlington in 1944. A tow hook or winch outlet can just be seen under the rear fuselage.*

German towns and cities, oil plants, troop and tank concentrations, airfields, and Germany's communications network. There would be many disturbed nights for people living close to Bomber Command airfields. Noise was not the only problem for these people — there was also the fear factor, the fear that a bomber with a full load of fuel and bombs might crash onto their farm or into their village during that most critical phase of an operation, the takeoff. Many an East Yorkshire family living in the vicinity of a bomber base felt that they were more likely to be killed by a RAF bomber than by a Luftwaffe bomb.

Fortunately, however, thanks to the expertise of the Bomber Command pilots, no such tragedy occurred in East Yorkshire in 1944. There were one or two nasty scares though. For example, on Tuesday 18 July the villagers of Barmston had a lucky escape when a crashing Halifax bomber narrowly missed their village as it dived into Bridlington Bay, a mere 100 yards beyond Barmston. The aircraft, MZ286/NP-X of 158 Sqn and piloted by F/Lt H.C. Monnier (RCAF), was on an operation to bomb troop concentrations at Caen in France. Monnier's aircraft had lifted off alright from RAF Lissett but something must have gone drastically wrong almost immediately after takeoff, for the bomber crashed into the sea just two minutes later. As the next Halifax up from Lissett, piloted by F/O W.R. Dennis, crossed the coast at Barmston, some of the crew could see the black shape of a Halifax in the sea, trapped in a mass of flames. The impact had ruptured the bomber's fuel tanks and as the petrol poured out it had ignited; there was no escape for the seven men on board 'X-X-ray'.

Then, on Monday 15 October, people in Lissett had an unpleasant shock when a massive explosion shook their homes. What had happened was that a 158 Sqn Halifax, LK850/NP-H piloted by F/Lt D.W. McAdam, was taking off from RAF Lissett at 0050 hrs bound for Duisburg in the Ruhr when the starboard outer engine failed. With a full load of bombs and fuel on board, McAdam realised that he could neither take off safely nor stop his aircraft in the length of runway ahead of him. He therefore retracted the undercarriage, which caused the Halifax to skid and screech along the runway before sliding off onto an area of grass. As the aircraft caught fire, six of the crew leapt from the escape hatches. The seventh member of the crew, the rear gunner, was trapped in his turret but was quickly rescued by his determined pilot. Two hours later, after fire had totally consumed the Halifax, the bomb load exploded. The power of the explosion destroyed another Halifax, MZ862/NP-K, which had been left on the grass following a collapsed tail wheel, and blasted debris over a wide area.

The autumn of 1944 and early winter of 1944-45 produced yet another hazard for East Yorkshire's bomber crews — fog. It was during this period that Carnaby's emergency landing ground quickly proved its worth, its extensive runway with the added benefit of FIDO helping out many a desperate bomber crew. FIDO was in use so frequently in a very foggy December that the airfield's petrol consumption for the month soared to an incredible 1,700,000 gallons, and there was a daily stream of LNER tanker wagons into the Carnaby siding to top up the FIDO storage tanks. The busiest time of all for RAF Carnaby was 22-26 December when almost 100 aircraft, mainly RAF Halifaxes and Lancasters but also including 13 USAAF B-17 Flying Fortresses, landed safely. These aircraft and their crews were all weather-bound until conditions started to improve on 27 December. The arrival of so many aircraft at Carnaby ELG was not in itself a problem, but the sudden presence of several hundred airmen provided RAF administrators in the region with a logistical headache. Accommodating and feeding the stranded bomber crews could not be done at RAF Carnaby, which had only very basic amenities. Therefore these airmen had to be transported to other RAF stations in East Yorkshire, with most of them making the short journey along the A165 to RAF Lissett.

Operation Rumpelkammer

The year 1944 had been a relatively quiet time for the people of East Yorkshire who were now looking forward to a much happier Christmas than they could have envisaged 12 months earlier. Then, early on the morning of Christmas Eve, something totally unexpected and most alarming happened — the unique sound of V-1 flying bombs was heard across the southern part of the region, but how could these weapons, with a range of only about 130 miles, have reached East Yorkshire?

The answer was that the flying bombs had been air-launched, (in a series of operations codenamed *Rumpelkammer*[21] by the Luftwaffe) from German bombers off the East Coast. Between 0500 and 0600 hrs, 45 Heinkel He 111H-22s of KG 53 from Schleswig Holstein in northern Germany each launched a V-1 when approximately 40 miles off the Lincolnshire coast between Skegness and Mablethorpe. Their target, however, was not Hull, but Manchester.

KG 53's operation got off to a bad start when 14 of the V-1s failed to cross the Lincolnshire coastline, disappearing somewhere over the North Sea. Of the remaining 31 V-1s, fewer than half detonated anywhere near Manchester. Three of the deadly weapons flew north-west instead of west before coming down in East Yorkshire, between 0545 and 0600 hrs. One dived to the ground at Willerby, on the western outskirts of Hull, where it exploded and did some damage to housing and the Springhead Pumping Station. A second fell harmlessly at South Cliffe, four miles south of Market Weighton. The third blew up as it crashed to earth at Barmby Moor, close to RAF Pocklington where a 102 Sqn Halifax was damaged. A fourth missile plunged into a mud bank at Reads Island in the Humber but failed to detonate. Four more V-1s came down in other parts of Yorkshire: at Sowerby Bridge near Halifax, Rossington near Doncaster, Grange Moor near Huddersfield, and on Midhope Moor near Penistone. The V-1 attack on the North had been a failure; it would not be repeated. To this day, however, an eyewitness swears that he saw one fly low down past Withernsea lighthouse, heading inland. Could this have been the one which crashed at Reads Island?

In fact, the missile could often be most dangerous to the carrier aircraft. In mid-December II./KG 53 lost 12 aircraft in two operations when missiles detonated prematurely shortly after take-off. This event halted operations for two weeks.

Despite the disturbing events early on Christmas Eve, Christmas Day 1944 would be a far more cheerful occasion than any of the previous wartime Christmases. The war overseas was progressing well for the Allies, while at home people across East Yorkshire felt less threatened from the air. There was now a growing belief that World War II would soon be brought to a successful conclusion and that Christmas 1945 would be celebrated with the world at peace.

Facts:
Other names by which the 'doodlebugs' were known to the Germans were:
Kirschkern — *Cherry stone*
Fi 103 — *the prototype name given by Gerhard Fieseler*
FZG-76 — *a deception name 'target device 76'*
Maikafer — *Maybug*
Kivic — *Hellhound*

[21] *'Junkroom'*

249: *A Fieseler Fi 103 (V-1) attached to the pylon under the wing root of the Heinkel He 111 carrier aircraft. This is an experimental model as it appears that most operational versions were carried under the starboard wing root. There was a complex procedure for starting the V-1's engine in flight which had to be started at a very precise point in the aircraft's flight pattern. It then took about 20 minutes to countdown to the moment of engine start on the missile, which was released about ten seconds later. If need be the pilot could jettison the bomb by pulling a large red lever fitted above his head in the cockpit.*

250: *After the launching sites in France had been overrun, the Allies found scores of abandone V-1s. This one is on display in Brussels after the end of the war.*

251: *Although not used by KG 53, this Heinkel He 111H-20 or H-22, found abandoned at Gatow at the end of the war, gives a good idea of the type of aircraft used to carry and launch the V-1. The major external difference to earlier models is the rotating dorsal turret, the clear glazing of which has been smashed on this particular machine. The 'cloud' camouflage was also used on V-1 carriers.*

252: *Mention must be made of the many Commonwealth airmen who flew from East Yorkshire. This is S/Ldr T.E. Eagleton DFC and his crew from the Australian 466 Sqn, based at Driffield, in front of their Halifax III, LW172/HD-F. The crew had just completed their first tour of operations, Eagleton his second, while the aircraft had done 91 missions. Five missions later, the aircraft crashed in fog two miles west of Driffield, on 9 April 1945, killing another crew. Popeye and Olive Oyl were two of the more uncommon bomber emblems.*

147

1945 - GISELA
The Luftwaffe's final fling and the last air raid on Hull

The final air battles over East Yorkshire in World War Two did not involve RAF night fighters defending the region against Luftwaffe bombers, but saw combat between returning RAF heavy bombers and Luftwaffe long-range night fighters, commonly referred to as 'intruders'.

A German long-range intruder force known as the *Fernnachtjäger*, a branch of the night fighting arm of the Luftwaffe, had first been established back in the summer of 1940. The early strategy of this force had been to attack RAF aircraft in the vicinity of their British bases as they were taking off or landing, at times when both aircraft and airfields would be displaying an array of lights.

Early *Fernnachtjäger* activity over Yorkshire involved Junkers Ju 88C *Zerstörer* (destroyer) aircraft of I/NJG 2 operating out of the airfield at Gilze-Rijen in Holland. First blood to the intruders over Yorkshire came on the night of Thursday 24 October 1940. It was approximately 2130 hours when *Fw* Hans Hahn flew his Ju 88 in low over Flamborough Head before circling the region in search of aircraft/airfield activity. As Hahn was heading towards York, he spotted a well-lit airfield to the north-west of the city. This was RAF Linton-on-Ouse where nine 102 Sqn Whitley bombers were preparing to take off on an operation to raid German Air Ministry buildings in Berlin. As P/O A.G. Davies and crew in Whitley P5073/DY-D became airborne at 2202 hours, they came under heavy fire from Hahn's Ju 88. The unsuspecting Whitley crew did not stand a chance against Hahn's devastating attack.

Davies struggled to force land his crippled bomber to the north of Linton, but the Whitley was too badly damaged for the pilot to make a controlled descent and it crashed near the village of Tholthorpe at 2210 hours. Only P/O Davies survived; P/O Murfitt (second pilot) and Sgt Scoular (observer) were both killed in the crash, while Sgt Wilson (wireless operator) and P/O Lee (rear gunner) both died later, on 2 November 1940.

This 102 Sqn Whitley was the first of 14 Yorkshire-based bombers to be shot down or forced down by German intruder aircraft between October 1940 and October 1941. Most of the action took place in the proximity of RAF airfields in North and West Yorkshire, but at about 1900 hours on Thursday 2 January 1941 combat took place off Withernsea and once again a 102 Sqn Whitley was on the receiving end of an intruder strike. The aircraft in question was Whitley T4227/DY-R, piloted by F/O D.C.F. Coutts and based at RAF Topcliffe in North Yorkshire. Heading east to bomb the German port of Bremen, the Whitley had just crossed the East Yorkshire coast at Withernsea when it was attacked by an enemy night

253 Above: This Junkers Ju 88R-1, Werk Nr 360043, D5+EV, of IV./NJG 3 was flown to Britain on 9 May 1943 by a German crew who were defecting to the British. It carried radar equipment of vital importance to the RAF. Seen here in early 1945 it still wears its original German camouflage and the 'Englandblitz' emblem carried by many nightfighters and intruder aircraft of the Luftwaffe. The heavy nose armament which posed such a threat to RAF bombers is clearly visible, although only the stubs of the radar antenna remain. Today the aircraft resides in the RAF Museum at Hendon.

fighter. Although the rear gunner on board the Whitley fought back hard, it was a one-sided contest and soon the shattered bomber was plunging into the North Sea approximately 30 miles out from Withernsea. There were no survivors. The victorious Luftwaffe pilot was again Hans Hahn, now promoted to *Oberleutnant* and this was his second *abschusse* (claim of one aircraft shot down).

So far, East Yorkshire's aircraft and airfields had not yet attracted the attention of I./NJG 2 pilots, with the one exception of a failed attack on an RAF training aircraft in the Driffield circuit during the night of 29/30 April 1940.

The I./NJG 2 intruder operations over Britain were beginning to pay off, as much of the RAF's night-training programme was suspended. Also, some Bomber Command aircrew were becoming psychologically unsettled at the sight of squadron aircraft being shot down so close to base. Then, in October 1941, and much to the surprise, but relief, of the RAF, Adolf Hitler called a halt to German intruder flights over England. Hitler argued that these operations had not resulted in any let-up in RAF bombing raids on Germany and that in future all Luftwaffe night fighters must concentrate on defending the Third Reich.

It was not until the night of 3/4 March 1945 that German intruder aircraft were again in action over Yorkshire, only this time East Yorkshire airfields and their bombers were in the forefront of *Fernnachtjäger* attacks. This was to be the Luftwaffe's final major operation of the war over Britain and was code-named *'Gisela'*.[22]

Shortly after noon on Saturday 3 March 1945, orders and details relating to the coming night's operation were received at 4 Group Bomber Command airfields in Yorkshire. The plan was for 200 Halifaxes from nine East Yorkshire bases (Breighton, Driffield, Elvington, Full Sutton, Holme-on-Spalding Moor, Leconfield, Lissett, Melbourne and Pocklington) and two West Yorkshire airfields (Burn and Snaith) to raid the synthetic oil plant at Kamen, a German town at the eastern end of the Ruhr industrial region. These Halifaxes were to be led by 33 pathfinder aircraft – 21 Lancasters and 12 Mosquitoes from 8 Group Bomber Command which would mark the target area with clusters of red and green flares. Take-off for the Halifaxes would be from 1800 hours.

First Halifax up, from RAF Elvington at precisely 1800 hours, was a 347 (Tunisie) Sqn aircraft piloted by A/C M. Vidal. Throughout the next hour, Halifax after Halifax roared up into the evening sky before swinging south for Reading and then crossing the English coast between Beachy Head and Selsey Bill. Several 4 Group Halifaxes aborted the operation because of technical problems, but 181 made it to Kamen where the synthetic oil plant was bombed from 2153 hours. There was little opposition from German flak batteries or night fighters and all the Yorkshire-based Halifaxes reached the French coast on the return leg without loss. The bomber crews were quite relaxed now as they flew across the North Sea between Dunkirk and Oxford Ness, and headed for home. For several of the Halifax crews, however, a nasty shock awaited them as they flew the last leg of the night's operation, probably thinking more about the traditional eggs and bacon meal for returning bomber crews than of any danger from enemy night fighters. After all, they were over England now and only minutes away from their Yorkshire airfields.

But unknown to the Halifax crews, from around 2300 hours on 3 March wave after wave of Luftwaffe night fighter intruder aircraft had been taking off from bases in Holland and North Germany and heading out across the North Sea. The Luftwaffe plan was for the Junkers Ju 88G-6 long-range night fighters to fly as low as 150 feet over the North Sea, in an attempt to avoid radar detection, before climbing sharply to the approximate height of the returning RAF bombers as the latter headed for their airfields. They would then, in a freelancing operation, search for illuminated airfields and returning bombers with their landing lights switched on.

Apart from the 4 Group Halifax raid on Kamen, there had also been a major attack on the Dortmund-Ems Canal at Ladbergen by 212 Lancasters and 12 Mosquitoes of 5 Group, while 96 Mosquitoes from 8 Group had bombed Berlin and Wurzburg. Other Bomber Command activities during the night of 3/4 March included mine-laying in Oslo harbour by 5 Group Lancasters, mine-laying in the Kattegat by 1 Group Lancasters, diversionary flights towards the Frisian Islands by Halifaxes, Lancasters and Wellingtons from 7 Group, and signal jamming operations by a variety of aircraft from 100 Group. All told there would be around 600 RAF aircraft returning to their English bases during the early hours of Sunday 4 March. Consequently, the Luftwaffe intruder crews were anticipating rich pickings over East Anglia, Lincolnshire and Yorkshire.

Slaughter in the night

First of the East Yorkshire-based bombers to be attacked was Halifax NP916/C8-J, a 640 Sqn aircraft from RAF Leconfield. Piloted by P/O P.B. Manton, it had only just crossed the Suffolk coast when it was shot down near RAF Woodbridge, an emergency landing ground, at 0015 hours. Only the rear gunner, Sgt E.J.V. Thompson, survived the crash.

Next to come under fire was Halifax NR240/NP-N, a 158 Sqn Lissett-based bomber piloted by F/Sgt K.M. Anderson, an Australian. As this aircraft was overflying Norfolk, with navigation lights switched on to lessen the chance of a mid-air collision, mid-upper gunner Sgt George Tuohy warned that an unidentified aircraft without lights was following them. Suddenly, bright streams of tracer flashed past on

---

[22] *A girl's name*

Incident:
11 February 1945. Hptm Hans Felde of 1.(F)/123 made a reconnaissance flight over the Humber area in a jet-powered Arado Ar 234, 4U+DH, Werk Nr 140148, the first time jets had operated over East Yorkshire. This mission may have formed part of the planning for the Gisela attacks. Unfortunately for Felde he was shot down near Rheine on his return to Germany by a Tempest fighter of 274 Sqn flown by S/Ldr David Fairbanks. This was the first Ar 234 to be destroyed by Allied air forces, but at the time was thought to be an Me 262.

254: Keith Anderson's 158 Sqn crew, safely back at Lissett after surviving attacks by German intruder aircraft and a heavy landing at Middleton St. George after their return from Kamen on 3/4 March 1945. L-r: Sgt L. Lamb (wireless operator), Sgt G. Tuohy (mid-upper gunner), Sgt S.D. Till (rear gunner), F/Sgt K.M. Anderson (pilot), W/O L. Cooper (bomb-aimer), Sgt R.C. Mundy (flight engineer) and F/Sgt H. Lomas (navigator). Three members of the groundcrew kneel in front. (via Harry Lomas DFM)

255: Wreckage of F/Lt Rogers' Halifax NP-X was scattered far and wide over the Yorkshire Wolds near Sledmere Grange.

256: Six of these men were killed when 158 Sqn's 'X-X-ray' crashed. Also killed was P/O C.J.W. Muir who had replaced Sgt Hutchings as flight engineer in F/Lt Rogers' crew.

257 Above: *This 347 Sqn Halifax III PN167/L8-C, piloted by Lt Pillissier, was the first Free French aircraft to return safely to Elvington (at 0200 hrs) from the Kamen operation of 4 March 1945. The censor has blocked out the Perspex nose cone and removed both the H2S radar blister under the fuselage and Miquette's individual aircraft letter on the fuselage side.*

Facts:

By 1945 popular songs were beginning to take on a more lighthearted feel. Among the more popular were Don't Fence Me In, *sung by Bing Crosby and The Andrews Sisters and* Sentimental Journey *by the Les Brown Orchestra. Films were more about relationships, in particular the classic tearjerker* Brief Encounter *starring Trevor Howard and Celia Johnson. At war's end 20 Churchman's cigarettes cost 2/6 (12.5p), but attitudes to smoking were very different then.*

both sides of the Halifax. Pilot Keith Anderson immediately put the big bomber through a series of violent manoeuvres in an attempt to shake off their attacker. These tactics worked and 'N-Nan' was able to continue northwards towards the Humber, Holderness and home.

Abruptly, shortly after joining the circuit to land at RAF Lissett, a dramatic call was received from the airfield's control tower:

"All Luxsoap aircraft from Step-in. Bandits! Dogleg!"

This meant that enemy aircraft were in the vicinity, and that F/Sgt Anderson must now fly a diversionary route away from Lissett. As navigator F/Sgt Harry Lomas was working out a new course, some of the other crew members spotted a blazing aircraft, out of control and falling to earth about ten miles west of Lissett. This was another 158 Sqn Halifax, PN437/NP-X, piloted by one of the squadron's most respected and experienced captains, F/Lt C.A. Rogers. 'X-X-ray' had been attacked and set on fire by an enemy night fighter before crashing and disintegrating over the upper slopes of a Wolds dry valley near Sledmere Grange. The time was 0030 hours and there were no survivors.

There was also an intruder aircraft in the circuit at RAF Driffield. A 466 (RAAF) Sqn Halifax, NR250/HD-N piloted by P/O A.E. Schrank, was just minutes away from touchdown when a number of cannon shells blasted huge holes in the rear part of the bomber's fuselage, damaging the hydraulic system and starting a fire inside the fuselage. It was quite remarkable that only one member of the Halifax crew, mid-upper gunner Sgt P. Stuart, was injured in the attack, hit in one leg by cannon shell splinters. Three minutes later, the Junkers 88 night fighter closed in again but on this occasion it was seen in time for Schrank to put his aircraft into a steep dive to starboard and escape without any further damage or injury.

P/O Schrank's evasive action took his Halifax away from East Yorkshire and south over the Humber. With a serious fire in the fuselage, all fire extinguishers now exhausted, and only a few minutes flying time left as the fuel tanks were almost empty, Schrank had no alternative but to climb his aircraft and gain sufficient altitude for the crew to bale out. All seven men on board the blazing bomber were able to parachute to safety, at approximately 0040 hours, landing near RAF Waddington in Lincolnshire. Some books state that the abandoned Halifax flew on to crash at Friskney, a Lincolnshire village eight miles south-west of Skegness. However, an entry in 466 Sqn's Operations Record Book for 4 March 1944 clearly states that Schrank's Halifax crashed at Skellingthorpe, a village four miles west of Lincoln.

Back in the Lissett circuit, there was another attack on a 158 Sqn Halifax, MZ917/NP-R, an aircraft officially referred to as 'R-Roger' but popularly known as *Krazy Kate*. P/O W.P. Strachan (RAAF) was at the controls and preparing to land at Lissett when, at a height of around 1000 feet, his bomber was hit by a three to four second burst of cannon fire. With the port outer engine on fire and the possibility of other serious damage to his aircraft, Bill Strachan continued with his descent. Then, at a height of only 500 feet, the German night fighter attacked again, fortunately missing the crippled Halifax. Minutes later, at 0051 hours, P/O Strachan landed *Krazy Kate* and taxied clear of the runway before switching off the engines and checking out the condition of his crew. He quickly discovered that both his air gunners had been wounded; Sgt Alan Parish (mid-upper gunner) had been hit in the arm but would be alright, whereas Sgt Arthur Tait (rear gunner) had been critically injured by a cannon shell which had penetrated his chest, smashed a lung and then exited through his back.

The Ju 88 pilot responsible for the attack on Bill

Strachan's Halifax was still circling RAF Lissett and, as Arthur Tait was being extricated from the rear turret, swept in to make a number of low-level passes across the aerodrome, strafing aircraft on the ground, hangars, the control tower and even the ambulance on its way to pick up Tait.[23] It was a miracle that no RAF personnel were killed or seriously injured in this daring attack on RAF Lissett.

As P/O Strachan was making his dramatic return to Lissett, two other 4 Group Halifaxes were also in trouble over East Yorkshire. Halifax MZ133/ZA-X, piloted by W/O R.W. Poley, had just crossed the coast to the south of Bridlington and was heading back to RAF Melbourne when, at a height of 2,500 feet, it was attacked by an intruder aircraft. As cannon fire flashed past the 10 Sqn bomber, rear gunner F/Sgt R. Grayson opened up with his machine guns; he too missed his target. Then, after a violent corkscrew to port, Poley succeeded in losing the night fighter. Although 'X-X-ray' had not been hit during the combat, the aircraft did have a serious problem in that the main hydraulic feed line had burst. As this situation was likely to lead to a dangerous landing at base, W/O Poley opted instead to make for the long emergency runway at Carnaby, where the Halifax touched down safely at 0050 hours.

The other Halifax with problems was a 77 Sqn aircraft, NR210/KN-Z, piloted by New Zealander F/O J.M. Gaddes. As 'Z-Zebra' was coming in to land at RAF Full Sutton, it was attacked by one of the Ju 88 intruders. A burst of cannon fire smashed the rear turret of the Halifax, wounded its occupant F/Sgt H. Mustoe and put the aircraft's intercom system out of action. Although the runway lights at Full Sutton had been switched off, P/O Gaddes was determined to land his bomber rather than risk a diversion to another airfield. This he successfully achieved, at the second attempt, at 0055 hours. The enemy night fighter then strafed the airfield but little damage was done and there were no casualties.

Between 0100 and 0115 hours another four of East Yorkshire's Halifaxes were shot down. The first to be attacked, NA680/L8-H of 347 (Tunisie) Sqn, was overflying Lincolnshire when it was hit by cannon fire from an enemy night fighter. Five members of the crew parachuted to safety but Capt P. Lacou (pilot), who was on his very first operation, and Sgt P. Masson (flight engineer) perished when their bomber crashed near Cranwell in Lincolnshire at 0105 hours.

Five minutes later, a 466 (RAAF) Sqn Halifax came under attack as it approached RAF Driffield. Halifax NR179/HD-C, piloted by F/O A.P. Shelton, was as low as 150 feet when the airfield's runway lights went out and the pilot was instructed to divert to RAF Pocklington. Then, just minutes from the runway, 'C-Charlie' was hit by a well-directed burst of cannon fire which hit and set on fire the port outer and in-

[23] Despite some books stating that Sgt A. Tait had been 'mortally wounded' on 4 March 1945, Arthur Tait recovered from his terrible injuries, but only after lengthy spells in hospitals at Driffleld and Northallerton.

258: The wreckage of 347 Sqn's 'O-Orange' which crashed near Sutton-upon-Derwent at 0115 hours on Sunday 4 March 1945.

259: The regular crew in front of Halifax III MZ917/NP-R, known as Krazy Kate, from 158 Sqn at RAF Lissett and which was written off after the events of 4 March 1945. L-r: Sgt J.R. Wakefield (bomb-aimer), Sgt E.H. Richards (wireless operator), Sgt A. Parrish (mid-upper gunner), F/O W.P. Strachan (pilot), F/Sgt C. Keeton (navigator), F/O R. Stow (flight engineer) and Sgt A. Tait (rear gunner). For the Kamen operation, navigator Keeton was suffering from a heavy cold and was replaced by P/O D.H. Mackirdy, a Canadian.

260: Air warfare over the East Riding did not only involve operational aircraft. It also involved much pilot training and one of the more important bases for this was at Blackburn Aircraft's factory and airfield at Brough. No 4 Elementary Flying Training School was located there and one of the principal instructors was Mr Thomas Richardson, who had been a member of Hull Aero Club since 1929. From 1935 he was a flying instructor there and when the club was forced to move from Hedon at the outbreak of war, he went to Brough. From 1941 until 1945, for four days a week, he served as an unpaid instructor giving initial flying instruction to would-be RAF pilots. Awarded the MBE in 1943 for these services he was eventually released from this task on 3 January 1945 as the letter of appreciation from Air Marshal Babington shown here notes.

```
Telephone No.:                    HEADQUARTERS, FLYING TRAINING
  READING 60103, 60471, 60881.                  COMMAND,
Telegraphic Address               ROYAL AIR FORCE,
  "PER ARDUA, READING."
                                      SHINFIELD PARK,
Your Reference —
                                        READING, BERKS.
My Reference — FTC/C.70248/P(34)
                                      3rd January, 1945.


Dear Richardson,

        I have received information from
the Air Ministry that you are to be
released from your part time instructor
duties at No. 4 E.F.T.S., and I should
like to take this opportunity of expressing
my appreciation and that of the Royal
Air Force for the valuable service you
have rendered whilst employed on these
duties.

        The Air Officer Commanding No.51
Group and the Officer Commanding No. 4
E.F.T.S. have spoken very highly of the
manner in which you have given instruction
and how valuable your assistance has been
over a long and difficult period.

        I wish you every success in the
New Year and in years to come.

                        Yours sincerely,

                        P. Babington

                        P.BABINGTON,
                        Air Marshal.
T.E.RICHARDSON Esq., M.B.E.,
No. 4 E.F.T.S.
BROUGH.
```

261 Right: An RAF pupil pilot receives initial training from a civilian instructor.

262 Far right: The mainstay of most EFT Schools was the Tiger Moth, as shown here. The ground staff are obviously civilians, as at 4 EFTS at Brough, but it is not known if the picture was taken there.

153

ner engines. With the engine fires quickly spreading to the fuselage P/O Shelton, realising the hopelessness of the situation, ordered his crew to bale out.

First out, through the rear escape hatch, was mid-upper gunner F/Sgt G.D. Laing and he was quickly followed by navigator F/Sgt P. Hogan. Next to escape, from the rear turret was rear gunner F/Sgt V. Bullen. The aircraft's flight engineer, Sgt W.E. Welsh, hesitated at the escape hatch and although he did eventually jump he had left his exit too late and he plummeted to the ground before his parachute could open. P/O A.P. Shelton (pilot), F/Sgt G.W. Dixon (wireless operator) and F/Sgt R.R. Johnson were all trapped in the diving, blazing bomber and were killed as the machine crashed and exploded at Fridaythorpe on the Yorkshire Wolds.

Meanwhile, a 76 Sqn bomber was attacked as it came in to land at RAF Holme-on-Spalding Moor. Halifax NA584/MP-E, piloted by P/O P. Oleynik, was hit by a sudden burst of cannon fire, one of the shells striking mid-upper gunner F/Sgt W.T. Maltby. P/O Oleynik immediately switched off his aircraft's lights and headed for the emergency landing ground at Carnaby, where he landed 'E-Easy' at 0110 hours. The landing was rather eventful. Unknown to Oleynik, a tyre on the port side had been shot through and as the Halifax touched down it swung off the runway before crashing into a steam roller and then hitting another aircraft. Six members of the crew emerged virtually unscathed from the broken Halifax but F/Sgt Maltby's injuries were far more serious than first realised and he died shortly afterwards in RAF Carnaby's Sick Quarters.

Five minutes later, 347 (Tunisie) Sqn lost a second aircraft during the early hours of 4 March. This was Halifax NR235/L8-0, piloted by S/Ldr J. Terrien, one of the squadron's most experienced captains. While approaching their home base at Elvington, Terrien and his crew had the unnerving experience of seeing Shelton's bomber go down in flames. Seconds later their own bomber was attacked. Soon, both starboard engines were on fire with flames licking their way along the wing towards the fuselage. Six of the Frenchmen parachuted to safety, but the unfortunate Terrien was unable to get out before 'O-Orange' lurched into a steep dive. The Halifax crashed and broke up near Sutton-upon-Derwent with its brave pilot still on board.

Soon afterwards, there was an attempt to destroy the control tower at RAF Carnaby. This is how the attack was recorded in the station's Operations Record Book:

"At 0130 hours, an attempt was made by a low-flying Ju 88 to bomb the Control Tower – two containers of anti-personnel bombs were released, falling about 50 and 300 yards from the tower. Owing to the low altitude at which they were released, the containers did not have time to open and buried themselves harmlessly without exploding, being removed later by the Bomb Disposal Squad without incident".

The next 4 Group bomber to be attacked was a 76 Sqn Halifax, MZ680/MP-R, piloted by P/O H. Bertenshaw. This aircraft was circling the squadron's base at Holme-on-Spalding Moor when instructed to carry out a dog-leg. P/O Bertenshaw flew his Halifax out to sea before heading south and eventually turning back inland over the Wash. As the bomber was flying north over Lincolnshire, several cannon shells exploded in the starboard wing starting an uncontrollable fire. Fortunately on this occasion all seven men on board were able to parachute to safety as their aircraft dived into the ground near the Lincolnshire village of Cadney at 0136 hours.

Back over East Yorkshire, there was still considerable confusion caused by the continued presence of intruder aircraft. This resulted in several returning 4 Group aircraft being confronted with blacked out runways and ordered to divert to alternative airfields. One such bomber was Halifax HX322/ZA-V of 10 Sqn, piloted by Canadian F/Lt J. Laffoley, 'V-Victor' had already made two unsuccessful attempts at landing and was approaching the runway at RAF Melbourne for the third time when the 'Bandits' call

263: *This poor quality picture is the only one known of 466 Squadron's Halifax III, NR179/HD-C, taken before it was shot down. On 4 March, piloted by P/O Shelton, and just minutes away from its home base at RAF Driffield, it was hit by a German intruder. The yellow stripes across the fins were to assist in formation-keeping as the Halifax squadrons of 4 Group began to take part in daylight raids.*

264: *This is how the events of 4-5 March over East Yorkshire were reported to the general public in the* Daily Mail. *Needless to say, a degree of optimistic 'spin' is apparent in the tone of the article, which attempts to minimise the enemy action. No mention is made of the RAF aircrew and aircraft lost — the real victims of the attack.*

4-The Daily Mail, March 5th, 1945

Piloted Planes Over North-East

MUCH MACHINE-GUNNING, SLIGHT CASUALTIES

GERMAN piloted 'planes, for the second night in succession, raided England last night, but the scale of the attack was not so heavy as on Saturday night when six of the raiders were shot down.

Last night the raiders were met by a constant A.A. barrage as they crossed the East Anglian coast. As they flew in from the sea they dropped flares which were quickly shot down.

Flying low over an East Anglian town one raider dropped a number of small bombs. Two exploded above a roof where babies were sleeping. They escaped injury, although smothered with plaster. The only casualty was a woman who received cuts.

The official statement says that in the period between dawn yesterday and 7 o'clock to-day there has been enemy air activity directed against Northern and Southern England. Damage and casualties have been reported.

MANY ROOFS "PEPPERED"

Cannon shells whistled through the air at a north-east town in the early hours of Sunday morning, when, during the night, and for the first time since Christmas Eve, the town experienced a raid. It was another typical nuisance raid, and many incidents of a minor nature and over a widely scattered area were reported. No bombs were reported to have fallen in the town and while there were some remarkable escapes, no serious injury has been reported.

In many instances when the alert sounded, inhabitants ignored the ruling, regarding the black-out regulations. Many still maintained their dim-out coverings. Some of the broad thoroughfares came in for cannon and machine gun fire as the enemy 'planes swept low. The firing was in a haphazard manner.

On one housing estate considerable fire occurred. Roofs were peppered, windows broken, and ceilings cracked and escape from injury in so many instances was nothing short of miraculous.

In the town two policemen were cycling home when they were caught in a spray of bullets. One was grazed on the forehead by a splinter of cement, and another had a torch in his pocket flattened by fragment. One of the officers stated "I was with my pal, cycling home, when some thing hit him in the pocket. All it did was to flatten out his torch. We continued our journey and put out a couple of fires caused by incendiary bullets."

ONE SHOT DOWN CLAIM

Cannon shells penetrated the roof of a detective-sergeant's house, boring their way through a bedroom ceiling and ricocheting to caused other internal damage. There was a five years old evacuee from Harrow in the house at the time.

Later enemy 'planes swooped low and there was a crashing of glass as windows were shattered and pieces of masonry were knocked about the streets.

Civil Defence personnel were instant in their response and outside one first-aid post an ambulance in readiness was hit and a bullet found in the driver's seat Wardens in some districts, had a special job of work to do going round with instructions that people should not handle cannon shells and bullets which they might find and which might have been of the explosive type.

Rocket-firing anti-aircraft guns along the coast opened up and it is claimed that in the district one enemy intruder was shot down.

The town had a further alert on Sunday evening.

BANK WALLS PITTED

Incidents were also reported from country areas on Saturday-Sunday night, but the only victim was a calf in a field.

At another north-east town the walls of a bank were pitted when a 'plane machine-gunned it, but no windows were touched A tracer bullet went through a stationer's shop. A cannon shell bounced off a bridge, went through the woodwork of a cabin, through a chest of drawers and into a coal bucket and riddled it with holes.

In another district, next door to a butcher's shop, the window of the house was riddled with tracer bullets, but no one was injured. Bullets were also found on an estate which had previously suffered from enemy action.

VEHICLES ATTACKED

Two N.F.S. vehicles responding to calls, were attacked by an enemy fighter. Both incidents occurred in the country. In one a crew of four in charge of L.P. Barmby, were attending to a fire when the enemy machine swooped down and opened fire. The crew flung themselves to the ground and all escaped injury. In the second instance a mobile dam unit was proceeding to another fire. The fire-fighting vehicle continued its journey while under fire and the fields on either side were hit.

Some miles away other firemen were shot at and, while in one case the driver of a fire tender was injured, a despatch rider with the N.F.S. turnout was fortunate to escape more serious injury when a bullet hit his lip.

Another town suffered from cannon-fire, the greenhouse of the police superintendent was damaged.

On a country road leading from the suburbs of a north-east town, a motorist experienced a wonderful escape when a machine-gun bullet crashed through the windscreen of the car. The driver was uninjured.

155

was received and the runway lights went out. After a twenty minute dog-leg, F/Lt Laffoley brought in his aircraft for a fourth time only to find that Melbourne's runway lights were still out. Directed north of RAF Dishforth, the pilot again found a blacked out airfield.

The young Canadian pilot had just started another dog-leg when a Ju 88 swept in to rake the Halifax with cannon fire. Almost immediately the whole of the starboard wing was ablaze; the eight-man crew had to get out — and get out very quickly. Out of the rear escape hatch went F/Sgt S. Hamilton (navigator), P/O W. Kay (mid-upper gunner) and P/O H.V. Palmer (second pilot). As these three airmen floated safely to earth, they had the depressing experience of seeing their Halifax diving steeply and blowing up on the ground with their five comrades still on board. 'V-Victor' crashed at Spellar Hill near Knaresborough in North Yorkshire at 0140 hours.

Nemesis at Dunnington Lodge

At 0200 hours, ARP wardens reported that an aircraft had crashed in the Elvington area, only this time it was one of the Junkers Ju 88G-6 intruder aircraft. This particular night fighter had already been involved in a number of dramatic incidents over East Yorkshire, first attacking 158 Sqn Halifaxes in the Lissett circuit, next targeting a 102 Sqn Halifax as it approached RAF Pocklington, and then strafing the airfield's buildings and bombers on the ground. The Ju 88 had then flown towards York, at a dangerously low height, before making a tight turn to port in preparation for a strafing attack on RAF Elvington. This time, however, the pilot paid the price for his daring and overconfidence, a wing tip clipping a tree and then the aircraft hitting Dunnington Lodge alongside the B1228 before crashing and disintegrating at the nearby Dunnington/Elvington road junction.

So violent was the crash that only two of the four German airmen on board could be identified. They were radar operator *Ofw* Hugo Böker and wireless operator *Fw* Gustav Schmidt. Sadly, as the Ju 88 struck Dunnington Lodge it killed three civilians in the building, Mrs Ellen Moll, her husband Richard and their daughter-in-law Mrs Violet Moll.

Later, it was revealed that the German aircraft which crashed after hitting Dunnington Lodge was a Junkers Ju 88G-6 D5+AX (*Werk Nr* 620028) and that the pilot had been *Hptm* Johann Dreher, *Staffelkapitän* of 13./NJG 3. A most experienced bomber pilot and holder of the *Ritterkreuz* (Knight's Cross), Dreher had only recently transferred to night fighters and had little experience of high speed, low-level flying in the dark. The fourth German to die in the crash was flight engineer *Fw* Martin Bechter.

As a result of the arrival of Dreher's Junkers 88 in the Elvington circuit, Halifax NR229/H7-D of 346 (Guyenne) Sqn had to be diverted away from its Elvington base to RAF Croft in North Yorkshire. As the bomber pulled off the runway a Ju 88 roared in low across the airfield, blazing away with all guns. Thankfully, however, there were no casualties and little damage was done in this daredevil attack.

Minutes later, the crew of 158 Sqn's 'N-Nan' had a hair-raising experience as F/Sgt K.M. Anderson landed their Halifax at Middleton St George, a RCAF Lancaster base in County Durham. Diverted away from RAF Lissett on account of intruder activity and low on fuel, Keith Anderson persuaded the Canadians to switch on their runway lights just long enough for him to land his bomber. In a heavy landing, Anderson's Halifax slewed off the runway, the port undercarriage collapsed, and the aircraft finished up embedded in a soft grassy area alongside the runway. The seven crew members had only just climbed out of the wrecked 'N-Nan' when a Ju 88, clearly vis-

Facts:
The last German aircraft to come down on British soil in World War II was a Junkers Ju 88G-6, which crashed on 4 March 1945 near Elvington in East Yorkshire.

265: *Dunnington Lodge. Dreher's Junkers 88 struck the upper part of this building before plunging to the ground. Most of the wreckage finished up at a road junction just to the left of the nearest car in the distance. It is thought that Dreher mistook the headlights of a passing car for aircraft landing lights and misjudged his height.*

266: *A crashed Junkers Ju 88G, clearly showing the deadly upward firing 'Schräge Musik' ('oblique music', a German term for jazz) cannons behind the cockpit area. (Goss/Rauchbach Archives)*

267 Right: Hptmn *Johann Dreher, pilot of the Junkers 88 which crashed after hitting Dunnington Lodge on Elvington Lane during the early hours of 4 March 1945. (Goss/Rauchbach Archives)*

268 Far right: *The 'Englandblitz' emblem of the Luftwaffe nightfighter force.*

ible in the bright moonlight, came in low across the airfield in an ineffective strafing attack.

The last 4 Group bomber to be attacked on the ground during the *Gisela* operation was Halifax MZ751/ZA-J of 10 Sqn. This aircraft, piloted by F/Lt Brian Davies, had been diverted away from RAF Melbourne and made a safe landing at RAF Leeming at 0200 hours. F/Lt Davies was taxiing his Halifax around the perimeter of the airfield when a low-flying Ju 88 unleashed a stream of cannon shells which exploded across the taxi track in front of the bomber. Then, to the Halifax crew's utter amazement and great admiration, a young WAAF driving a small truck arrived alongside the now stationary aircraft. She collected Davies and his crew and then calmly drove them across the airfield to the Watch Office for de-briefing.

While searching for RAF aircraft and airfields, some of the low-flying Ju 88s had fired their cannon and machine guns at East Yorkshire towns and villages. Here are just a few such incidents as recorded by the ARP during the early hours of 4 March 1945:

> 0110hrs: A German plane machine-gunned Norwood, Beverley and windows at No 4 were broken. A post-box was damaged.
> 0115hrs: Superficial damage caused by cannon shells at Cottingham.
> 0130hrs: Superficial damage caused by cannon shells at Willerby.
> 0135hrs: Cannon shells at Cherry Tree Lane, Beverley. Damage to Nos 35 and 40.
> 0145hrs: Cannon shells fired at Hull Road, Woodmansey. Houses and furniture damaged and also telephone wires.

Cannon shells were also fired into the streets of Hull. Again, there was little damage and no casualties. Also, several small anti-personnel fragmentation bombs were dropped, one cluster fell at High Stonehills Farm to the north of Barmston and another along Gransmoor Road near Lissett. Luckily, however, most of them failed to explode.

By approximately 0230 hours on 4 March 1945 the German night fighters participating in the *Gisela* operation over England had re-crossed the English coast and were heading home. Nationwide, the RAF had lost 24 aircraft (13 Halifaxes, nine Lancasters, one B17 Flying Fortress and one Mosquito) during the Gisela offensive. Nine of the Halifaxes shot down were 4 Group aircraft based in East Yorkshire and another two were training aircraft from 1664 HCU at RAF Dishforth in North Yorkshire. It had been an eventful and damaging night for RAF Bomber Command.

Nor had 3/4 March 1945 been a particularly auspicious night for the Luftwaffe. They had lost 21 of their Junkers Ju 88 long-range night fighters: three crashed in England, four failed to return (believed lost over the North Sea), six crashed on the continent, and another eight crashed after their crews had baled out. Another 12 of the *Gisela* Ju 88s were severely damaged, some in combat, while others were the worse for wear after heavy landings. Many crews had had to bale out over the continent because their aircraft were running out of fuel. One of the Ju 88s with a fuel shortage problem was the aircraft of *Major* B. Ney, *Gruppenkommandeur* of IV./NJG 3, the man who had led the intruder force over East and North Yorkshire. Ney suffered the indignity of having to bale out over northern Germany and the agony of breaking his back on landing. Bertold Ney would never walk again.

157

Where were our fighters?

Three important questions remain with regard to the events of 3/4 March 1945. Why, on a clear moonlit night, were the Halifax air gunners unable to defend their aircraft more adequately against attacks from the Ju 88 night fighters? Why wasn't there a strong RAF night fighter presence over Yorkshire during Gisela? Why did so many Ju 88s fail to return or crash on the continent due to empty fuel tanks?

The first of these questions is easily answered. From the time the bombers received the 'Bandits' alert their air gunners were most vigilant, peering into the bright moonlight for any signs of pursuing night fighters, but the technique used by some of the German pilots made it quite impossible for the RAF gunners to spot an attacker. What happened was that the Ju 88 pilot skilfully manoeuvred his aircraft into a position under a bomber and then fired an oblique cannon, known as *Schräge Musik* ('jazz music') upwards into the bomber's engines, fuel tanks and underbelly.

A lack of RAF night fighter cover over Yorkshire for the returning Halifaxes can be put down to important changes in RAF Fighter Command strategy. During 1944, major night raids on the region by Luftwaffe bombers were considered to be virtually at an end, and so the night fighters which had patrolled the coast from the Tees to the Humber from their bases at Catterick and Scorton were moved elsewhere. At the time of Gisela, the only night fighter squadron left in Yorkshire was 456 (RAAF) Sqn equipped with Mosquito XXXs at RAF Church Fenton. But there was a problem; Fighter command had decided to move 456 Sqn from RAF Church Fenton to RAF Bradwell Bay in Essex. Shortly before 2200 hours on 3 March 1945, the squadron's groundcrew and their equipment had left by train for the Essex coast. Aircraft and their crews were to follow on the morning of 4 March after a squadron 'thrash', a dance with liberal quantities of liquid refreshment in the Officers' Mess.

"The impossible has happened!" is how an entry in 456 Sqn's Operations Record Book succinctly introduces the drama which was about to unfold at RAF Church Fenton during the early hours of 4 March. With enemy intruder aircraft active over East and North Yorkshire, an urgent call came from 12 Group Fighter Command HQ at Watnall at 0100 hours *"... to ask if we could do anything"*.

Although the fighter station no longer had any groundcrew or essential equipment, within a little over one hour five 456 Sqn Mosquitoes were airborne and on the trail of the so far unchallenged German intruders. Regrettably, however, most of the Ju 88 night fighters had by now turned for home and only one of the Mosquitoes made contact with the enemy. This was the aircraft crewed by F/O W.A. McLardy (pilot) and F/O R.A. Woodman (navigator-radar) which was in combat with a Ju 88 off Holderness. Shots were fired by both aircraft but neither scored any hits; contact was then lost.

It had been a chaotic night at RAF Church Fenton, but the small number of 456 Sqn personnel still at the station had certainly lived up to the squadron's motto: *'Press on, regardless'*.

"The British had jammed our radio beacons"

Finally, with regard to Gisela, what explanation can be put forward for the loss of so many of the IV./NJG 3 Ju 88s over the North Sea and in crashes on the continent due to empty fuel tanks? Although deteriorating weather conditions, especially strengthening winds, over the North Sea may have contributed to a hazardous return leg for some of the Ju 88 crews, it is interesting to note a comment made by *Lt* Arnold Döring after he had eventually located an airfield in North Germany:

> *"... the British had jammed our radio beacons so that we could not get a fix on them ... I could not orientate myself".*

From Döring's observation we can reasonably conclude that RAF systems for jamming or re-transmitting German radio navigational systems were most likely responsible for several of the IV/NJG 3 losses at the conclusion of the Gisela operation, 3/4 March 1945.

The last civilian deaths

Between Gisela and the end of the war there were just two further *Fernnachtjäger* intruder operations over East Yorkshire and the Humber. These were, however, very minor attacks and involved just one or two enemy aircraft. First, during the night of 4/5 March 1945, a Junkers Ju 88G-6 of IV./NJG 2, piloted by *Fw* Rudi Morenz, attempted to shoot down a Halifax bomber as it came in to land at RAF Pocklington. The combination of fire from the airfield's light AA guns and the appearance of a Mosquito night fighter quicklyn resulted in Morenz swinging his Ju 88 away from the Pocklington area and heading east over the Yorkshire Wolds to cross the coast near Hornsea and escape out over the North Sea. Morenz returned, however, on 17 March to claim a Lancaster and a Halifax shot down near Pocklington.

The second of these small-scale intruder operations occurred on the night of Saturday 17 March 1945 and resulted in bombs falling on East Yorkshire for the last time in World War Two. Only one aircraft was involved in this final attack of the war; this was a Junkers Ju 88G-6, 4R+MR, piloted by *Ofw* Heinz Hommel of III./NJG 2, and based at Marx in North Germany. Although this was essentially an intruder operation to destroy RAF bombers, Hommel's Ju 88 did carry two AB 500 missile containers, each of which

269 Right: Lt Arnold Doring of 10./NJG 3 who was flying his Ju 88G-6 over East Yorkshire in the early hours of 4 March 1945. He used his upward firing cannon to shoot down two 1664 HCU Halifaxes near Dishforth, before using the nose armament to strafe a train on the East Coast main line and houses in Filey Road, Scarborough causing some damage and wounding one person before returning to base.

270 Far right: The commemorative plaque to the victims of Ofw Heinz Hommel's attack, located on the side of Messrs Boyes' store on Holderness Road in Hull, the site of the old Savoy Cinema.

271: Hommel's logbook records he dropped two AB 500 weapons containers, each holding 37 SD 10A anti-personnel bombs similar to those shown here during his attack on 17 March 1945.

[24] *By a bitter irony, the area around Morrill Street had also witnessed the first civilian deaths caused by bombing in Hull, on 24 August 1940.*

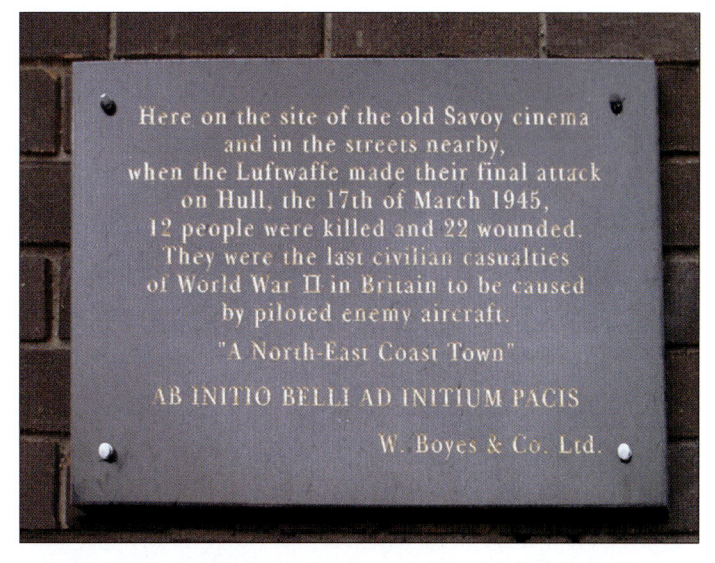

was almost seven feet in length and contained 37 SD 10A anti-personnel fragmentation bombs. When dropped from the aircraft, these containers opened up to release the individual bombs, each of which was 21.5 inches long, 3.4 inches wide and weighed 10kg.

At 2136 hours, air raid sirens sounded across Hull and Holderness after radar stations in the region had detected unidentified aircraft off the Humber. Surprisingly, when Hommel's bombs fell on East Hull fourteen minutes later there were still large numbers of people thronging the streets. The 74 anti-personnel bombs landed on Holderness Road, Morrill Street[24] and Holland Street. Fortunately, most of them fell harmlessly on uninhabited property which had already been wrecked by high explosive bombs, while many others failed to detonate. Sadly, however, one cluster exploded close to the Savoy Cinema on Holderness Road, blasting lethal jagged pieces of shrapnel into a crowd of people walking along the footpath. There were 12 fatalities, including four children, while a thirteenth person was killed inside a house adjacent to another cluster. Another 22 people were seriously injured in the raid. These were the last British casualties of the war to result from an air raid by a piloted aircraft.

To complete his evening's work Hommel then claimed a Lancaster shot down over the Humber at 21.55. In fact only one aircraft was lost in the area that evening, namely Lancaster Mk I NG132/BQ-F2 of 550 Sqn, killing the pilot, F/O A.C. Lockyer of the RNZAF and five of his crew, on their first flight since joining the squadron. Sgt T. Drawbridge was the only survivor. The aircraft crashed at Sunk Island (according to available records at about 1800hrs) which is a good way from Pocklington where Rudi Morenz claimed his two kills. Either Morenz misidentified his location, or the time of the crash was wrongly recorded. If the time is correct, then the interception took place during twilight which seems unlikely — darkness was the necessary cloak of invisibility for the German intruders. On balance it seems more likely that Hommel was the victor.

159

Air Raid on N.E. Town

12 KILLED, 22 IN HOSPITAL

In a north-east town on Saturday night hundreds of people began to leave cinemas to make their way home.

An enemy 'plane flew low over the town and dropped containers of small fragmentation bombs. They fell on a road crowded with pedestrians and traffic, causing a number of casualties, 12 people being killed and 22 admitted to hospital suffering from serious injuries.

Only superficial damage was done to nearby shops and houses. The area is one which has been the target of the enemy on previous occasions, when larger calibre bombs had caused much structural damage.

Quite close to the incident is a first-aid post, but unfortunately this was closed and none of the personnel were on duty. The injured people were taken to another casualty post.

CONGESTED STREET

One of the injured was a prominent local British Legion official who was travelling down in a motor car. A bomb exploded at the rear of the car and he received shrapnel wounds in the thigh and behind the ear. The driver suffered from flying glass.

A 'bus carrying a full load of passengers pulled up and escaped damage and none of the passengers was injured.

A local Press photographer was travelling on the road in his car when he saw a flash in the sky, followed by the noise of several explosions. Later he came across inert figures lying in the road and gave valuable assistance by taking injured children to the casualty post.

The police rendered splendid service and hurried ambulances to the scene, and were ably helped by civilians.

Difficulty was experienced by the civil defence services in getting to the scene. People anxious about families, relatives, and friends, rushed into the street, which was further congested by 'bus and other traffic.

SON'S ESCAPE

Mr and Mrs Martin were returning home after having completed arrangements at a club for a concert to be held in aid of a war comforts fund. An amateur tenor vocalist, Mr Martin and his brother were known as the Martin Brothers. He had composed a popular song "Just tell me the truth." A previous concert had been interrupted, but a sum of £28 had been raised, and Mr Martin's intention was to increase it to £50.

He and his wife were walking home arm-in-arm when they were caught in the shower of bombs.

Their son left a cinema to return home and travelled by 'bus. As he reached the corner of the street, the bombs exploded and he ran into a shelter for safety. He afterwards learned of the fate of his parents who according to family calculations, must have been only a short distance away from him when they were killed. Mr Martin was a lorry driver employed by a local transport contractor. He was a member of a rescue squad and was driving in London during the daylight bombing, carrying supplies to various hospitals. His excertions had an effect upon his health and for a time he had to rest. Mrs. Martin was one of a family of 10, five of whom are serving in H.M. Forces, one in the Navy, and one is in the Woman's Land Army.

TRIED TO SAVE BOY

Mr John Reed (71), a retired docker, lost his life in an attempt to protect a boy. Running from his house, he was crossing a side street when there was a burst of shrapnel. He flung himself on the boy. Both fell and were killed.

Mr Stanley Duncan (21), formerly a clerk in the medical officer's department home on leave for the first time since receiving a commission, was fatally injured.

A mother of month-old twins was killed, as were Mr Walter Coggle (60), and Mr Ollenshaw (49), two boys aged 12, and a girl aged two.

The injured include children from eight to 16 years of age, Mrs Lilian Winter was taken to hospital and her two-year old child was treated at a first-aid post.

Herbert Thorsden, who with his wife, was injured by shrapnel and taken to hospital, was a member of a Home Guard Rifle Club.

REPAIRERS AT WORK

The repair squads were at work the whole of yesterday carrying out temporary repairs to shops and houses. Windows had been blown out and some of the brickwork at the rear of houses was demolished. Armed with mops and pails, women in some terraces were swilling throughout the morning. Some casualties occurred outside these houses.

A cinema in the neighbourhood received only slight damage. The manager said the hall was closed, therefore it was incorrect to state the bombs fell as people were leaving that cinema.-

---

272: *Despite the late date in the war, with victory clearly in sight, Hull was still treated only as 'a north-east town'. Reading this report from a contemporary newspaper it would appear that Hull had ceased to exist. Photos taken of a grim-faced Churchill visiting the city after the 1941 Blitz may indicate that he had some connection with this.*

Right: *This illustration depicts Ofw Heinz Hommel of III./NJG 2 in his Junkers Ju 88G-6, 4R+MR, just after releasing his bombs over East Hull at about 2150 hours on Saturday 17 March 1945. Five minutes later he claimed a Lancaster bomber shot down which crashed at Sunk Island.*

Larger size prints of this illustration suitable for framing are available either from the publisher or direct from:
Aeroprints
113 East End Road
East Finchley
London
N2 0SU
Tel: 0208 444 4510
or visit their website at:
www.aeroprints.co.uk
where a wide variety of aviation prints can be seen.

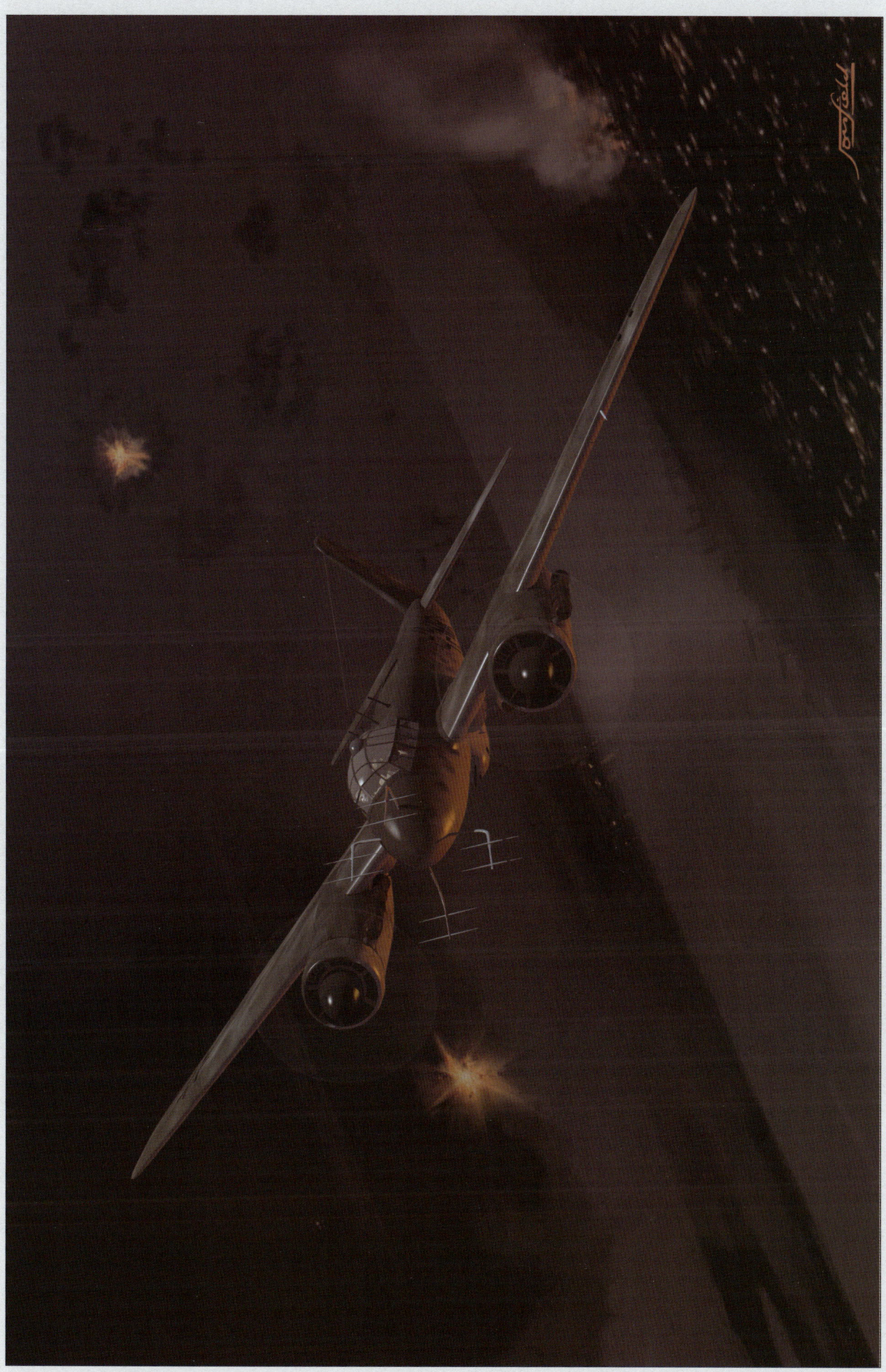

Junkers Ju 188E-1, W.Nr 260175, Z6+GK of 2./KG 66 which crashed near the Humber Lightship off Spurn Head on 2 October 1943 while avoiding flak. No pictures of this specific aircraft are known to exist, so this is a reconstruction based on pictures of other aircraft of the unit.

Arado Ar 234B-2, 8H+BH, of 1.(F)/33, as flown by Oblt Planck on a reconnaissance mission over Hull on 4 April 1945. This was almost certainly the last Luftwaffe mission over East Yorkshire, possibly over the British mainland, in World War II. The Werk Nr is shown as 140474, but is not confirmed. 140466 and 140476 also both flew with 1.(F)/33.

ILLUSTRATIONS NOT TO SAME SCALE

The final flight?

Air raid sirens sounded across Hull and Holderness for the last time on Monday 19 March 1945, but this was a false alarm. There was, however, one more Luftwaffe mission over Hull — at breakfast time on 4 April 1945. This was almost certainly the last flight by a Luftwaffe aircraft over East Yorkshire. So far this has passed unnoticed by historians, probably because the aircraft involved was an Arado Ar 234 jet, 8H+BH, of 1.(F)/33 on a high-altitude reconnaissance mission flown from Wittmundhafen by *Oblt* Planck (now *Professor Emeritus*). As the extract from *Oblt* Planck's logbook shows, there was a great deal of shipping in the docks at the time. The flight was undetected and uneventful, but one questions what possible use it could have had at that late stage of the war.

Counting the cost

In the course of the war, Hull had experienced more than 800 air raid warnings and although bombs had fallen on only about one-tenth of these alerts the results of the Luftwaffe raids were devastating. Approximately 1,200 Hull people were killed in the raids and another 3,000 injured, while more than 86,000 out of 93,000 houses in the city were destroyed or damaged. Furthermore, many factories, schools, churches and shops had been wrecked or badly damaged, and there had been serious disruption to road and rail transport and to port activities. Elsewhere in Great Britain, most people were unaware of Hull's long and terrifying ordeal, for some reason the city only ever being referred to during BBC radio broadcasts and in newspapers as 'a north-east coast town'.

Outside Hull, Bridlington was the East Yorkshire town which suffered the most from Luftwaffe air raids. Bridlington was bombed on 30 occasions as a result of which 100 houses were destroyed or badly damaged, 24 people were killed and another 40 seriously injured. Elsewhere in East Yorkshire, there were fatalities in the Hedon-Bilton area (21), Withernsea (12), Hutton Cranswick (5), Hornsea (4), Pocklington (3), Beverley (2), Roos (2), and one each in Flamborough, Hessle, Aldbrough, Catfoss, Woodmansey, Brough and Patrington.

The air war may have ended for the civilians in East Yorkshire, but for aircrew stationed in the region their air war was far from over. For another month, 4 Group Halifaxes would continue with their bombing campaign against enemy targets. Lives would be risked; some would be lost as operations were carried out against Münster, Hamburg, Nuremberg and the heavily fortified island of Heligoland, which guarded the sea approach to the ports of NW Germany.

During the final phase of the air war against Germany, the emergency landing ground at Carnaby saw plenty of action. Many an RAF and USAAF pilot, flying an aircraft in difficulties, was greatly relieved to

273: This Arado Ar 234B was the first of its type to be captured by the British and was sent to Farnborough for tests. It wears an unusual camouflage, but is otherwise typical of the breed.

274 Below: this extract from Oblt Planck's logbook shows his reconnaissance mission over Hull and the Humber on 4 April 1945. His notes (not shown) of the shipping in Hull docks revealed some 27 vessels there with a gross tonnage of about 119,000 BRT.

163

see that massive runway near Bridlington. On 9 April 1945, there was a remarkable incident at RAF Carnaby which merits a special mention.

As a badly damaged and low on fuel Halifax of 58 Sqn Coastal Command, operating out of RAF Stornoway in the Outer Hebrides, landed with the aid of FIDO at 0620 hours, onlookers at Carnaby were astonished to see an airman hanging down from underneath the bomber's fuselage. Their astonishment quickly changed to grave concern when they realised that, as the aircraft's tail wheel touched down, the airman's head appeared to be scraping along the runway. As the Halifax rolled to a halt and a medical team rushed to the scene, it was discovered that the airman in distress was unconscious but still alive. He had been saved from serious injury by his oxygen mask and goggles, which had protected his face from friction with the ground.

What had happened was that while Halifax 'E-Easy', piloted by F/Lt R.N. Lawson, was attacking German shipping in the Skagerrak off the south coast of Norway, a photo-flash had exploded in the aircraft's bomb bay. A huge hole was blown in the floor of the plane through which the mid-upper gunner, F/Sgt J.F. Smith, had disappeared. As Smith fell through the hole, however, his parachute harness had snagged on a jagged piece of the damaged fuselage. The air gunner was then carried from the coast of Norway to East Yorkshire, about three hours flying time, suspended underneath the Halifax. It was incredible that Frank Smith was unhurt, apart from shock and the effects of exposure, and after 48 hours in RAF Carnaby's Sick Quarters he was able to return to his squadron in Scotland. It had been a miraculous escape for the young Coastal Command air gunner.

The final operation of the war for East Yorkshire's bomber crews came on Wednesday 25 April 1945, with a daylight raid on the heavy coastal gun batteries at Wangerooge, the most easterly of the Frisian Islands. There was great elation at most 4 Group Bomber Command bases as their Halifaxes touched down for the last time after action over enemy territory, but there was sadness at RAF Holme-on-Spalding Moor when two 76 Sqn aircraft failed to return, lost in a mid-air collision over the target area, and at RAF Elvington where 347 Sqn had lost one of its bombers, shot down by heavy flak. Of the 21 airmen on board the three Halifaxes which failed to return to East Yorkshire there was only one survivor, P/O G.W. Lawson, one of the 76 Sqn pilots.

It was so sad that 20 young airmen had lost their lives so close to the end of hostilities in the European theatre of war. All told, more than 55,000 airmen were killed and another 10,000 were shot down and captured while flying with Bomber Command in World War Two. Such was the high price paid by the aircrew of Bomber Command — most of them in their late 'teens and early twenties — for their courage, commitment and tenacity.

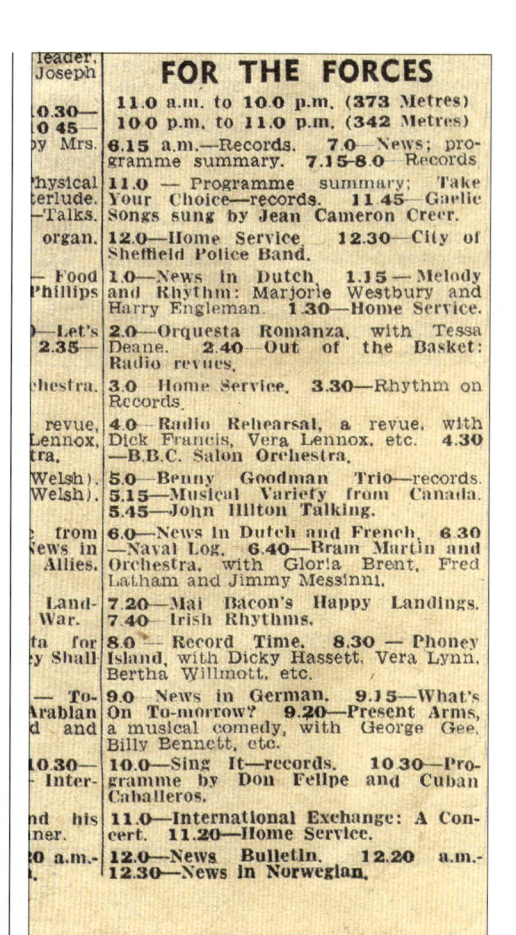

275: A typical wartime day's radio programmes, especially for the Forces. Apart from noting the numerous foreign language news broadcasts to the various Allies, it is probably true to say not much air time is given over to Gaelic songs these days.

276: Many advertisements of the time seem to be concerned about what 'a man' should or should not do. This one features a long-forgotten radio announcer and the benefits of Reckitt's Pine Bath Cubes. What the present Advertising Standards Agency would make of the 'dip in the Fountain of Youth' claim could be interesting!

Ship losses in the Humber and off the East Yorkshire coast due to enemy action

1939
10/9	SS *Goodwood*	Off Flamboro' Head	M
21/10	SS *Orsa*	"	M
22/10	SS *Whitemantle*	Off Withernsea	M
30/10	ML 109	Humber	M
4/11	SS *Canada*	Off Spurn Head	M
21/11	SS *Geraldus*	Off Sunk LV	M
24/11	SS *Mangalore*	Off Spurn Head	M
25/11	ML 111	"	M
26/11	SS *Pilsudski*	Humber	M
28/12	ST *Resercho*	Off Flamboro' Head	M

1940
29/1	SS *Stanburn*	Off Flamboro' Head	A/C
23/2	HMS *Benvolio*	Humber	M
10/5	SS *Henry Woodall*	Off Withernsea	M
16/8	SS *City of Birmingham*	Off Spurn	M
7/9	ST *Salacon*	"	M
9/9	HMS *Dervish*	Humber	M
12/9	SS *Gothic*	Off Spurn Head	M
17/10	FV *Albatros*	Humber	M
14/10	MS *Reculver*	Off Spurn Head	M
25/10	ST *Windsor*	"	M
25/10	SD *Carlton*	"	M
24/11	HMS *Gael*	"	M
28/11	HMS *Manx Prince*	Humber	M
28/11	SS *Sagacity*	Off Sunk LV	M
28/11	SS *Sheaf Field*	Off Spurn Head	M
29/11	HMS *Calverton*	"	M

1941
22/1	HMS *Luda Lady*	Humber	M
22/1	HMS *St. Cyrus*	"	M
4/2	SS *Gwynwood*	"	M
16/2	ST *Thomas Deas*	Off Spurn Head	M
26/2	*Monarch* (Lighter)	Hull	M
26/2	*Brakelu* (Lighter)	"	M
27/2	HMS *Remillo*	Humber	M
18/3	SS *Daphne II*	"	E Boat
20/3	HMS *Gloaming*	"	M
20/3	FV *Joan Margaret*	"	M
29/3	ST *Kimberley*	Off Flamboro' Head	A/C
31/3	HMS *Lord Selborne*	"	M
3/4	HMS *Bahram*	"	M
11/4	HMS *Yorkshire Belle*	"	M
11/4	HMS *Othello*	"	M
15/4	MV *Aquila*	Hull	A/C
4/5	SS *Royston*	Humber	A/C
7/5	HMS *Susarion*	"	A/C
7/5	SB *Ril Ida*	Hull	A/C
8/5	HMS *Silicia*	Humber	M
8/5	SB *Delite*	Hull	A/C
8/5	SB *Ladore*	"	A/C
8/5	SB *Whitakers No. II*	"	A/C
8/5	Ketch *Welcome Home*	Hull	A/C
12/5	SS *Fowberry Tower*	Humber	A/C
10/6	HMS *Pintail*	Humber	M
10/6	SS *Royal Scot*	"	M
4/7	HMS *Akranes*	Bridlington Bay	A/C
23/7	SB *Omfleet*	Hull	M
6/9	HMS *Strathborve*	Humber	M
7/9	ST *Ophir II*	Off Spurn Head	M
3/11	SS *Marie Dawn*	Humber	A/C
15/11	SS *Corhampton*	"	A/C
7/12	SS *Welsh Prince*	"	M
8/12	ST *Lord Shrewsbury*	Humber	M
12/12	SS *Dromore Castle*	"	M
21/12	SS *Benmacdhui*	Off Spurn	M
26/12	*Henriette* (Free French)	Humber	M
27/12	SS *J. B. Paddon*	Off Hornsea	A/C

1942
30/1	HMS *Loch Alsh*	Humber	A/C
2/2	HMS *Cape Spartel*	"	A/C
2/2	HMS *Cloughton Wyke*	"	A/C

1943
3/10	HMS *Meror*	Humber	M

1944
13/2	HMS *Cap d'Antifer*	Humber	E/B

Note:
This list shows mainly British-registered vessels, with only the more important foreign-registered ships to be lost in the area. It does not show the large number of other vessels which were damaged by enemy action, but not sunk.
In this book the focus is upon the operations of enemy minelaying and anti-shipping aircraft off the Humber and the East Yorkshire coast (which caused numerous casualties) and the British countermeasures, but in fact the vast majority of several thousand mines laid in the North Sea were placed there by German U-boats and naval surface vessels.

Abbreviations

FV	Fishing Vessel
HMS	His Majesty's Ship (Royal Navy)
ML	Motor Launch (Royal Navy)
MV	Motor Vessel
SB	Sailing Barge
SD	Steam Drifter
SS	Steamship
ST	Steam Trawler
M	Mine
A/C	Aircraft

277: *Although mostly based in more western parts of Yorkshire, it was not unusual for numbers of Canadian airmen and their aircraft to seek emergency refuge in East Yorkshire after some of the more harrowing bombing missions. This is Ron Craven and his crew from 408 Sqn, based at Linton-on-Ouse north-west of York. Their Halifax Mk VII PN230/EQ-V, Vicky the Vicious Virgin, took part in 16 missions with the same crew before being replaced by a Lancater.*

278: *As the war shuddered to a stop, the once-mighty Luftwaffe was reduced to near impotence as the fuel supplies ran out, leaving many serviceable aircraft sitting uselessly on their airfields, no longer able to menace the RAF bombers, either over Germany or the British bases. Here Junkers Ju 88 and Messerschmitt Bf 110 nightfighters, still fitted with 'reindeer antlers' antenna, await scrapping.*

279: *By May 1945 the only German aircraft flying over Britain were those under test by the victors, but another form of warfare had also been waged from East Yorkshire — over the air waves. With several 500ft high masts and 800kw transmitters, BBC Ottringham was the most powerful radio station in Europe when it was completed in 1943, specifically to beam messages to the Resistance movements. Covering 95 acres, it was closed in 1959 and subsequently demolished — by a German ex-prisoner of war.*

280 Above: Halifax III NA222/C8-O of 640 Sqn awaits scrapping with many others in the post-war run-down. NA222 crashed on the night of 18-19 March 1945 and was sent to 29 Maintenance Unit for repair, but was later sold for scrap. The aircraft wears the highly visible tail markings applied to 4 Group's Halifaxes as they went over to daylight tactical bombing in support of the Allied invasion forces in Europe.

EPILOGUE
Emptying the bomb dumps

On Monday 7 May 1945, news came through of Germany's unconditional surrender to the Allies, with a result that British Prime Minister Winston S. Churchill and the new United States President, Harry S. Truman, decided that Tuesday 8 May should be a public holiday and celebrated as VE (Victory in Europe) Day.

At East Yorkshire's airfields, the celebrations started during the night of 7 May, with the beer flowing freely and all the popular wartime songs being sung with great gusto. Some airfields also held spectacular pyrotechnic displays, with flares, signal rockets and Very Lights being substituted for fireworks. In his book *One Wing High*, former 158 Sqn navigator Harry Lomas tells the story of how at RAF Lissett one group of airmen wanted to highlight the occasion with the most dramatic plan of them all; to set fire to one particular Halifax which had always been plagued with technical problems. Somehow, however, news of this master plan leaked out and someone in a position of power made sure that it would not come to fruition; RAF police dog teams patrolled the Halifaxes throughout the night!

RAF personnel also celebrated that night at the radar stations in the region; at Staxton Wold, Bempton, Easington and Patrington; at Catfoss's Central Gunnery School, Carnaby's emergency landing ground, and at the Air-Sea Rescue station in Bridlington Harbour.

On VE Day itself, many groundcrew, aircrew and airfield administrators left their stations to join in the celebrations in the pubs and streets of neighbouring villages and towns. There, the flags, banners and streamers provided a rich splash of colour, so welcome after the grey days of wartime. There were street parties, parades, bonfires, and church bells rang out across the land — not to warn of enemy invasion but to signal and welcome peace in Europe.

For the bomber crews it was a time of mixed emotions. Their lives had been on the line every time they had taken off on an operation. Also, they had frequently witnessed scenes of utmost horror; of bombers blowing up or suddenly becoming diving infernos, after being hit by flak or gunfire from night fighters, and of aircraft colliding and spiralling down. Harry Lomas, veteran of more than 20 operations from RAF Lissett, summed up the feelings of many of the bomber men on VE Day with the following poignant words:

"...*the festivities held a measure of restraint. The general feeling of thankfulness at having lived to see this day were inevitably tempered with thoughts of those who had not survived, especially those with whom we had been personally involved.*"

Throughout the rest of May there was much flying to be done from the former Bomber Command airfields in East Yorkshire. Daily, Halifax after Halifax would take off with their bomb bays full of bombs of various sizes. The routine was for the aircraft to fly out over Flamborough Head and when about 90 miles out over the North Sea to drop their unarmed bombs into a designated area of deep water. Soon, the bomb dumps in the region would be empty.

Next, in June, came the disposal of the Halifax bombers themselves, followed by a conversion programme for aircrew staying with their squadrons in preparation for flying new types of aircraft under the auspices of RAF Transport Command. By now, the closely-knit, seven-man crews had been broken up as most Australian, Canadian and New Zealand crew members had left their squadrons, and the services of bomb aimers and air gunners were no longer required. One squadron, 640, had already been disbanded, its Halifaxes being transferred to 466 Sqn at RAF Driffield. Before the squadron left RAF Leconfield, 640's Halifaxes carried out a memorable flypast over the nearby market town of Beverley, whose public houses had provided precious moments of relaxation for 640's battle-weary bomber crews. Then, on the day of the transfer of aircraft to RAF Driffield, 640's pilots flew their Halifaxes out to sea before coming in over Flamborough Head and making a spectacular, low-level pass in formation close to the seafront at Bridlington. Finally, they flew low over the emergency landing ground at Carnaby before bringing in their Halifaxes for the last time.

Before East Yorkshire's Halifaxes were finally disposed of, there were several flights, popularly known as 'Cook's Tours', over some of Bomber Command's most heavily bombed targets in Germany. For the former bomber men this was another occasion filled with mixed emotions. As they overflew such cities as Berlin, Cologne and Essen they could not help but be shocked by what they could see below — scenes of utter devastation. Any sensitive feelings aroused by these scenes were tempered somewhat by the knowledge of what had been done to British towns and cities by the bombers and missiles of the Third Reich.

By early July 1945, practically all of the former 4 Group Bomber Command Halifaxes had been flown from their East Yorkshire bases to airfields at High Ercall in Shropshire or Clifton on the outskirts of York. From there, most of them would go for scrap, while a relatively small number would enter the commercial market. One Halifax which had a temporary reprieve was 158 Sqn's Halifax III LV907/NP-F, *Friday the 13th*. This aircraft, a veteran of 128 operations from RAF Lissett, was put on display in London's Oxford Street during the summer of 1945. Then, Friday too was scrapped with only the bomber's operations tally panels — a hand-painted bomb symbol representing each operation flown — being preserved for posterity in the Royal Air Force Museum at Hendon.

Of the Halifaxes converted for civil transport, one had flown 51 operations from East Yorkshire. This was Halifax III NR 169/HD-T, *Waltzing Matilda*, of 466 (RAAF) Sqn and based at RAF Driffield. Appropriately, this aircraft was flown to Australia for civil operations but was eventually scrapped in 1948.

The only East Yorkshire airfields to retain their Halifaxes were Driffield, with 466 (RAAF) Sqn's Halifax VIs and Elvington with the Halifax IIIs of 346 and 347 (Free French) squadrons. Elsewhere in the region, airfields were seeing the arrival of Short Stirlings, Consolidated B-24 Liberators and Douglas C-47 Dakotas of RAF Transport Command. After a period of crew conversion training, it was on to the Middle East or Far East for East Yorkshire's former bomber squadrons. There, they would be primarily involved in troop transporting operations.

On 6 August 1945, a USAAF Boeing B-29 Superfortress named *Enola Gay* dropped an atomic bomb on the Japanese city of Hiroshima. Three days later, B-29 *Bockscar* dropped a second atomic bomb, this time on the Japanese city of Nagasaki. Such was

281: Halifax III LV907 Friday the 13th *on display on Selfridges' roof in London in summer 1945. The artwork on this battered original aircraft bears comparison with that on the re-constructed Halifax in the Yorkshire Air Museum at Elvington.*

the extensive devastation of the two cities that it came as no surprise when, on 15 August, it was announced that Japan had surrendered. After six long years of death, destruction, hardship and suffering, World War II was at last over.

In East Yorkshire, world peace signalled the end for the region's three remaining Halifax squadrons. In September 1945, 466 (RAAF) Sqn was disbanded at RAF Driffield, on 25 October 346 (Guyenne) Sqn left RAF Elvington to be followed soon afterwards by its sister squadron at Elvington, 347 (Tunisie) Sqn. These two Free French squadrons were allowed to fly their Halifaxes home to France in recognition of their brave and committed contribution to RAF Bomber Command's air war against Germany. Sadly, however, one 347 Sqn aircraft, L8-Q, crashed near the village of Deighton, four miles south-west of Elvington, shortly after takeoff; two of the crew were killed.

Within about one year of the war ending, only four of East Yorkshire's former Bomber Command airfields remained open, those at Driffield, Elvington, Full Sutton and Leconfield. Apart from the closure of most of East Yorkshire's bomber airfields, the Heavy Conversion Unit at Riccall was also shut down, as was the vast emergency landing ground at Carnaby, the fighter station at Hutton Cranswick, and the Central Gunnery School at Catfoss. Some of East Yorkshire's airfields were given a new lease of life, as Thor nuclear missile sites, during the Cold War period of the late 1950s and early 1960s, but that is another story.

282: Cocooned Halifaxes of 10 Sqn stand forlornly at RAF Melbourne as they await disposal.

Facing the enemy

It was the late summer in 1945 and we were on our way back to Hull after a day at Aldburgh, a small village on the Holderness coast.

Mal and me had enjoyed ourselves, climbing the mud cliffs and playing football on the beach, on the areas where mines had been cleared, with a local lad who lived with his grandma on the cliff top, called, funnily enough, Cliff. We were fairly exhausted after pedalling half way home against a strong head wind, so we stopped for a rest and sat on a wall at the corner of a farmyard.

After a few minutes we saw two German prisoners-of-war, in their green patched uniforms, walking down the road towards us.

We kept a forced conversation going to cover our uneasiness.

"Goot afternoon".

"Good afternoon".

At last I was face to face with a German, in fact two Germans, and I remembered my secret vow that I made to myself four years previously as an angry eleven-year old.

One prisoner was a small dark man wearing army spectacles, the other one was tall and blond with pale blue eyes. A typical Kraut I thought to myself.

"You haff been cycle riding?" *the typical Kraut asked.*

He could speak very good English and we started talking together, and we learnt that they worked at the farm nearby. I asked them when they expected to be repatriated back to Germany. The blond German's voice faltered:

"I vish if I can to stay in England as my vife and two boys were killed in ze raids on Koln".

My heart went out to this man who had lost his family and was a prisoner in an alien land and from that moment my hatred was blunted.

John-Cottrell Smith's diary

169

283: Looking east-north-east along what was the emergency landing ground at Carnaby. It is now an industrial estate.

284: A Sea King helicopter from RAF Leconfield on exercise with Filey's two lifeboats during Filey RNLI's Lifeboat Day, 3 August 2002. Piloted by F/Lt Martyn Williams, the helicopter hovers over the offshore lifeboat with coxswain Malcolm Johnson at the helm. Other crew members in the Sea King were winchman F/Lt Mark Vickery, F/Lt Peter Binstead (co-pilot) and Sgt James Lyne (radar operator).

285: One of the attractions in the Yorkshire Air Museum at Elvington is this re-constructed Halifax which carries the nose artwork of the most famous of East Yorkshire's World War II bombers, Friday the 13th.

Facts:

East Yorkshire based bombers took part in nine raids on Berlin, losing 92 Halifaxes (7.8% of those dispatched) in the process and 487 men. 226 became prisoners; four evaded.

10 Sqn (Melbourne) went on eight Berlin raids. 10 aircraft lost.

76 Sqn (Holme-on-Spalding Moor) went on eight Berlin raids. Five aircraft lost, one crashed.

77 Sqn (Elvington) went on seven Berlin raids. 15 aircraft lost, one crashed. Suffered the highest casualty rate of 4 Group.

78 Sqn (Breighton) went on seven Berlin raids. 12 aircraft lost, one crashed.

102 Sqn (Pocklington) went on seven Berlin raids. 13 aircraft lost, three crashed.

158 Sqn (Lissett) went on eight Berlin raids. 15 aircraft lost, one crashed.

466 (Australian) Sqn (Leconfield) went on six Berlin raids. Seven aircraft lost.

640 Sqn (Leconfield) went on five Berlin raids. Two aircraft lost, three crashed.

Postscript

Today, some 60 years on from the events described in this book, there is still great interest in those distant wartime days. From former RAF personnel and their families, from local people who have their own personal memories of the air war over East Yorkshire in World War Two, and from young people who have heard about 'the war' from older relatives.

Many of the RAF personnel based in East Yorkshire between 1939 and 1945 have re-visited the region, some on a regular basis, to attend reunions and memorial services or simply to see again the places which had become their homes during the war years. Some have travelled from Australia, New Zealand, Canada, South Africa, France and Poland. Many have been disappointed to discover that their former airfield no longer exists – some have been returned to agriculture, as at Catfoss, Hutton Cranswick and Lissett, while others have had industrial estates built within their perimeters, as is the case at Carnaby and Holme-on-Spalding Moor. Part of what was RAF Pocklington is also now an industrial estate, although the former Bomber Command airfield retains a link with flying in that the Wolds Gliding Club is based their. Breighton also has a flying club, plus a collection of vintage aircraft. Any ex-77 Sqn airmen returning to Full Sutton will find that a prison now stands on their former bomber base.

Across at Leconfield, most of the former RAF fighter/bomber airfield has been taken over by the Army School of Mechanical Transport where soldiers are trained to drive a variety of vehicles. The RAF retains control of the rest of the airfield, which is the home of 202 Sqn's 'E' Flight, a SAR (Search and Rescue) unit flying Sea King HAR 3 helicopters. Men and women who crew these aircraft do a fantastic job and their rescue operations, over both land and sea, have saved many lives. Their flying skills and superb professionalism can often be witnessed by the general public as they carry out exercises with local lifeboats and coastguards.

Up the A164, things are very quiet now at what was RAF Driffield. The runways and control tower were demolished several years ago, but the four hangars and most of the buildings in the south-east corner of the airfield are still there. Directly in front of the old Station HQ building stands a memorial to the fourteen people who lost their lives following the Luftwaffe raid on the bomber station, 15 August 1940. Unveiled at a ceremony on 19 August 1990, this memorial is a poignant reminder of what happened at RAF Driffield on that fateful summer's afternoon during the Battle of Britain.

One airfield in the region which is no longer used by the RAF but which remains very much alive is Elvington which now houses the Yorkshire Air Museum, one the most popular tourist attractions in the region. With its restored control tower and fine collection of aircraft, vehicles, weapons and RAF memorabilia, it is an excellent living memorial to the Bomber Command airmen who flew on operations against the enemy in World War Two. Just inside the main gate, there is a memorial to 77 Sqn personnel who lost their lives during the war, while in nearby Elvington village one can see a memorial to the Free French airmen of 346 (Guyenne) and 347 (Tunisie) squadrons who failed to return from operations during the final year of the war. Elvington's very long runway, extended to around 10,000 feet for use by United States nuclear bombers in the 1950s, is still there and is often used by enthusiastic individuals attempting various land speed records.

An East Yorkshire RAF station which played such an important part in the defence of the North of England during the war years, RAF Staxton Wold, is still operational today, although much less conspicuous on the Wolds skyline than its World War Two predecessor. Since the reorganisation of local government in 1974 the radar station is now in North Yorkshire.

Some former RAF personnel who have returned to the region over the years have done so for a very special personal reason. This is why Arthur Tait, former rear gunner with 158 Sqn at RAF Lissett, was in the Elvington area on 18 June 1993. We have already seen how Arthur had been close to death after Bill Strachan's *Krazy Kate* was badly shot up by a Junkers 88 in the Lissett circuit early on 4 March 1945. To an outsider, it seems quite incredible that Arthur was in the Elvington area to pay his respects to the man who almost killed him on that Sunday morning, Johann Dreher, the German pilot who was dead within minutes of inflicting such terrible injuries on Arthur Tait.

Outside Dunnington Lodge alongside the B1228 road to Elvington village, Arthur met up with a former Luftwaffe crewman, Herbert Thomas, who had flown as a navigator with 2./NJG 2. The two former adversaries were there to lay wreaths at the unveiling of a memorial to the seven people – four German airmen and three local civilians – who had been killed when Johann Dreher's Ju88 crashed into Dunnington Lodge on 4 March 1945. At the simple ceremony, Arthur Tait was representing the RAF Air Gunners' Association while Herbert Thomas was there on behalf of the Luftwaffe Nightfighters' Association. For Arthur Tait, the occasion was a time for compassion, not one for gloating, argument or recrimination.

John Goldby DFC, who had served with 78 and 640 squadrons in World War Two also had a very personal reason for visiting Filey in the summer of 2000. John had been the bomb aimer on board the burning Halifax bomber which ditched in Filey Bay on 11 December 1942. When John arrived in Filey on 11 July 2000, it was the first time that he had been in the town since that memorable December evening in 1942. It was a very special, personal moment for

171

John to look out across the bay to where his Halifax had ditched off Bempton Cliffs, and to see where its aircrew had been brought ashore at Coble Landing. While in Filey, John met four local men – Dick and Jim Haxby, David Baker and Bob Watkinson – who had all seen the crippled Halifax crossing the coast at Filey and then dipping down to the sea. Before coming to Filey, John and Jean Goldby had been in Beverley for a reunion of former members of 640 Sqn, an event which included a visit to the squadron's wartime airfield at Leconfield and to the squadron's memorial in the grounds of St Mary's Church at Beverley.

Similarly, former RAF pilot Peter French returned to the scene of his personal wartime drama on Saturday 29 July 2000. Peter was the pilot of the Airspeed Oxford, lost in dense fog over East Yorkshire before making a hair-raising forced landing at East Leys Farm, Grindale, on 16 January 1944. After revisiting the field in which it is thought he landed on that remarkable Sunday in 1944, Peter was taken on a flight over the area by a pilot from the British Skysports Paracentre, which operates from an adjacent field. As they recreated the final minutes of Peter's wartime flight, flying in from the North Sea over the mighty chalk cliffs along the north side of Flamborough Head, mist was rapidly descending on the area, just as it did on that winter's afternoon in January 1944.

Finally, on a cold and windy Sunday morning in September 2001, I attended the annual 158 Sqn memorial service held in Lissett churchyard. It was essentially a service of remembrance, to remember not just the 851 airmen who had lost their lives while serving with 158 in World War Two but also former members of the squadron who had died in peacetime. It was noticeable while listening to former pilot H.N. 'Bluey' Mottershead DFC reading the Roll of Honour – a list of ex-158 Sqn personnel who had passed on since the last service and reunion – that every person who had served with the squadron in whatever capacity was being remembered. The list of names included aircrew, groundcrew, air controllers, WAAF's… no one had been overlooked. The survivors, wearing their medals with pride, had come from far and wide. Some were very old and frail now, but remained undeterred by the bitterly cold wind blowing across the East Yorkshire countryside. The service was moving, but so were the cries of recognition as old comrades met up once again, more than half a century on from their grim wartime days at RAF Lissett. I was an intruder in their midst, yet felt privileged to be in such company and to experience the strong feeling of comradeship which permeated the proceedings.

The service at Lissett was typical of squadron association ceremonies which are held up and down the country every year. Whatever the squadron, whatever the command, the feelings of everyone present at such gatherings are best summed up in four words: *"we will remember them".*

We should also remember the innocents caught up in the ferocity of war from the air. These were the civilians who lost their lives as a result of air raids, and a special thought for the children who would never live long enough to understand the meaning of the word 'Peace'.

286: The RAF Memorial at Catfoss which was generously donated by Robinson's Builders Merchants who now occupy part of the site.

287 Below left: Arthur Tait (left) former 158 Sqn rear gunner, with Herbert Thomas, ex-Luftwaffe nightfighter observer, seen at the memorial outside Dunnington Lodge dedicated to the seven people killed there early on 4 March 1945. (York Evening Press)

288 Below: Together for the last time. Old warriors George Tuoby (left) and Harry Lomas who served in the same 158 Sqn Halifax in World War II. They are shown at Lissett after the memorial service on 9 September 2001. Sadly Harry died the following March.

289 Right: Retribution III. The ruins of the Reichstag in Berlin, late 1945. The city was visited nine times by bombers from East Yorkshire.

East Riding Airfields in 1945

- ● Bomber airfield
- ● Fighter airfield
- ● Training airfield (Catfoss)
- ▲ Emergency landing ground (Carnaby)
- ◆ Heavy Conversion Unit (Riccall)
- ✕ No 4 Elementary Flying Training School (Brough)
- ★ Bomb storage field (Cottam)
- ✚ Air Sea Rescue station (Bridlington)
- ❖ Radar station
- ❖ Radar station (under Royal Navy control)
- ▼ V-1 impact point

INDEX

Entries in **bold** are illustrations

Evacuees 6, **19**

LUFTWAFFE UNITS
1.(F)/33: **162**, 163
1.(F)/123 98, 149
1.(F)/Aufkl.Gr 124: 32
KG 1: 92
KG 100: 138, **140**
KG 2: **100**, 101, **103**, 104, 110, 112, 113, 119, **120, 121, 122, 126**, 128, 129, 132, **134**, 138
KG 4: 27, **30**, **91**
KG 26: **24**, 54, 66, **76**, **78**
KG 3: 28
KG 30: **30**, 32, **34**, 39, **43**, **44**, 49, **55**, **57**, **58**, 59, **60-62**, 63, 65-68, **69**, **70**, 71, 72, **73**, **75**, 90, 138
KG 4: 27, 28, 35, 71, 98
KG 40: 113
KG 53: 90, 92, 146
KG 54: 138
KG 55: 78, 92, **97**, 101
KG 66: 133, 138, **162**
KG 77: 90, 106
KGr 106: **77**, 95, 104, **105**, **108**
Kü.Fl.Gr 406: **23**, **25**
Kü.Fl.Gr 506: 110
NJG 2: 67, 148, 158, **161**
NJG 3: **148**, 156, 157, 158
ZG 76: 54, 66

NAMES
Abel, *Uffz* Georg 36
Agnew, F/O R. 138
Alderson, Thomas Hopper 59, 67, **69**, 71
Allison, Sgt J.W. 35
Anderson, Alfred William 67
Anderson, F/Sgt K.M. 149, **150**, 156
Apitz, *Fw* Helmuth 32
Appleby, Ken 50
Ash, LAC B. 58
Askew, Sgt R.E. 127
Atkinson, Eric 50
Auernhammer, Ofw 90
Bachmann, *Oblt* Werner 63
Bailey, Sgt G.E. 114
Baker, David 115
Bamford, Sgt W. 114
Banister, Sgt T.H. 54
Baumann, Oblt 90
Baumbach, *Lt* Werner 66
Beazley, P/O H.J.S. 35
Bechter, *Fw* Martin 156
Beguin, Lt 104, 109
Beisser, *Ofw* Engelbert 101
Bell, F/O J.S. **28**
Bellof, *Lt* Rudolf 95
Bellringer, Charles 142
Benn, Sgt G.W. 54, **56**
Berridge, Sgt H.W.W. **54**
Bertenshaw, P/O H. 154
Beubler, *Lt* Gunther 133
Beuting, *Fw* Harald 95
Beveridge, P/O 104, 109
Bihr, *Fw* Rudolf 65
Bines, P/O C.A. 138
Bintley, W/C Bruce **113**
Blackwell, Sgt H.B. 139
Blake, Robert 46
Bleek, *Fw* Hans 110
Blome, *Lt* Werner 95
Böker, *Ofw* Hugo 156

Böning, *Uffz* Heinrich 129
Boy, *Lt* Werner 104, 105
Bradshaw, F/Lt C.J. 120
Bradshaw, J.W.H. 49
Bradshaw, Mrs Joyce 127
Bradshaw, Sgt 104
Bradshaw, Ted 32, 63, 127
Bray, W.S. 'Billy' 141
Brewster, P/O J. **28**
Bright, Sydney 120, **126**
Brimble, Sgt John **62**
Brockless, George **51**
Brownlie, P/O I.M.R. 40, 52
Bullen, F/Sgt V. 154
Bunch, F/O D.C. 120
Burnard, F/Sgt F.P. 32, **52**
Cameron, F/Sgt D.C. 132
Cammish, William 'Codge' **117**
Cammish, Frank 'Tosh' **117**
Cappleman, Geoffrey 115
Cardwell, Mrs Eveline 35
Carter, P/O P.E.G. 46
Casson, P/O Lionel 'Buck' **42**, **52**
Chalupa, P/O S.J. 68, 70, 71
Cheshire, Leonard 27, 50, **142**
Chunn, Sgt 92
Churchill, Winston S. 35, **36**, **37**, 39, 40, 68, 99, 167
Clarke, Sgt Harry T. **127**
Clay, Mary 67
Clay, Mrs 67
Clay, PC Percival 67
Clay, Rachael 67
Cockburn, Dr Robert 142
Coleman, Christopher 95
Coleman, Sgt G.E. 114
Colley, Brian 63
Colley, PC James 63
Colwe, *Uffz* Hans-Ulrich 129, **130**
Comrie, F/Sgt W.P. 130
Cornelius, *Oblt* Alfred 112
Cooper, W/O L. **150**
Corre, F/O J.H. 138
Cottrell-Smith, John 17, 80, 83, 86, 168
Court, Rodney 115
Coutts, F/O D.C.F. 148
Coutts, P/O Desmond 50
Cowles, F/O G.H. 128
Cox, Sgt 98
Cunningham, F/Lt John 'Cat's-Eyes' 100
Davies, F/Lt Brian 157
Davies, P/O A.G. 148
Decker, *Gefr* Hermann 92
Dennis, F/O W.R. 145
Diamond, Dr David 94
Dickson, Sgt J.S. 127
Dietsch, *Ofw* 92
Dixon, F/Sgt G.W. 154
Donder, *Fw* Otto 95
Doorly, P/O E. 109
Döring, *Lt* Arnold 158, **159**
Downes, P/O J.H. **103**, 104, 106
Drawbridge, Sgt T. 159
Dreher, *Hptm* Johann 156, **157**, 171
Dundas, John 41
Dundas, P/O Hugh 'Cocky' 32, 41, 46, **52**
Dupee, Sgt O.A. 54
Dymock, Sgt J.M. 112
Eagleton, S/Ldr T.E. **147**
Ehemann, *Gefr* Arno 132
Ellston, Mr & Mrs 92
Elsdon, F/O Thomas 44
Ender, *Fw* Gerhard 92
Erber, *Ofw* Karl 101
Ernst, *Ofw* Rudolf 28, **30**
Etherington, Inspector 35
Evers, *Uffz* Werner 49, **61**, 63
Fairbanks, S/Ldr David 149

Felde, *Hptm* Hans 149
Ferry, P/O 101
Fewster, Ernest 99
Fischer, *Uffz* Albert 133
Fitzsimmons, Sgt 98
Folkes, F/O Thomas 24
Fouracre, Able Seaman Percy 133
French, F/Lt Peter **136**, 172
Fridel, *Uffz* 92
Friedrich, *Ofw* Heinz 32
Fruth, *Uffz* Friedrich 127
Fuchs, *Uffz* Robert 129
Furcht, *Lt* Helmut 28
Furse, F/O D.C. **103**, 104, 106
Fussnecker, *Fw* Otto 104
Gabriel, Helmut **130**
Gaddes, F/O J.M. 152
Galbraith, Sgt T.R. 114
Gates, Ernest 59
George VI, HRH **36**
Gillam, F/Lt D. **46**, **52**
Gobel, *Gefr* Johann 63
Goddard, F/Lt 54
Goldby, Sgt J.L. 5, 114, **116**, 171
Grayson, F/Sgt R. 152
Gregory, Sgt 67
Griffin, Sgt J.J. 46
Griffiths, Capt G.C. 53
Grimstone, LAC J. 58
Günther, *Uffz* Helmut 101
Gutow, *Fw* Bernard 65
Habel, *Gefr* Herbert 32
Hacker, *Uffz* Otto 104
Hahn, *Fw* Hans 148
Hallowes, Sgt James 24
Hamilton, F/Sgt S. 156
Harland, Mr 68
Harnett, F/O T.P. 54
Harris, Air Marshal Sir Arthur 101, 110
Hartel, *Ofw* Martin 28
Haussner, *Oblt* Rolf 113
Haxby, James 115, **117**
Haxby, Richard 115, **117**
Hayward, Gordon 62
Head, F/O G.M. 54
Hedler, *Oblt* Helmut 101
Hefele, *Oberstlt* Hans **30**
Heir, *Fw* Heinz 74
Hellyer, F/Lt R. 46
Henneske, *Fw* Georg 63
Hildrew, Clara 39
Hill, P/O A.M. 112
Hill, Sgt 130
Hitler, Adolf 38, 149
Hodgkinson, Sgt A.J. 54
Hoffman, *Ofw* Alfred 90, **94**
Hogan, F/Sgt P. 154
Hommel, *Ofw* Heinz 158, **161**
Hopewell, Sgt J. 49, **52**, 58, 62
Hopfer, *Fw* 90
Howard, Horace 49
Howe, George 31
Hoy, S/Ldr W. 128
Hudson, ACW Marguerite 58
Hulme, Sgt **132**
Hülsmeyer, Christian 11
Hunter, Charles **22**
Ibbitson, Frank 58
Jackson, Philip 95
Jastrzebski, P/O Franciszek 70
Jenkins, F/Lt J.G. 130
Jenkinson, Thomas 'Tint' **117**
Johnson, Amy 21
Johnson, F/Sgt R.R. 154
Kälber, *Uffz* Fritz 104
Kalle, *Uffz* Jakob 90
Kaminski, *Gefr* Johannes 92
Kappenberg, *Uffz* Hans 101
Kay, P/O W. 156

Keele, F/O B.R. **122**, 128
Keeton, Sgt C. **152**
Keller, *Fw* Hugo 68
Kenski, *Uffz* Heinrich 63–66
Kinder, *Fw* Karl 95
Koch, *Oblt zur See* Friedrich-Wilhelm 28
Körfer, *Lt* Armin 106
Kowalski, *Fw* Günter 101
Kratz, *Oblt* Rudolf 49
Kruczinski, *Uffz* Werner 68
Kuberka, *Fw* Gustav 101
Kugler, *Uffz* Karl-Heinz 104
Kuhnapfel, *Uffz* Artur 36
Kursch, *Uffz* Severin 65
Küster, *Ogefr* Horst 120
Lacey, Sgt James H. 'Ginger' 73
Lacou, Capt P. 152
Laffoley, F/Lt J. 154
Laing, F/Sgt G.D. 154
Lake, P/O D.M. 54
Lamb, Sgt L. **150**
Lambie, P/O W.G. 54
Land, Sgt I.J. 127
Langford, Robert 99
Lawrence, P/O A.G. 104, 106
Lawson, F/Lt R.N. 164
Lawson, P/O G.W. 164
Laycock, P/O H.K. **52**
Le Conte, W/O E. 128
Leather, F/Lt W.J. 31
Lee, P/O 148
Leng, Sgt Maurice 72
Lewald, *Fw* Heinz 120
Lewis, Col Isaac 22
Lockyer, F/O A.C. 159
Loft, PC Thomas H. **23**
Lomas, F/Sgt Harry **150**, 151, 167, **172**
London, *Gefr* Willi 92, **94**
Long, P/O F. H. 27
Lorenz, *Ogefr* Rudolf 92, **94**
Lovell, F/O A.D.J. 35
Lovett, F/Lt R.E. 46, **62**
Ludwig, *Uffz* Siegfried 129
Lund, P/O J.W. 31
Lupton, Sgt 40
Machon, Miss P. 59
Magie, *Uffz* Franz 90
Mahé, W/O Yves 104, 106
Main, Sgt A.D.W. 35
Mallinson, Herbert 135
Maltby, F/Sgt W.T. 154
Manton, P/O P.B. 149
Marchbank, W/Cdr S.J. 130
Marples, P/O R. 28, **46**, **52**
Marshall, Norman 62
Masson, Sgt P. 152
Materne, *Uffz* Hermann 101
Maul, Sgt 92
McAdam, F/Lt D.W. 145
McCarthy, S/Ldr Joseph 142
McCheaney, Sgt 92
McClymont, Sgt 127
McKinnon, Sgt L.H. 114
McLardy, F/O W.A. 158
McNay, Sgt Alexander L. 46, 53, **62**
Megginson, Irene 65
Megginson, Jack **51**
Megginson, Nellie 71
Miles, Sgt J. 127
Miller, P/O R. 28
Mischalla, *Uffz* Sylvester 101
Moberley, F/O G.E. 32, 45, 54
Moll, Mrs Ellen 156
Moll, Mrs Violet 156
Moll, Richard 156
Monnier, F/Lt H.C. 145
Moog, *Hptm* Heinrich 95
Morenz, *Fw* Rudi 158
Moss, Sgt Olive 132

174

Mottershead, H.N. 172
Mühlen, *Lt* Karl-Heinz **103**, 104
Müller, *Fw* Heinrich 92
Müller, *Gefr* Heinz 104
Müller, *Ofw* Karl 120
Mümler, S/Ldr Mieczyslaw 40
Mundy, Sgt R.C. **150**
Munro, S/Ldr Les **142**
Murfitt, P/O 148
Murray, P/O Thomas **42**, **52**
Muschiol, *Uffz* Alfred 120
Mustoe, F/Sgt H. 152
Neige, *Uffz* Walter 32
Neumeyer, *Uffz* Arnulf 65
New, LAC K.E. 58
Ney, *Maj* Bertold 157
Nicholls, Inspector 68
Nicholson, Agnes Annie 39
Nightingale, Sgt F. 54, **56**
Oechler, *Uffz* Heinz 36
Oleynik, P/O P. 154
Owen, Jack 31
Owich, *Uffz* Helmut 90
Palmer, P/O H.V. 156
Pankuweit, *Uffz* Hugo 128
Parish, Sgt Alan 151
Parkin, Evelyn 71
Parkin, Walter 71
Parnall, F/O D.G. 35
Parrish, Sgt A. **152**
Parry, Sgt T.R. 112
Paterek, Sgt Edward 70
Patrick, G.W. 116, **117**
Pausch, *Uffz* Erwin 133
Peake, P/O R. 112
Peissert, *Oblt* Edgar 95
Perrin, LAC 132
Pétain, Marshall 39
Phillipson, Sgt J. 100
Pilger, Fritz **130**
Pillisier, Lt **151**
Piontek, *Uffz* Oskar 74
Planck, *Oblt* 163
Plant, Sgt 92
Podbielski, *Oblt* Friedrich-Franz 73
Pohl, *Fw* Robert 65
Poley, W/O R.W. 152
Pollok, *Uffz* Christian 101
Porter, Richard 99
Potter, Mabel 39
Powell, Royston 81-82
Przibilla, *Uffz* Bruno 101
Quodt, *Uffz* Wilhelm 95
Rahl, *Uffz* Josef 128
Raisbach, *Ofw* Hermann 28, **30**
Rautenberg, *Uffz* Willi 68
Ray, W/O D.W. 128
Reid, F/Lt William 142
Reinelt, *Uffz* Günter 92
Reis, *Uffz* Anton 120
Reüthe, *Uffz* Max 113, 128, 129
Rhodes, P/O 67
Richards, Sgt E.H. **152**
Richardson, Thomas E. **153**
Riede, *Lt* Wolf-Dietrich 65
Rieme, *Fw* Heinz 95
Riley, F/Lt W. 68, 70
Rivaz, P/O R.C. 42, 50
Robinson, Edward **22**
Robinson, F/O J. 68
Robinson, S/Ldr Marcus 27, 46
Rogers, F/Lt C.A. 151
Rogers, Gunner P. 39
Rohloff, *Hptm* Kurt 35
Ross, Colin 115
Roth, *Gefr* Hans
Rudd, John 50
Rumpf, *Hptm* Alfred 110
Rumpff, *Fw* Helmut 132

Russell, Sgt M.A. 113
Russo, F/Sgt 101
Rutter, P/O Robert **62**
Sadler, Joseph 83
Saltzgeber, P/O 59
Salz, *Uffz* Arno 120
Satchell, S/Ldr W.A.J. 40, 68, 70
Sawyer, G/C Tom 144
Schakat, *Uffz* Bruno 92
Schieting, *Ofw* 90
Schindler, *Gefr* Willi 104
Schmidt, *Fw* Gustav 156
Schneider, *Oblt* Anton 101
Scholz, *Lt* Heinz 110
Schopf, *Fw* Georg 92
Schramm, *Fw* Gustav 67
Schrank, P/O A.E. 151
Schreiber, *Fw* Willi 90
Schröder, *Hptm* Heinz 28
Schröder, *Oblt* Karl 92
Schröder, *Ofw* Hans-Karl 90
Schürleien, *Ogefr* Willi 129
Scott, Lt 32
Scott, P/O 104
Scott, Sgt D.S. 54, **62**, 64, 65
Scoular, Sgt 148
Seal, F/O H.D. 106
Seitz, *Fw* Eugen 28
Sewell, George 31
Shannon, S/Ldr David 142
Scharnbacher, *Lt* Josef 101
Shaw, Esther 68
Sheen, F/O Desmond 23
Shelton, F/O A.P. 152
Sheperdson, Ernest 53
Siddle, Mr & Mrs 78
Sigsworth, William 31
Sikorski, General Stanislaw 41
Singleton, F/Lt J. 120
Sinz, *Lt* Helmut 95
Skalski, P/O Stanislaw 41
Skelton, Bill 62
Sleath, Sgt A. 42
Smethurst, Gunner Edward H. **32**
Smith, F/Sgt J.F. 164
Smith, P/O D.S. 27, 46
Smith, P/O R.A. 28, 41
Smith, S/Ldr Roddick 92
Spear, Betty 71
Spielmanns, *Uffz* Willi 128
Staveley, Alan 62, 96
Stelter, *Uffz* Heinz 101
Stephen, Sgt 104
Stevens, P/O Richard 90
Stiegler, *Ogefr* Kurt 132
Stieglitz, *Gefr* Hans 92, **94**
Stoll, *Fw* Wilhelm 113
Stow, F/O R. **152**
Strachan, P/O W.P. 151, **152**, 171
Stuart, Sgt P. 151
Sullivan, Miss 68
Sutton, P/O J.R.G. 31
Tait, Sgt Arthur 151, **152**, 171, **172**
Tanner, Lt Cdr Peter 133
Terrien, S/Ldr J. 154
Teschke, *Uffz* Helmut 92
Tholen, *Oblt zur See* Paul 90
Thomas, Herbert 171, **172**
Thompson, Sgt E.J.V. 149
Till, Sgt S.D. **150**
Tilley, PC Harold 127
Timoney, P/O 59
Toeltsch, *Uffz* Hubert 129
Topham, P/O J.G. **54**
Townsend, F/Lt Peter **24**
Tranmer, Lesley **126**
Trodler, Rudolf **130**
Trousdale, F/Lt Richard 92
Truman, President Harry S. 167

Trumann, *Ogefr* Heinrich 63
Tuohy, Sgt George 149, **150**, 172
Turner, Ms 111
Turner, Clifford 31
Unglaube, *Uffz* Hans 120
Urban, *Uffz* Heinz 133
Vidal, A/C M. 149
Vinyard, Sgt F.F. 76
Vogel, *Gefr* Gerhard 95
Volz, *Uffz* Wolfgang 101
Von Kidrowski, *Ofw* Karl 74
Von Lorentz, *Uffz* Ludwig 63
Von Weg, *Lt* Siegfried 132
Wainwright, Charles 39
Wainwright, Gertrude 39
Wakefield, Sgt J.R. **152**
Walker, P/O W.L.B. 28
Wallace, Sgt R.V. 134
Waller, Mr 68
Waller, W/O G.A. 128
Walsh, Sgt J.P. 41
Walther, *Flgr* Robert **61**, 63
Walz, *Fw* Willi 101
Wapniarek, F/Lt Stefan 70
Wareing, Sgt P.T. **52**
Watkinson, Robert 115
Watkinson, Thomas **22**
Watkinson, William **22**
Watson, Henry 49
Watson, James & Dorothy 71
Watson, P/O K.T. 114, **116**
Weber, *Fw* Alfred 28
Weitz, *Fw* L. 98
Welsh, Sgt W.E. 154
Westenra P/O 12
Westmoreland, Sgt T.E. 41, **52**, 54
Whitfield, Mr 68
Wick, *Maj* Helmut 41
Wiefer, *Ofw* Alfons 95, 96
Wiffen, Leslie 48, 59
Wilensen, *Uffz* Heinrich 127
Wiles, Mr and Mrs 39
Williams, Capt A.H. 53
Willson, F/Lt J.E. 120, **123**, **124**
Willson, P/O Wynne 92
Wilmer Sgt H.J. 106
Wilmer, Sgt H.J. 104
Wilms, *Uffz* Hermann 24
Wilson, Sgt 148
Wingenfeld, *Stabsfw* 92
Winn, F/Lt 101
Wolff, *Uffz* Franz-Georg 68
Wolk, *Stabsfw* 128
Woodman, F/O R.A. 158
Worsdell, F/O T.P. 54
Wright, P/O 92
Wülf, *Gefr* Heinrich 92
Wyvill, P/O 92
Young, Sgt A.K. **132**
Zenkel, *Ofw* Fritz 67

ORGANISATIONS
Air Transport Auxiliary **21**
Auxiliary Territorial Service **20**
Keyingham Home Guard **19**
Observer Corps **8**
Womens' Land Army **20**

PLACE NAMES
Aalborg 32, 44, 67, 68
Aldbrough 6, 23, 35, 163
Atwick 14, 27
Auburn 63
Augsburg 99
Bainton 76
Bannial Flat Farm 24
Barmby
  Newlands Farm 130
Barmby Moor 146

Barmston 53, 145
  Hamilton Hill Farm 63
  High Stonehills Farm 157
Beeford 27
Bempton Cliffs 12, 115
Berlin 130, 149, 168, **173**
Beverley 72, 78, 110, 157, 163
  ARP Control 68
Bewholme 39, 129
Bishop Burton 78
Bordeaux 42, 99
Brandesburton 92, 129, 130
Brantingham 78
Breighton 130, **133**, 171
Bremen 99, 110
Bridlington 23, 27, 39, 46, 67, 68, 141, 163
  Britannia Hotel **71**
  Byas Avenue 49, 59
  Carlton Road 74
  Hamilton Road 90
  Hilderthorpe Road **40**
  Lamplugh Road 92
  New Burlington Road 90
  Oxford Street 68
  Prince Street **67**, 68
  Promenade 92
  Quay Road **73**, 74
  Reservoir 58
  Seamer Road 48
  St Anne's Road 33
  St Alban Road **56**
Brough 14, 110, 163
Buckton 53
Burton Agnes
  Home Farm 59
Burton Fleming 27, 133
Carnaby **139**, **140**, 145, 152, 154, 164, 169, **170**, 171
Catfoss 11, 27, 28, 90, 127, 163, 169, 171, **172**
Catwick 92
Cologne 110, 130, 168
Coneysthorpe 106
Cottam 11
Cottingham 71, 157
Crockey Hill 104
Deighton 169
Dortmund 130
Driffield 11, 24, 27, 32, 42, 44, **48**, 49, **57**, 58, **60**, 67, 71, **72**, 99, 113, 169, 171
  Eastburn Farm 59
Duggleby 73
Duisburg 130
Dunnington 127
Dunnington Lodge **156**
Dusseldorf 130
Easington 13, 112
East Bewholme 127
East Carlton Farm 35
Elvington 139, 169, **170**, 171
Essen 110, 130, 168
Filey 12, 40, 45
  Carr Naze 71, 95
  West Avenue 67
  Filey Bay 115
Flamborough 163
Flamborough Head 27, 28, **29**, 35, 42, 45, 76, 98, 112, 141, 142, 143, 148
Flixton Carr
  Carr House Farm 116
Folkton Wold 139
Fordon 132
Fraisthorpe 65, 71
Frankfurt 130
Fridaythorpe 154
Full Sutton 169, 171
Gainsborough 109
Gelsenkirchen 130

175

Grindale 137
  East Leys Farm 137
Halsham 14
Hamburg 40, 99, 130, 163
Hatfield 129
Head Farm, Flamborough 40
Hedon 14, 71, 90, 129, 163
  Paull Road 72
Heligoland 163
Hessle 163
Holme-on-Spalding Moor 99, 113, 154, 171
Hornsea 6, 14, 40, 53, 78, 90, 129, 133, 163
  Belgrave Drive 112
  Cliff Road 112
  Eastgate 112
Huggate 76
Hull 14, 27, 28, 71, 76, 78, **79**, **84**, **85**, 87, 100, 101, 119, 128, 138, 163
  Alexandra Dock **84**
  Anlaby Road 113
  Bellfield Avenue 72
  Bilton Grove 113
  Blenheim Street 92
  Buckingham Street 27, **94**
  Campbell Street 113
  Carden Avenue 113
  Carlton Street 71
  Chapman Street 27
  Derwent Street **85**
  Eastbourne Street 71
  Ellerby Grove **83**
  Ellis Terrace, Holderness Road 90
  Ferensway **94**
  Franklin Street **88**
  Hedon Road 73, 110
  Hessle Road 110
  Holderness Road 113, 159
  Holland Street 159
  Kirklands Road 90
  Margaret Street 92
  Marlborough Avenue 92
  Maybury Road 72
  Morrill Street 71, 159
  Park Avenue 92
  Prospect Street **89**
  Queen's Gardens **37**, **126**
  Rustenburg Street 71
  Scarborough Street 110, **111**
  Silverdale Road 72
  Spring Bank West 90
  St Andrew's Dock 110
  Staveley Road 113
  Sutton Road 72
  Tunis Street 113
  Victor Street 27
  Victoria Dock 92
  Walker Street 113
  Hull Bridge 130
Humber 125
  Ferry **22**
  Lightship 138
  Reads Island 146
Hunmanby 27, 45, 74, 78, 127, 133
  Hall **64**
  Simpson's Avenue 141
Hutton Cranswick 78, 163
  RAF Station 100, 169, 171
  Rotsea Farm 71
Immingham 81
Kamen 149
Kelk 76
Kelleythorpe 59
Kiel 99
Kilham 90
Kilnsea 14, 17
Ladbergen 149
Leconfield 8, **9**, 24, 27, 28, 32, 35, 41, 44,
68, 73, 98, 113, 149, 169, 171
Lindholme 137
Linton-on-Ouse 73
Lissett 127, 139, 145, 171
Londesborough 71
Long Riston 92, 129, 130
Lorient 99
Lübeck 101
Lund 27
Manchester 146
Mannheim 40, 99
Mappleton 90, 119
Market Weighton 96
Meaux 71
Melbourne (RAF Station) 154
Milan 42
Millington 96
Münster 163
Muston 120
Nafferton 53
Newbald 71
North Dalton 130
Nuremburg 130, 139, 163
Osnabrück 116
Ottringham 68, **69**, **70**, **166**
Patrington 68, 78, 92, 101, 163
  GCI Station 112, 128
Paull 90
Peenemünde 130
Pocklington 99, 130, **132**, 152, 156, 158, 163, 171
Preston 14, 90
Reighton 32, 127
  Dotterel Inn 62, 127
Riccall 169
Rise 14
Roos 129, 163
Rostock 101
Rudston 133
Saltend 27, 28
Scarborough 35, 46, 78
  Gasworks **47**
  Purnell's Wood 59
  Seamer Road 59
Seaton 119, 129
Sewerby 90
  Hall Farm 71
Skeffling 119
Skellingthorpe 151
Skerne 27
Skipsea 11, 27, 35, 39, 40, 71, 127
Sledmere Grange **150**, 151
South Cliffe 146
South Frodingham 78
Speeton 95
  Millholme Farm 95
  Southfield Farm 49
Spurn Head 14, **16**, 23, 67, 77, 92, 122, 129, 138
  Lighthouse 133
Staithes 95
Staxton Wold **10**, 11, 24, 28, 32, 77, 96, 116, 171
Stillingfleet 27
Sunk Island 14, 90, 159
Sutton-upon-Derwent **152**, 154
Tholthorpe 148
Thornaby 68
Thwing 90
Tibthorpe 49
Turin 114
Ulrome 40
  Vicarage Farm 27
Walkington 78
Wangerooge 164
Wawne 90
Weaverthorpe
  High Barn Farm 71
Welwick 14
Willerby 78, 146, 157
Winestead 92
Withernsea 6, 28, 31, 90, 91, 110, **111**, 148, 163
Withernwick 119
Woodmansey 90, 157, 163
York 90, **107-109**
  Baedeker raids on 101

RAF UNITS
1 Armament Training School 11
10 OTU 27, 114
10 Sqn **113**, 130, 152, 154, 157, **169**, 171
101 Sqn 113
102 Sqn 8, 24, **25**, 27, **29**, 42, 44, **47**, **57**, 72, **113**, 130, 132, 139, 148, 156, 171
104 Sqn 99
129 Sqn 98
133 (Eagle) Sqn 101, 109
143 Sqn 138
1448 Rota Calibration Flight 12
1459 Flight 101, **102**, 109
1484 (Bombing) Gunnery Flight 113, **122**
1502 Beam Approach Training Flight 113
151 Sqn 90, **91**
158 Sqn **131**, **132**, 139, 145, 149, **150**, 151, **152**, 156, 167, 168, 171, 172
1652 HCU 114
196 Sqn 113
2 (Coastal) OTU **123**, 127
202 Sqn **170**, 171
218 Sqn 144
219 Sqn 45, 54, 66, 120
249 Sqn 35
25 Sqn 112, 120
29 Sqn 67
253 Sqn 101, **102**, **105**, 106, 109
255 Sqn 90, 92, **97**, 98
256 Sqn 92
264 Sqn 138
38 Sqn 40, **41**
302 Sqn 40, **42**, 68, **70**, 71
303 Sqn 73
316 Sqn 127
346 (Guyenne) Sqn 156, 168, 171
347 (Tunisie) Sqn 149, **151**, **152**, 154, 164, 168, 171
405 (RCAF) Sqn 99
406 (RCAF) Sqn 100, 101, 104, 106, **118**
41 Sqn 35
43 Sqn 24
456 Sqn 158
458 (RCAF) Sqn 99
46 Sqn 23
466 Sqn 113, 139, **147**, 151, 152, **154**, 168, 171
501 Sqn 41
550 Sqn 159
58 Sqn 164
64 Sqn 76
604 Sqn 100, **119**, **121**, 28
605 Sqn 66
607 Sqn 66
608 Sqn **26**
609 Sqn 41
610 Sqn 100
611 Sqn 31
616 Sqn 8, 10, 24, **26**, 27, 28, 32, 41, **42**, **43**, 45, **51**, 54, 59
617 Sqn 141, 142
640 Sqn **131**, 149, **167**, 168, 171
72 Sqn 11, 23, 66
73 Sqn 44, **52**, **55**, 59, 72, **75**
74 Sqn 27
76 Sqn **129**, 154, 164, 171
77 Sqn 8, 24, **39**, 40, 42, 44, **57**, 72, 130,
139, 152, 171
78 Sqn **114**, 130, **133**, **140**, 171
79 Sqn 66
942 Balloon Sqn **15**

USAAF UNITS
2nd Gunnery Tow Target Flight **145**
422nd NFS **141**
425th NFS 141

BIBLIOGRAPHY
Space allows only a short list of primary souces:
RAF Documents
AIR 25 RAF Group ORBs
AIR 26 RAF Wing ORBs
AIR 27 RAF Squadron/Flight ORBs
AIR 28 RAF Station ORBs
AIR 40 Air Intelligence Reports
AIR 50 RAF Squadron Combat Reports
AIR 25/221: 12 Group Fighter Command
AIR 26/105: 73 Wing
AIR 27/145: 10 Sqn
AIR 27/305 and 307: 25 Sqn
AIR 27/424: 41 Sqn
AIR 27/494: 51 Sqn
AIR 27/495: 133 Sqn
AIR 27/545: 58 Sqn
AIR 27/629: 73 Sqn
AIR 27/653: 76 Sqn
AIR 27/655 and 658: 77 Sqn
AIR 27/660 and 662: 78 Sqn
AIR 27/807 and 811: 102 Sqn
AIR 27/1019: 151 Sqn
AIR 27/1049: 158 Sqn
AIR 27/1360: 219 Sqn
AIR 27/1511: 253 Sqn
AIR 27/1518: 255 Sqn
AIR 27/1553: 264 Sqn
AIR 27/1661: 302 Sqn
AIR 27/1676: 307 Sqn
AIR 27/1742: 346 Sqn
AIR 27/1743: 347 Sqn
AIR 27/1791: 406 Sqn
AIR 27/1802: 410 Sqn
AIR 27/1900: 456 Sqn
AIR 27/1925: 466 Sqn
AIR 27/2006: 1459 Flight
AIR 27/2050: 578 Sqn
AIR 27/2084: 604 Sqn
AIR 27/2109: 611 Sqn
AIR 27/2126: 616 Sqn
AIR 27/2128: 617 Sqn
AIR 27/2157: 640 Sqn
AIR 28/125: RAF Carnaby
AIR 28/139: RAF Catfoss
AIR 28/221: RAF Driffield
AIR 28/391: 1 RAF Regiment School, Filey
AIR 40/2398: AI 1 (k) Report 267/1940
AIR 40/2406: AI 1 (k) Reports 380 and 381/1941
AIR 40/2410: AI 1 (k) Report 85/1942
AIR 50/13: 25 Sqn
AIR 50/18: 41 Sqn
AIR 50/31: 73 Sqn
AIR 50/84: 219 Sqn
AIR 50/97: 253 Sqn
AIR 50/98: 255 Sqn
AIR 50/116: 302 Sqn
AIR 50/168: 604 Sqn
AIR 50/173: 611 Sqn
AIR 50/176: 616 Sqn
RAF Museum & Air Historical Branch — Aircraft Accident Record Cards
Luftwaffe Documents — Logbooks via Goss/Ketley/Schell
Civil Defence Documents – County Archives, Beverley